SPIRITUAL TREASURES

Courtesy: Vedanta Society of Northern California

Swami Turiyananda reading his mail at Marina,
San Francisco, 1900

SPIRITUAL TREASURES

LETTERS OF SWAMI TURIYANANDA

Translated, Edited, and
with a Biographical Introduction by
Swami Chetanananda

Advaita Ashrama
(Publication Department)
5 Dehi Entally Road
Calcutta 700 014

Published by
Swami Mumukshananda
President, Advaita Ashrama
Mayavati, Pithoragarh, Himalayas

First Published in St. Louis, 1992
First Indian Edition, January 1994
3M3C

ISBN 81-85301-24-7

Printed in India at
Swapna Printing Works Private Ltd.
52 Raja Rammohan Ray Sarani
Calcutta 700 009

CONTENTS

Preface	7
Biographical Introduction	11
Section I: Letters translated from Bengali	29
Section II: Letters written in English	231
Glossary	277
Index	285

PUBLISHER'S NOTE

The life of an illumined soul is always refreshing and invigorating. It is the life that inspires life. Swami Turiyananda's life and message were saturated with God-consciousness. About him, his guru Sri Ramakrishna remarked, 'He is a yogi according to the Gita.' The swami was also well-versed in Vedanta and yoga scriptures. Through his correspondence with some of the monastics and lay devotees, he shared his life's experiences as well as his wisdom of the scriptures.

Over many decades Swami Turiyananda's letters, most of which were written in Bengali and the rest in English, have been a source of unfailing inspiration and guidance to earnest spiritual seekers. Swami Chetanananda of the Vedanta Society of St. Louis has performed a great service by translating and editing these valuable letters, and publishing them in the book *Spiritual Treasures: Letters of Swami Turiyananda.*

We are indebted to the Vedanta Society of St. Louis, 205 South Skinker Boulevard, St. Louis, Missouri 63105, U.S.A., for granting us the exclusive rights to the publication and circulation of this book in India. The Vedanta Society of St. Louis continues to hold the copyright.

1 January 1994 PUBLISHER

TRANSLATOR'S PREFACE

"When I receive a letter from you, I get a picture of your mental state, and I answer it through inspiration, without much thought." In this way Swami Turiyananda, a disciple of Sri Ramakrishna and a knower of God, answered his letters. Apart from his personal experiences, these letters contain the quintessence of the Upanishads, Bhagavad Gita, Bhagavatam, Yoga-sutras, Bhakti-sutras, Yoga Vashistha Ramayana; the teachings of the mystics, such as Tulasidas, Suradas, Ramprasad, Hafiz, and Kabir. Turiyananda's letters also shed light on the teachings of Sri Ramakrishna and Swami Vivekananda and include many personal reminiscences of them. Swami Turiyananda did not write any books or articles. Once he said to a monk, "Whatever I have to give to the world, that I have given through my letters."

Every spiritual aspirant, at some time or other, passes through a "dark night" in the spiritual journey from an egocentric life to a God-centred life. According to the mystics, during this "dark night," or *kala-ratri*, the spiritual aspirant encounters subtle, unseen enemies, such as lust, anger, greed, delusion, pride, and jealousy. It is veritable warfare. Many aspirants are trapped by maya and yield to temptation. This moral or spiritual death is more painful than physical death. However, Swami Vivekananda said, "True greatness consists not in rising, but in rising every time we fall."

Life means struggle. No one can make progress, either in material life or spiritual life, without struggle. Spiritual progress rarely moves in a straight line: it goes up and down. Suppose a person wants to go to the top of Mount Everest. He will cross one peak of the Himalayas, then he will come down to a valley, and then again he will climb another peak. Although he may seem to come down after each climb, he will be progressing upward overall. So it is with spiritual life.

After joining the monastery, Swami Turiyananda passed through a dry spell which he later described: "When I was young and living in the Baranagore Math, once I was in a very despondent mood. I could not meditate. I was then pacing back and forth on the roof. Suddenly there was a rift in the cloud, and out came the full moon in all its majesty. All darkness was dispelled, and the whole landscape was flooded with light. It struck me. It flashed in my mind that I am the Light, the Spirit. My Light gives light to the whole world. Then all my melancholy disappeared."

Once an old monk, who was very close to Swami Turiyananda, told me, "Whenever you feel a dry spell, depression, or stagnation in spiritual life, please read the letters of Swami Turiyananda; you will get a boost instantly." His words are true. I translated those letters which contain spiritual instructions, as well as his personal reminiscences. Moreover, I included forty-one letters which were originally written in English; most of them were published in the *Prabuddha Bharata*.

Since Swami Turiyananda's death in 1922, several swamis of the Ramakrishna Order have translated some of his letters into English, either in part or in full, in the *Prabuddha Bharata*, *Vedanta Kesari*, and *Vedanta and the West*. I am indebted to the ground work of those swamis, especially to Swami Pavitrananda who translated some excerpts (not complete letters) in *Vedanta and the West*. Whenever Swami Turiyananda quoted from the Gita and Upanishads, I used Swami Nikhilananda's translations which are published by Ramakrishna-Vivekananda Center, New York.

I am thankful to the President of Udbodhan Office, Calcutta, for giving me permission to translate *Swami Turiya-*

nander Patra into English. I am grateful to the Vedanta students who helped edit and type the manuscript.

Nowadays people are tired of listening to sermons and exploring religion through the intellect. Some are also very sceptical about organized religion. They want to experience God directly. In this context, mysticism will play a vital role in the forthcoming century. A real mystic is he who has touched Reality, as did Swami Turiyananda. That is why his words are so powerful and penetrating. I am sure readers will enjoy the mystical aspects of ancient Vedanta revealed in this book, *Spiritual Treasures*.

Chetanananda

Courtesy: *Vedanta Society of Northern California*

Swami Turiyananda, Calcutta (?) c. 1911

SWAMI TURIYANANDA

(A Biographical Introduction)

Before daybreak a teenage boy was bathing in the Ganga in north Calcutta when he saw something floating near him. Some people on the shore saw it and shouted: "Crocodile! Crocodile! Come out quickly!" The boy immediately rushed towards the shore and, standing in knee-deep water, thought to himself: "What are you doing? You repeat day and night, *Soham! Soham!* I am He! I am He! And now all of a sudden you forget your ideal and think you are the body! Shame on you!" Right away he went back into the deep water and continued his bathing. Fortunately, the crocodile left without harming the boy.

This fearless boy, Harinath Chattopadhya, was to become Swami Turiyananda. He was born on January 3, 1863, in north Calcutta. His mother died when he was three years old, and he lost his father at twelve, so he was brought up by his elder brother and sister-in-law. From his very childhood Harinath was inclined to austere spiritual life. He did not care much for secular education, and therefore did not finish the entrance examination. However, he attended Bible class regularly, and at home he studied many Sanskrit books on Vedanta philosophy. He wrestled in the gymnasium and could do one hundred push-ups and five hundred deep knee-bends at a stretch. He told his friends that he would not marry and that he would lead the life of an ascetic.

Harinath first met Sri Ramakrishna at Dinanath Basu's house in Calcutta when he was thirteen or fourteen. He described this meeting in his letter of September 19, 1917, which is included in this book. His second meeting with the Master took place in Dakshineswar sometime in 1879 or 1880. After that he became a frequent visitor, and the Master began to train this young disciple. One day Harinath said to the Master: "Sir, whenever I am here I feel very elated and spiritually roused, but as soon as I return to Calcutta the mood completely disappears. Why does that happen?" "How can it be so?" replied the Master. "You are Hari-das, the servant of Hari [the Lord]. Is it possible for you to live without remembering the Lord?"

Gradually Harinath became familiar with the Master and began to ask him all sorts of personal questions. "Sir," he asked one day, "how can one become completely free from lust?" Sri Ramakrishna replied: "Why should it go, my boy? Give it a turn in another direction. What is lust? It is the desire to get. So desire to get God and strengthen this desire greatly." Sri Ramakrishna's way of teaching was simple, natural, and very effective. He did not ask his disciples to mortify themselves. He said, "The more you go towards the east, the farther you will be from the west." The more you increase your love for God, the more your lust, anger, and jealousy will decrease.

Sri Ramakrishna taught Harinath not to look down upon women, but rather to respect them as the manifestation of the Divine Mother. The Master gave special instructions to him regarding meditation and other spiritual disciplines. Harinath was attracted by monistic Vedanta and was trying his utmost to attain nirvana through self-effort. While he was absorbed in his Vedantic sadhana (hearing, reflecting, and meditating) and studying the works of Shankara, he stopped visiting the Master. One day the Master visited Balaram's house in Calcutta and sent for Harinath. When the boy arrived, the Master inquired about his welfare and then said with great emphasis: "Nothing can be achieved—neither knowledge, nor devotion, nor direct spiritual experience—without God's grace. . . . Well, is it an easy matter to realize that lust and gold are unreal, and to have the firm conviction that the universe is eternally nonexistent? Is it possible without his compassion?"

After a while the Master went into samadhi. Gradually he regained his outer consciousness and sang a song from the *Uttara Rama Charitam*, where Hanuman tells the sons of Rama:

> O Kusa and Lava, why are you so proud?
> If I had not let myself be captured,
> Could you have captured me?

As the Master sang these words, tears began to trickle from Harinath's eyes. Referring to this incident, Harinath later said: "That day I got a lesson that was forever imprinted on my mind. From that day on I understood that nothing can be achieved without God's grace."

On another occasion, Sri Ramakrishna said to Harinath: "What is there in the scriptures? They are like sheets of paper with a shopping list on them. The list is useful only for checking off the items once purchased. When you have done that, the list is thrown away. So you should check your knowledge, your devotion, and consult the scriptures to see whether they agree. It is said, 'When you have the knowledge of the Absolute, the scriptures are worth only a straw.'"

Everything is not in the scriptures; a personal example is necessary. It is life that inspires life. Sri Ramakrishna through his sadhana made a perfect mould of divine life and taught his disciples how to cast their own lives accordingly. Ordinary teachers teach religion, but teachers like Buddha, Christ, and Ramakrishna give religion. Later, Harinath reminisced about his days with the Master in the temple garden of Dakshineswar:

Ah, those days at Dakshineswar were like heaven itself! From morning till one o'clock in the afternoon everyone would be busy picking flowers and making other preparations for worship until the poor were fed. In the meantime Sri Ramakrishna would discuss spiritual subjects, and the devotees would listen to him with rapt attention. Even his fun and jokes were related to God. There was no other topic.

Everything culminated in his samadhi [transcendental state of consciousness]. After lunch, Sri Ramakrishna would rest for a short period and again would speak on spiritual matters. At vesper time he would go to the temple of Mother Kali and fan her a little. He would become God-intoxicated there and would return to his room reeling in a state of ecstasy. He used to ask those of us who were practising spiritual disciplines under his guidance, "Tell me, do you feel divine inebriation when you meditate in the mornings and evenings?" At night Sri Ramakrishna slept very little. He used to get up and wake those who were sleeping in his room, saying: "Don't sleep too much! Wake up and meditate!" Again he would lie down a short while and then rise before dawn and chant the name of the Lord in his inimitable sweet voice. The disciples would sit and meditate in their own way. Now and then the Master would go to them and correct their posture.

An hour of congregational singing in the company of the Master would fill us with such exuberant joy that we would feel transported, as it were, into an ethereal region. But now even meditation fails to evoke that celestial bliss, or even a semblance of it. That bliss would stay with us continuously for a week. We used to feel intoxicated, though we did not know why or how. Who would believe it? It is difficult to convince anyone. Yet I must speak out.

> The ordinary man seeks nirvana because he has suffered. But he does not know the tremendous joy in divine communion.

To live with Sri Ramakrishna was a great education. He taught the disciples how to attain perfection in service as well as samadhi. Harinath later recalled:

> One day at Dakshineswar the Master said to me: "Go to the Panchavati. Some devotees had a picnic there. See if they have left anything behind. If you find anything, bring it here." I went and found an umbrella in one place, a knife in another place, and some other articles. I gathered them up and took them to the Master. The knife had been borrowed from him. I was just placing it on the shelf when he said: "Where are you putting it? No, not there. Put it underneath this small bedstead. That is where it belongs. You must put everything in its proper place. Suppose I need the knife during the night. If you put it anywhere you please, I will have to go around the room in the dark, stretching out my arms in search of it, wondering where you put it. Is such service a service? No! You do things as you like and thereby only cause trouble. If you want to serve properly, you should completely forget yourself."

Sri Ramakrishna prayed, "Mother, may these children of mine surpass me in spirituality." There is a saying, "Welcome defeat at the hands of the son or disciple." The disciples, like their guru, explored various aspects of spiritual life. Harinath once said: "I have meditated much on the teachings of the Gita, which contain the essence of all scriptures. Sri Ramakrishna said that I was a monk according to the precepts of the Gita."

After The Master's Passing Away

Sri Ramakrishna passed away at the Cossipore garden house on August 16, 1886. The disciples then moved to Baranagore and founded the Ramakrishna Monastery. In the early part of 1887, they took their monastic vows under the leadership of Swami Vivekananda. Harinath then became Swami Turiyananda. From 1887 to 1896, Swami Turiyananda lived as an itinerant monk and travelled extensively in the northern and western parts of India. Later he graphically described his days of austerity as well as his personal experiences:

> Formerly my nerves were very fine, and I had great powers of explaining things. Whenever anyone asked me a question, I could see everything from its very origin to its outer expression—I could see from what motive he spoke and why. And in a single word of mine there was a flood of light.
>
> I used to observe absolute silence during the Navaratri [nine days during Durga Puja]. I would feel a sort of intoxication and my mind would become one-pointed. I have done what one being born a man should do. My aim was to make my life pure. I used to read a great deal—eight or nine hours daily. I read many Puranas and then Vedanta, and my mind finally settled on Vedanta. . . .
>
> I travelled widely in the early days. I went towards the Narmada, alone, without a pice with me, and I slept anywhere. I went via Allahabad, Chitrakut, Rewa, and Jabbalpur—all on foot. Whenever I travelled I kept a place of pilgrimage in mind and found my way by asking people. I went next to Hardwar, Rishikesh, Uttarkashi, and so on. I thought of not coming down from the mountains. I lived happily in the Garwal hills, totally forgot the existence of the world, and aimed only at God-realization. I meditated

and read a great deal. But Swamiji made me come down. I met him at Meerut. Some seven or eight of us lived together at Delhi. Then Maharaj [Swami Brahmananda] spoke of visiting Jawalji and asked me to accompany him. So I went with him to Jawalji, Gopinathpur, Baijnath, Pathankot, Multan, Gujranwala, Montgomery, and so on. And then we came down to Bombay via Karachi. At Bombay we met Swamiji as he was about to embark for America. . . .

I stayed for some time at Mount Abu. From there I went to Ajmere and Pushkar and then to Vrindaban where I stayed for six months. The next six months I passed at Lucknow. Then I went to Ayodhya. At Ayodhya, Mahapurush [Swami Shivananda] met me and asked me to come to the Alambazar Math.

Though I travelled much, I also studied much along the way. At Vrindaban I studied a great many devotional scriptures. It is not good to wander much if you do not at the same time continue your spiritual effort.

In the Jagannatha Temple at Puri, a sound suddenly came to my ears and my heart was filled with a great joy, so much so that I felt as if I were walking in the air. The sound continued in various strains. My whole mind was transported. I then remembered what I had read of anahata dhvani [the music of the spheres] and I thought it must be that.

One night at Ujjain I was sleeping under a tree. A storm came and suddenly someone touched me on the body. I got up, and at once a branch fell where I had slept.

When I first read the verse [of Narahari's] in which it is said that life is meant for the realization of jivanmukti [liberation-in-life], I leapt in joy. For that indeed was the purpose of my life.

"The first door of Yoga is the control of speech, nonacceptance of gifts, nonexpectation, desirelessness, and love of solitude." This verse had a great influence on me. Formerly I used to talk much, but when I read it I thought, "What! I have not entered even the first door of Yoga!" and I resolved that I would control my speech. I did not talk with anyone, lived by myself, and acted as I thought best. . . .

It was Shankara who moulded my life. Before I came to the Master, a single verse of Shankara's used to lift me a step up and give me a flood of light. . . .

Once I was sitting alone by the Ganga after my companions had left. I began to meditate and after some time it struck two o'clock. Then someone suddenly said, "Come, let us go home." These words seemed to club me on the head. I understood that they had come from my mind itself. There was really no home. But the mind had been thinking that there was a home where I was to return. I then determined that I would destroy this tendency of the mind.

Oh, those days are coming back to my mind. While I lived at Srinagar Ghat, I used to rise very early and bathe. Then I would sit in meditation and afterwards read. At eleven, I would rise and take an hour to procure some food. Then I would again begin meditation and japam. And thus I spent every day. It was there that I committed eight Upanishads to memory. I would meditate on every verse I read, and what an indescribable joy it was! I used to read the commentary of Shankara and the gloss of Jnanananda. And much further light used to come through meditation.

Vedanta says that a knower of Brahman becomes fearless. Fear originates from duality. Because an illumined soul experiences the nondual Brahman, he is never afraid. Once in the Himalayan region (Tihiri-Garwal), Turiyananda was living in a thatched hut with a broken door. One night he heard the villagers cry "Tiger! Tiger!" He immediately put some bricks behind the door to protect himself from the tiger. Just then he remembered the lines of a scripture which declare that even death runs away by the grace of the Lord. His awareness of the Atman awakened and defeated the body-idea. He kicked the bricks from the entrance door and sat for meditation.

Towards the later part of 1896, Swami Turiyananda returned to Calcutta. Swami Vivekananda returned to Calcutta from the West in early 1897, and founded the Ramakrishna Mission on May 1, 1897. Swami Turiyananda travelled to various places in India with Swami Vivekananda and wanted to pass his days in austerity. But Swami Vivekananda intervened: "Brother, can't you see I have been laying down my life, inch by inch, in fulfilling the mission of the Master till I am on the verge of death? Can you merely stand looking on and not come to my aid by relieving me of a part of my great burden?" Swami Turiyananda could not refuse the entreaties of their leader.

In America

In June 1899 Swami Turiyananda left for America with Swami Vivekananda and his Irish disciple, Sister Nivedita. On the boat, Swami Turiyananda asked Nivedita to teach him Western customs. She explained with an illustration. Picking up a knife, she held the sharp edge in her hand and gave the handle to the swami, saying, "Sir, whenever you give something to someone, always take the inconvenient and unpleasant side yourself, and give the convenient and pleasant side to the other."

After visiting England, Swamis Vivekananda and Turiyananda left for America on August 16, 1899. Soon after their arrival in New York, they went to Ridgely Manor, the country home of the Leggett family. They rested there for a few weeks. Gradually Swami Vivekananda introduced Swami Turiyananda to the Vedanta students in New York, and he was accepted with love because of his simple, meditative nature. Swami Atulananda, an American monk, later wrote, "He talked with fire and enthusiasm, and he would lose himself entirely in his subject, forgetting everything else for the time being." Swami Turiyananda was an illumined monk — full of purity and renunciation. He was a constant source of inspiration to the students. One day while walking on the street in New York, he shouted to a student, "Be a lion! Be a lion! Break the cage and be free!"

Swami Turiyananda carried on the Vedanta work in New York for a year, while Swami Vivekananda preached in California. Before leaving San Francisco, Swami Vivekananda said to the students: "I have lectured to you on Vedanta· in Turiyananda you will see Vedanta personified. He lives it every moment of his life. He is the ideal Hindu monk, and he will help you all to live a pure and holy life."

Miss Minnie C. Boock, a student of Vedanta from New York, offered a property of 160 acres in northern California for a retreat. When Swami Vivekananda returned to New York in June 1900, he accepted the offer and asked Swami Turiyananda to manage the project. Turiyananda was hesitant to assume the responsibility. However, Swami Vivekananda persuaded him by saying: "Don't trouble yourself about lecturing. You just live the life. Be an example to the devotees. Let them see how men of renunciation live. . . . Go and establish the Ashrama in California. Hoist the flag of Vedanta there. From this moment destroy even the memory of India. Mother will do the rest."

Swami Turiyananda arrived in Los Angeles on July 8, 1900, and became the guest of the Mead sisters at their

Pasadena home. After a couple of weeks he moved to San Francisco, and on August 2 he left for the retreat with a dozen enthusiastic men and women. They travelled by train to San Jose, then by four-horse stage to Mount Hamilton, and thence by a private horse carriage some twenty-two miles over narrow mountain roads to the San Antonio valley. The swami named the retreat "Shanti Ashrama."

Ashrama life began under primitive conditions—no running water, no electricity, and no bathroom facilities. There were snakes, scorpions and tarantulas all around. They had to bring water from a distance of six miles and lived on vegetarian food. Moreover, there was no food store nearby. Swami Turiyananda found himself in a wilderness with all these people dependent upon him. He felt disheartened, and he complained to the Divine Mother: "Mother, what have you done? What do you mean by this? These people will die. No shelter, no water—what shall they do?" Mrs. Agnes Stanley immediately said to him: "Swami, why are you dejected? Have you lost faith in her? You have less faith than even Baby [Ida Ansell]." After saying this, she emptied her purse in his lap.

The swami now saw a glimpse of the enterprising American mind. These students belonged to the old stock of pioneers and were not cowed by hardships. Swami Turiyananda was delighted to hear the bold words of his student. He said to her: "You are right. Mother will protect us. How great is your faith! Your name henceforth will be *Shraddha* [one who has firm faith in God]."

Ordeals and hardships continued in that remote, rugged mountain region. However, the students had found a wonderful teacher of Vedanta, who had the power to raise their minds to the higher realm of spirituality where they could forget their body consciousness. In the beginning they had only one small cabin and a shed, and their first meal was boiled rice and brown sugar. After supper they gathered round a campfire, and the swami chanted: "We meditate on the adorable and effulgent light of Brahman who has produced this universe. May he enlighten our understanding."

All of the students and the swami worked hard to build Shanti Ashrama. At first they built the meditation cabin, and then gradually more cabins for the members. Although there was a daily routine in the Ashrama, there were no formal rules.

One day someone proposed framing some rules. The swami replied: "Why do you want rules? Is not everything going on nicely and orderly without formal rules? Don't you see how punctual everyone is—how regular we all are? No one ever is absent from the classes or meditations. Mother has made her own rules. Let us be satisfied with that. Why should we make rules of our own? Let there be freedom, but no license. That is Mother's way of ruling. We have no organization, but see how organized we are. This kind of organization is lasting, but all other kinds of organization break up in time. This kind of organization makes one free: all other kinds are binding. This is the highest organization; it is based on spiritual laws."

Swami Atulananda wrote about Swami Turiyananda's way of teaching in the Shanti Ashrama:

> Be yourself, and be strong. Realization is only for the strong, the pure, and the upright. Remember that you are the Atman. That gives the greatest strength and courage. Be brave; break through the bondage of maya. Be like the lion; don't tremble at anything. Swamiji has taught you that every soul is potentially divine. Realize your own divinity, then you will realize that all souls are divine. A cloud obscures the sun. We say, "There is no sun." But the

sun always shines. So the cloud of ignorance makes us believe that we are weak human beings. But the sun of the Atman is always shining. Remove the cloud of ignorance, and the Atman will reveal itself in your heart. When you realize that, then you are a man. Otherwise you are no different from beasts.

And when asked how this can be realized, he answered: "Through meditation. Meditation is the key that opens the door to Truth. Meditate, meditate! Meditate till light flashes into your mind and the Atman stands self-revealed. Not by talk, not by study—but by meditation alone the Truth is known."

It was in this same spirit of trusting in God alone that the swami was very strongly opposed to all planning. There also he used almost the identical language: "Why do you plan? Why are you scheming? Why do you look so far ahead? Let Mother plan. Her plan comes true. Human planning is all in vain if she does not consent. She knows what will happen. The future is an open book to her. Live in the present; make the best of your time and opportunities. Don't think of the future. Know for certain that Mother's will shall come to pass. Trust in her. Only try to love her sincerely. Give yourself to her. Let her do with you as she wishes." But on one occasion he added, "Trusting in Mother does not mean idleness. Try to know her will, and then be up and doing like a man. Don't you see? I am never idle. The mind must be occupied in some way or another. If you don't do physical work you must use your mind—read, study, or meditate. And don't spend your time in idle gossip. Gossip breeds mischief. If you talk, talk of the Lord."

Of reading, Swami Turiyananda gave us the advice to read only books written by men of realization. When he found a lady student studying a book of New Thought, he told her, "Go to the source. Don't waste your time reading the ideas of every fool who wants to preach religion. There are thousands of books on religion. You cannot read them all. Therefore select the best. Only those who have realized the truth can speak with authority. Otherwise it is the blind leading the blind. Both come to grief; both fall into the ditch. Only the true guru can lead us right, and the true guru is he who knows Brahman."

Once a student versed in Christian Science asked: "Is it not our duty to keep our body healthy?" "Yes," said the swami. "But from the highest standpoint, body itself is the great disease. We want to go beyond the idea of body and to realize that we are the Atman. It is the love for our body that stands in the way to our realization of that higher state where we can say: 'I am not this body. I am the Atman. The body is an illusion.' As long as we love the body we cannot realize the Self, and we shall be born again and again. But when we love the Atman then we become indifferent towards the body. And when all love for the body goes, liberation will come very soon."

One of the students was psychic. One day Swami Turiyananda found her practising automatic writing. Making her mind passive, she sat with a pencil in her hand, and automatic writing would begin. The hand would begin to move and write, and our friend would see afterwards what was written. In that way beautiful things would be written on the paper. But when the swami saw her thus engaged, he rebuked her severely. "What is this foolishness?" he called out. "Do you want to be controlled by spooks? Give up that nonsense. We want *mukti,* liberation. We want to go beyond this world and all worlds. Why should you want to communicate with the departed? Leave them in peace. It is all maya. Get out of maya and be free!"

To live with Swami Turiyananda was a constant joy and inspiration. It was also an education, for one was learning all the time. And we all felt that spiritual help came through him. Sometimes gentle, sometimes the "roaring lion of Vedanta," the swami was always fully awake. There was not a dull moment in the Ashrama.

In the early part of 1902, Swami Turiyananda's health broke down. He went to San Francisco for treatment and afterwards returned to Shanti Ashrama. He then decided to visit India. He handed over the responsibility of the Ashrama to Gurudas (later, Swami Atulananda) and left for India on June 6, 1902. When he arrived in Rangoon, Burma, he heard of Swami Vivekananda's passing away. Grief-stricken, he reached Calcutta. After a short stay at Belur Math, he left on a pilgrimage to Vrindaban to practise spiritual disciplines.

Last Years in India

Swami Turiyananda spent most of the remaining years of his life in the northern part of India—Nangol, Gadamukteshwar, Rishikesh, Uttarkashi. Although he had lived in America for three years, Western affluence and influence had not affected his life of austerity and renunciation. As usual, he followed the ancient ideal of a Vedanta monk:

Roaming ever in the grove of Vedanta,
Ever pleased with his beggar's morsel,
Wandering onward, his heart free from sorrow,
Blest indeed is the wearer of the loin-cloth. (Shankara)

When his health again broke down, he stayed in the Ramakrishna Centres of Kankhal, Almora, Puri, and Calcutta. In spite of his fragile health, he taught the greatest teachings of Vedanta to the monks and the devotees. His illuminating conversations are recorded and translated in *Spiritual Talks*, and his inspiring letters are translated and edited in this present book.

In February 1919 Swami Turiyananda moved to Varanasi and lived there till his passing away. Wherever he was, he would hold classes on the scriptures. He was a wonderful conversationalist and inspired people to a higher life through his conversations. Once someone asked: "Swami, how is it possible always to speak on holy subjects? Don't you ever get exhausted?" To this the swami replied: "You see, I have lived this life from my youth; it has become part and parcel of me. And the Divine Mother keeps the supply filled up. Her store can never be exhausted. Whatever goes out, she at once fills up again."

Swami Turiyananda was really an awakener of souls. One day he encouraged a young man to lead a contemplative life instead of roaming here and there: "Musk grows in the navel of the musk deer, but the animal does not know it. Hence it becomes mad in the search of its perfume, running here and there; but all in vain. Similarly we run about and exhaust ourselves — till we gain the knowledge of the divinity, which is always within us."

In 1911 the swami developed diabetes, but he tried to forget it by following the teaching of his Master, "Let the body and the affliction take care of themselves; O my mind, you dwell in bliss." Towards the end he got a carbuncle on his back, for which he had to undergo surgery several times. Yet, in none of the operations did he allow himself to be under chloroform. He simply withdrew his mind from the body and asked the surgeons to do the surgery. The swami's actions amazed his doctors.

Later, the swami explained this phenomenon: "Do you know how it is? In the Bhagavad Gita we read, 'Wherein established in the bliss of his inmost being he is not shaken even by the heaviest sorrow.' This verse is explained by Shankara as follows, 'A man of realization is not shaken even by the pain caused by the application of a sharp weapon.' Two ideas are brought out here. First, Shankara shows that a perfect yogi has extraordinary control over his mind. Second, he shows that such a man remains in a state far beyond the control of nature."

Swami Turiyananda passed away on July 21, 1922. The night before his death, he said to his attendants, "Tomorrow is the last day." Towards the end, he chanted: "Om Ramakrishna, Om Ramakrishna," then he asked his attendant to help him sit up. With folded hands he saluted the Master and drank a little holy water. He then expressed his life's experience: "Everything is real. Brahman is real. The world is real. The world is Brahman. The life force is established in Truth. Hail Ramakrishna! Hail Ramakrishna! Say that he is the embodiment of Truth, and embodiment of Knowledge." He then recited, with Swami Akhandananda, an Upanishadic mantram: *Satyam jnanam anantam Brahma* — Brahman is Truth, Knowledge, and Infinity. Slowly he closed his eyes, as if merging into Brahman. It was 6:45 p.m.

Truly, Swami Turiyananda justified his name (turiya = transcendental, ananda = bliss). He tasted the bliss of transcendental Brahman and he shared that bliss with each and all. Like a true mystic, he silently transformed many lives in the East and the West. In America he told his Vedanta students: "You have been bitten by the cobra. The poison will have its effect. You will never be your old selves again. The Master has accepted you." One student asked, "If I fall?" Swami Turiyananda replied, "If you fall, you will fall in the lap of Mother, and you will get up again and try again." What an assurance!

Courtesy: Vedanta Society of Northern California

Swami Turiyananda reading his mail at
Shanti Ashrama, California, c. 1901

SECTION I

Letters Translated from Bengali

Swami Turiyananda at Shanti Ashrama,
California, c. 1901

1

Belur Math
Howrah, India

Dear Harimohan,

I have just received your letter after a long time. What kind of illness did you have? Is it that chest pain again? Always be careful. A careful person is not subject to grief. Never forget that. *Prarabdha karma* [the past actions which have begun to yield results] cannot torment a person who is always alert. . . . What are you studying nowadays? Never give up study of the scriptures, and at the same time practise meditation steadily on a regular basis. A pure life is very rare; so always watch the purity of the heart. Never think that you are safe, and always take refuge in God. . . .

Your well-wisher,
Turiyananda

2

Belur Math
Howrah, India

Dear Harimohan,

I have just received another letter from you. Happy to learn that you are keeping well. Please take care of your health. It is better to use your energy in the recollectedness of God than to consume it in repeated ailments. . . . Don't be upset at the behaviour of K. Babaji. There is very little education in that sect, as a result they are narrow and superstitious. You lead your life in your own way and pray for others' welfare. It is meaningless to wrangle and quarrel with anyone. It is very good that you have been studying the Gita. The Gita is the quintessence of all the scriptures. Arjuna became free from doubt and delusion after hearing the Gita, and whoever reflects on the Gita will certainly get the same result. Never give up studying the Gita. Accept my love and blessings.

Your well-wisher,
Turiyananda

3

Belur Math
Howrah, India
14 November 1898

Dear Harimohan,

Perhaps you know that I arrived here [Belur Math] from Almora on the last Vijaya day. While leaving Almora I received your letter, but could not answer it. Please accept my Vijaya greetings. . . . Always be vigilant in spiritual life. Don't be over-daring in any matter. Overconfidence leads to disaster. Know for certain: "Where there is fear, there is victory."* I hope you remember *Maniratnamala*, or a Garland of Pearls [a Vedanta treatise by Shankara in the form of questions and answers]. Vain is your studying the scriptures and futile your association with the holy, if you cannot absorb the teachings and apply them in your life. Reflect on why I am saying all these things to you, and then never hesitate to do what you think to be right.

Your well-wisher,
Turiyananda

P.S. "The good soon turns to bad. As milk curdles easily and never becomes milk again; so once a person becomes bad, he does not become good again." [Saint Tulasidas]

*A Bengali saying which means that a spiritual aspirant can avoid becoming entrapped if he is fearful of the temptations of maya.

4

America

Dear S—,

What is the matter with you? Why do you weep so much? Why do you want to sleep? "Who sleeps happily?" "A man of samadhi." [*Maniratnamala,* 4] True sleep comes when one is established in samadhi. Does one get any rest if he always thinks about himself? Let the mind jump; it will be calm later when it is exhausted. Don't inquire about the rascal mind — that is the best way to deal with it. What do you know about your worthlessness? Why are you so worried about yourself? There are many spiritual seekers in America. If you will agree to come here, I can arrange it. Please let me know. I am not joking. There are so many things to do here. When a person does not have anything to do, he thinks about himself and at last can't do anything. How long will you think about yourself? Enough! Now try to think of others. Come here. Everything will take care of itself.

Please accept my love and greetings and convey them to others,

Your well-wisher,
Turiyananda

5

Vrindaban, India
28 December 1902

Dear Harimohan,

I have received your kind letter. I am pleased to hear that the society which you formed is running smoothly and the boys are holding their zeal. I hope Shuddhananda is managing the society with success.

Know for certain: Human character is formed through true sympathy and love, and not through erudition or intellectualism. If you have real feeling for others, and if your life is pure, stainless, and unselfish, then the Divine Mother will make the impossible possible through you. Mere scholarly lecturing does not bear any result. This is the secret. . . .

Your well-wisher,
Turiyananda

6

Rishikesh
19 January 1906

Brother Sharat [Swami Saradananda],

Just now I have received your kind letter. It is hard to describe your kindness. "A friendless man is indeed wretched" — this saying is utterly true. In this awful world, a person should have at least someone with whom he can freely share his feelings and get rest. He who has no such friend is truly unfortunate. In fact, when I think of you in this respect, I consider myself fortunate. . . .

It was in this Rishikesh during our itinerant days where we experienced so much joy. Again, it was here that we passed our days with worries and anxieties in fear of losing Swamiji! [At that time Swami Vivekananda was so sick that he was close to death.] And now we simply count the days since Swamiji has passed away leaving us behind — such is the ruthless decree of the Lord! Accept my pranam and love.

Your servant,
Turiyananda

7

Gadamukteshwar
Meerut, U. P.
4 February 1908

Dear Vishuddhananda,

Yesterday I received your detailed letter. Some time ago I heard about you from X. I am glad to know that you are practising spiritual disciplines in Varanasi and keeping well by the grace of God. You have received initiation from Holy Mother [Sri Sarada Devi, the wife of Sri Ramakrishna], so there is nothing to fear. Now surrender yourself joyfully to God and live without worries.

Bondage is not outside. It is within. Bondage is in one's own mind, but it mistakenly appears to be outside. One can understand this clearly when one's mind becomes pure through good karma and God's grace. But intellectual understanding is not enough to get rid of bondage. It is through the grace of the guru and intense self-effort that one becomes free from bondage.

Needless to say, you are fortunate. Realizing the impermanency of the world, you have renounced it for the eternal treasure — this indicates that you are indeed fortunate. Moreover, you have received the blessings of Holy Mother. You intend to go on a pilgrimage and practise spiritual disciplines in a solitary place — that is a good resolution. Furthermore, you have received Holy Mother's permission. Never forget her advice to be careful about your health. Holding the Master in the heart, wherever you go there is no fear. All places are his. Is there any place where he is not? So don't worry. Fulfill your desire, freely travelling in holy places and practising spiritual disciplines in solitude. No one will object to this.

You have written about being entangled in work; such apprehension of yours, it seems to me, is baseless. There is nothing wrong in doing work; otherwise how can one have the purification of the mind? It is when one works that one is tested: How much craving for the result of action does one have? How desireless is the mind? How much selfishness has gone and how much still remains? All this can be known only through the performance of work. When divine love dawns in the heart, one no longer considers work as mere work — it turns into worship. That is real devotion.

In the beginning of spiritual life, one should practise both — work and worship — focusing the mind on the Ideal. Later, such a time will come, by God's grace, when there will be no difference between meditation and action. Everything will be transformed into worship, for God pervades everything. However, holding the Lord in your heart, do what you think best. Because both are equally good — either performing unselfish action in the monastery or practising spiritual disciplines in a solitary holy place.

Never think you are weak. You may be weak, but the One you have taken refuge in is all-powerful. Therefore, deem yourself strong in his strength. When one is firmly convinced that God is his all in all, he feels an upsurge of supreme strength in his heart.

May your devotion, faith, and longing for God continually increase; may you be immersed in his thoughts and attain fulfillment in this life — that is my prayer. What else is there to write?

Yours,
Turiyananda

8

Gadamukteshwar
Meerut, U.P.

Dear X,

I received your letter yesterday. I heard about you previously from Swami Shivananda, and now I am pleased to learn that you have decided to sever all worldly ties and intend to devote your whole life to the worship of God. It is good and extremely important to have longing for God, but it is not good to be impatient and despondent because one does not have calmness of mind. One should consider oneself blessed just to remain thirsting for the Lord. Is it not his immense grace that he has brought you away from worldly life and given you the inclination for sadhana [spiritual disciplines]? Now, whether your mind becomes calm or not depends on him. It is enough that he is making you practise spiritual disciplines. Pray to the Lord that he may keep you engaged in spiritual pursuits. Why should you pray for peace of mind?

Sri Ramakrishna used to talk about the hereditary farmer. A hereditary farmer continues to plough the land, without caring for drought or rain. He has no other occupation than farming. Likewise, go on chanting God's name and consider yourself to be blessed. Offer your happiness and misery, peace and restlessness to God. Be content in whatever way he keeps you. Pray to him so that you can continue your sadhana, then peace will come automatically.

Is God something like spinach or fish in the market that you can buy at a price? Is there any end to sadhana? Or can anyone attain God through it? Depending on him, stay at his door — that will be enough. His grace flows of itself. None can attain him by practising breath control or any other spiritual disciplines. The one who has attained God has done so through God's grace. Know it to be a great blessing if God allows you to remain waiting at his door. Spiritual practices mean that one should call on God sincerely, uniting the mind and speech. Never allow any theft in the chamber of your heart [that means no hypocrisy]. That is enough. He will get the rest done through you if needed.

With my best wishes,
Turiyananda

9

Dear X,

I see you could not grasp the purport of my last letter. It was not my intention to tell you that you should not practise any spiritual disciplines. What I wanted to tell you is this: God cannot be attained through spiritual disciplines [otherwise he would be like a market commodity] except through his grace — this is the conclusion of all scriptures and illumined souls. And may you never be proud of your sadhana. Surrender yourself fully to him. It is needless to be afraid lest you deviate from the spiritual path due to restlessness of the mind.

Sri Ramakrishna used to say, "The more you go towards the east, the farther you will be from the west." The more you concentrate on devotional practices, the more worldly feelings will dissipate from your mind. What good is it to invite trouble through imagining that which has not yet come? Death is inevitable in the future; for that reason, does anybody commit suicide out of fear? If you are always worried about hypothetical obstacles, your work will suffer and you will gain nothing. Have this faith: "I have taken refuge in God. All my obstacles and problems will go away. How can there be any danger for me?" No matter whether you are weak or strong, there is no other way than to surrender to God. This much I know; if you know something else, please try it. "If one takes one step towards God, God comes ten steps towards him." This is what I have heard all my life and have also experienced to some extent. But you have written contrary things, which are not right. God is omniscient and knows us inside and out. If you do not have this faith, I don't understand how you can practise spiritual disciplines. Let your mind be extremely restless for God and for nothing else — observe this carefully. The hereditary farmer makes his living only from farming and not from any other trade.

> Whom else should I call upon, O Shyama?
> The child calls upon the Mother alone.
> I am not a child of such a Mother
> That he will call Mother to each and all.
> If the mother spanks the child,
> The child cries, "mother, mother,"
> Even though he is shoved away
> He still cries, "mother, mother."

This attitude appeals to me.

You have asked, "Does practising spiritual discipline depend on one's own power?" My answer is: It is not within one's own power. When one understands this, one finds no other way than self-surrender and grace. You have written very incoherently. Be thoughtful. Unfurling the sail means to go on practising spiritual disciplines and nothing else. If your mind does not want to see the face of God, punish yourself either by twisting your ears or by any severe method. *Abhyasa*, or practice, means to attempt to place an idea repeatedly in the mind; this attempt has to be done with faith and love. Living in solitude, one can see one's mind well, and that helps to adopt methods to control it. Sannyasa [the life of renunciation] means complete self-surrender to God and no inner hypocrisy. This is the supreme objective of human life.

Yours,
Turiyananda

10

Varanasi
19 July 1911

Dear X,

I received your letter of Ashar 27 [July 1911] a few days ago.

I am pleased to know that you have a wish to become a "perfect man." I fervently pray that you can attain perfection in this very life. . . . If your desire is genuine, it will be fulfilled some day. There are many obstacles if you want to do anything good, but that does not mean you will have to give up. The more you face obstacles, the more you should make an effort to overcome them. It is good to increase your longing, but it must be wholehearted.

If you do not have holy association outside, then engage your mind with the association of the Lord who is within you. If you can make the inner companion your very own, then you don't need much association with outsiders. He who is within you is Satchidananda [Existence-Consciousness-Bliss Absolute]. If you think of him, you will not be inert matter. Wholeheartedly take refuge in that all-loving Lord. He will make you understand everything. He is omniscient and he does everything knowing our inner thoughts.

Your well-wisher,
Turiyananda

11

Ramakrishna Sevashrama
Kankhal
25 March 1912

Dear Suresh [Swami Yatiswarananda],

I received your letter of March 8, but could not answer earlier for various reasons. . . . Whatever you have written about yourself, I think, has been a correct diagnosis of the problem. It is not only true for yourself, but it is the same for all. We obstruct the path of our progress by limiting ourselves with rules. Of course, I am not saying that there is no need for rules. It is important to know when rules are necessary and when they are not.

"For a sage who wants to attain yoga, action is said to be the means; but when he has attained yoga, serenity is said to be the means." [Gita, VI.3]

With great effort we invoke the deity in an image; yet we immerse the image after the worship. It is like a change of arrangement according to the change of situation. But, undoubtedly, it is difficult to ascertain. This is certain: If we can surrender ourselves fully to the Lord, we will not have to repent for anything. By God's grace everything will be all right. Don't worry. Take refuge in God. Take refuge in God.

With my love,
Turiyananda

12

Dear X,

It is needless to say: Serve your father.

"Service to the father is the way to heaven; it is the greatest religious rite and the highest form of spiritual practice. If the father is pleased, all the gods become propitious." This is the injunction of the Hindu scripture. You have accepted the religion of service — to do good to all beings is your duty, what to speak of service to your father!

I am sorry to hear that you are not having any holy company, but what can you do? The holy of holies dwells in your heart; now try to get more attracted to him. He will make everything favourable for you. . . . Behave well with your relatives, otherwise your religion of service will be falsified. To see God in all beings is the main objective.

Your well-wisher,
Turiyananda

13

Ramakrishna Sevashrama
Kankhal
6 April 1912

Dear Sri —,

I received your letter dated March 29, and am glad to know that you are physically well. I am both surprised and saddened to learn that your mental conflict is "a great problem." I am astounded that you have to ask why parents are called "supreme teachers." I am filled with pity, because you were born in a Hindu family and have seen how people offer oblations to their parents, saying, "Service to the father is the way to heaven; it is the greatest religious rite and the highest form of religious practice. If the father is pleased, all the gods become propitious." And now you consider your parents equal to the street people! What spiritual degeneration!

You have mentioned "common intelligence." All beings have common intelligence, no doubt, but man is endowed with special intelligence; and for that reason he is higher than animals. "Eating, sleeping, fear, and sex — in these regards man is absolutely similar to animals; but knowledge distinguishes man from animals. Men devoid of knowledge are equal to animals." [*Hitopadesha*]

Children are born from their parents, are taken care of by them, and are raised by them through the promptings of parental instinct — this is seen in the animal world. But the case of man is altogether different. As you have mentioned, one should try to pay back the debt to one's parents by serving them — this sense is absent among the animals. In the animal kingdom, when young ones learn to take care of themselves, their relationship with their parents ceases. This is not the case in the human world. Among animals, training ends with learning to eat and to keep themselves alive. Whereas among men, learning continues not only in this entire life but also in the life to come. It is this knowledge of the hereafter that makes man a devoted son or loving father. God, out of compassion, created the Vedas so that we can endow ourselves with scriptural wisdom, which makes the unknown known. Man needs scripture and animals need instinct. Therefore, if we want to be considered human beings, we should abide by the scriptures. Krishna said in the Gita:

> He who discards the injunctions of the scriptures and acts upon the impulse of desire attains neither perfection nor happiness nor the Supreme Goal. Therefore let the scriptures be your authority in determining what ought to be done and what ought not to be done. Having learnt the injunctions of the scriptures, you should do your work in the world. [Gita, XVI.23-24]

True, all cannot become versed in the scriptures; so one should have faith and love for the teachers who know the scriptures. As soon as this faith and love dawn in a person, he easily attains the wisdom of the scriptures. Faith and love are gifts of God, no doubt, but one can have them by associating with the holy and by giving service. The Lord himself has said it in the Gita: "Learn it by prostration, by inquiry, and by service. The wise, who have seen the Truth, will teach you that knowledge." [Gita, IV.34]

It is true that when a person sees God in every being, all distinctions cease to exist for him. He becomes same-sighted. Then service to the parents and service to the street people become one and the same, for the same God resides in all. But that realization is far away. That highest knowledge arises from devoted service to parents, teachers, and saints. Until that knowledge comes, one should respect one's parents as great teachers; and it is through their grace that we become fit to attain supreme knowledge. Enough for today.

With love and good wishes,
Turiyananda

14

Kankhal
8 April 1912

Dear Tejnarayan [Swami Sharvananda],

I have received your letter of March 31. I am pleased to know that your activities are going well. Spiritual instructions will undoubtedly bear good results if a person teaches sincerely, without any selfish motive and according to his knowledge and the promptings of the indwelling Lord. Moreover, he should come down to the level of his students and try to understand the purport of their questions and then answer in such a way that they may get benefit from it.

A spiritual aspirant lacks nothing if he has genuine love for God and if he prays to him sincerely. The omniscient Lord makes everything favourable to him. Humility is a great aid to self-improvement. The Master used to say, "Water accumulates in a low place, whereas it flows down from a high mound." All virtues come to a humble person. Humility is a wonderful quality, and the Master has endowed you with that. I believe that the Master will do many great things through you. Go on doing your duty to the best of your ability and knowledge, and never mind the consequences. Leave them all at the feet of the Lord. He is the embodiment of goodness and will do nothing but good. If one sets his mind on God, need he fear going astray? He is the polestar of our life. He is the goal, he is the means, and he is the consequence.

Truly, the vow you have taken has no end. The Lord is in its beginning, middle, and end. There is no other refuge but him. In this vow — "When you lie down, think that you are prostrating yourself to the Mother; when you sleep, think that you are meditating on her; and while taking food, think that you are offering an oblation to Mother Shyama." In this vow — "Whatever you hear through your ears is a mantram of the Mother, for Mother Kali is verily the whole alphabet and in every letter she resides." In this vow — "In glee does Ramprasad sing that the Divine Mother is in every being; and when you roam about in the streets, think that you are circumambulating the Mother." Here the matter ends. This is the way one observes this vow. If one keeps it in mind, he has no more chances to slip. The Divine Mother is everything. . . .

What you have written about the Gita seems to be true, but is not really so. Sridhar Swami might have understood it in that manner, so he wrote a commentary on the Gita accordingly. Shankara's commentary contains a preponderance of knowledge. He transcended the world, so to him it appeared like that. The Advaita [nondualism] of Sri Ramakrishna and Shankara are not different. They are the same, only they appear to be different in their modes of application.

I shall try to write about this in another letter when I get a detailed letter from you.

Swamiji's letters are something wonderful! I cannot find words to describe the feeling I had while going through them. They are perfect illustrations of nonattachment. On the approach of evening, the divine child [Swamiji] returned to his abode. He was engaged in play throughout the day, but later did not remember it anymore. He always remembered the Divine Mother, so his attitude was "Mother, I am coming."

With love,
Turiyananda

15

Kankhal
25 April 1912

Dear Sridhar [Swami Nirupamananda],

I have received your letter of April 19. I don't know whether you understood the purport of my previous letter.

Why did you write such a strange thing? Why do you consider yourself little higher than an animal? You have so much devotion in your heart; you are fortunate and far superior to many. One should not think oneself worthless. Know that you are protected by God and that he is your very own — only then will you make progress. The Master used to say that he who thinks himself "good-for-nothing" becomes "good-for-nothing." Swamiji also advised in the same vein and forbade people to think lowly of themselves. The Master taught us to think that we belong to God. Practise intensely that you are offering your body and mind to God. This will do you good.

Your well-wisher,
Turiyananda

16

Kankhal
29 April 1912

Dear Sri —,

I have received your letter of April 21. . . . It is good that you have decided to stay at the Yogashrama for a few days. But don't be restless; rather maintain a calm and composed attitude. Always cultivate the recollectedness of God within, although it is very difficult to do. Circumstances, no doubt, tend to cut off that flow of recollectedness; but even then don't neglect to strengthen your practice of remembrance. Rather, continue your practice wholeheartedly.

"The more a tree is shaken by the storm, the more its roots become firm" — keep this precept always in your mind. The greater the difficulties and obstacles, the greater the need for perseverance. Indeed, by God's grace everything becomes favourable. What is wanted is patience, steadiness, and unshakable faith. Have no fear. Take refuge in God and spend your days in constant remembrance of him. All good will come; there is no doubt of it.

I shall stay here two or three months more. Don't worry. Wherever the Lord keeps you, that will be for your good. He knows best. Leave everything to him and don't forget him — that is your duty. It is his responsibility where and in what condition to keep you and what he will make you do. For your part, just see that you may not forget him. If you practise this continually for some time, everything will become easy. Pray wholeheartedly so that he may make you remember him constantly. He is omniscient. He answers the sincere prayers of our hearts.

Your well-wisher,
Turiyananda

17

Kankhal
5 May 1912

Dear Suresh [Swami Yatiswarananda],

I have received your letter of April 28. . . .

The principal books on Vedanta are: Upanishads, Bhagavad Gita, and Brahma- sutras, which are also called *Prasthanatraya*. One should have thorough knowledge of these three source books. Because there are many books on Vedanta, it is difficult to read them all. The *Panchadashi, Yoga Vashishtha,* and *Viveka-chudamani* are also famous Vedanta treatises. By studying the *Panchadashi* thoroughly, one can have a good grasp of non-dualistic Vedanta. Above all, one needs to practise sadhana. Experience of Vedantic truths is the most important thing, and that depends on sadhana. The study of the scriptures is only an indirect help.

With love,
Turiyananda

18

Kankhal
10 June 1912

Dear Sridhar [Swami Nirupamananda],

I was glad to receive your letter today after such a long time. . . .

You will always have the benefit of *sat-sanga,* or holy company. Try to have the company of that *Sat,* or Eternal Existence [Brahman] who is within you. And again one needs the association of holy people in external life — God will provide you with that. One should pray deeply and sincerely from one's inmost heart. Always be prayerful. The Lord will protect you. Have no fear. At present do your duty perfectly; again, when the Lord puts you to some other work, heartily submit to his will. Practise seeing God's will and power in all actions. By doing so you will be free from all worries. Whenever you have time, you should study the scriptures and practise meditation. Your thirst for learning is laudable, it will surely do you good.

With love and best wishes,
Turiyananda

19

Kankhal
18 July 1912

Dear S—,

I received your letter yesterday. . . .

Continue your spiritual practices as you are doing at present. Don't relax your efforts and concentration. The mind normally passes through good and bad conditions; don't let that keep you from performing your spiritual disciplines. As you go on with your practices, the condition of the mind will improve. No need to worry. Always cultivate holy thoughts and try to have uplifting conversations. Don't allow your mind to harbour impure thoughts. You are young; you should be particularly careful. Practise humility. You should neither jump with elation nor give in to depression. In short, try to have constant recollectedness of God and spend your days in humble submission to his will.

With love and best wishes,
Turiyananda

20

Kankhal
19 July 1912

Dear Sridhar [Swami Nirupamananda],

I just received your letter. . . .

If you think a little, you will see that nobody can function for a moment without talking. If one does not converse with others, one surely talks with one's mind. Thinking is nothing but talking to oneself. There is no escape from talking. Since this is the case, is it not better to chant the name of God than to talk about rubbish? When you are engaged in conversation with someone, you will have to talk on various topics, but when you are alone, why should you waste your thoughts on useless matters? It is better to think of the Lord. In order to be established in the recollectedness of God, one needs to practise japam.

Japam means the repetition of the Lord's name. Meditation is higher than japam. The Master used to say, "Japam is better than ritual; meditation is higher than japam; and the person who is perfect in meditation reaches the state of liberation." While practising japam one should think of God, considering the name and the person as identical. When one utters the name of a person, the form of that person manifests. The eternal One is within the heart, so one experiences bliss in meditation. Gradually when that feeling deepens, you will have realization. It comes slowly. Don't expect it in a day. It is no small thing to get joy in meditation.

If the desire for money arises in your mind, then discriminate in this way: What can money give me? Many have wealth, but are they happy? The Master used to say: "From matter comes material things. Matter cannot give you Satchidananda [Existence-Consciousness-Bliss Absolute]. One can buy food, clothing, and other things with money, but not God." This is all for today.

With love and best wishes,
Turiyananda

21

Kankhal
9 August 1912

Dear Sri —,

I have received your letter of August 4. . . .

You have asked a pertinent question. Your very question indicates your inner feeling, which shows that you are gradually making spiritual progress. It is hard to make one understand such a mystical subject through a letter, yet I shall try.

The *kundalini* [the coiled up energy at the base of the spine] is the Atman's *jnana-shakti,* or power of knowledge. She resides in every human being and is called Chaitanyamayi, Brahmamayi, and so on. She is asleep as it were in every being, and her place is in the lotus of *muladhara* — near the sacral plexus. There are six lotuses or spiritual centres in the human body, on which the yogis meditate. In addition, three nerves are also within the body: *ida, pingala,* and *sushumna.* When the kundalini becomes united with the Lord Shiva, or the Absolute, one attains illumination.

The abode of Lord Shiva is in the cerebrum. When the kundalini, coiled up like a snake, awakens and passes from the lowest centre through the sushumna to the brain and becomes united with Lord Shiva, a person then attains enlightenment. One can awaken the kundalini through yoga, worship, meditation, and various other processes. When she is awakened, one sees light, divine forms, and has many wonderful experiences. By the grace of the guru, sometimes she awakens of her own accord. The six lotuses are situated in the following areas: between the base of the sexual organ and the anus, at the base of the sexual organ, at the navel, at the heart, at the throat, and between the eyebrows. The six lotuses are called: muladhara, between the base of the sexual organ and the anus; swadhishthana at the base of the sexual organ; manipura at the navel; anahata at the heart; vishuddha at the throat; and ajna between the eyebrows. The three nerves are as follows: ida passes through the left side of the spinal column, pingala through the right side, and sushumna through the centre of the spinal column. The passage of the sushumna is closed; it opens when the kundalini is awakened.

This is all for today.

Your well-wisher,
Turiyananda

22

Kankhal
31 August 1912

Dear Tejnarayan [Swami Sharvananda],

I have received your letter of August 21. I am glad to hear all of your news. Life is full of troubles. Trouble will always remain, but the intelligent person can accomplish his work steadily in the midst of distractions. "That is real cleverness which serves to achieve men's objectives of this life and the next." . . .

If the mind is pure, everything becomes favourable and troubles cease. The root of all trouble is the mind. Everything becomes unfavourable for a person whose mind is crooked. As days pass by, I more and more clearly comprehend the meaning of the Master's saying, "One attains success in every form of spiritual discipline if he can make his mind and speech one." The greatest of all sadhanas is to unite the mind and the speech. When the inside and the outside do not coincide, all sorts of restlessness and trouble crop up. . . .

Let me tell you an incident that happened when I was in America. I was then staying in Montclair, New Jersey, at Mrs. Wheeler's residence. I heard that a middle-aged American woman was teaching pranayama [breathing exercises]. She would give two lessons and charge five dollars each. She introduced herself as Swami Vivekananda's student. Mrs. Wheeler invited her to her home to meet me. I talked to her on many subjects; she seemed to be a nice person. Later when I met Swamiji in New York, by the by I mentioned that woman to him. I asked him: "Is this woman your student? Is it proper that she is charging money and doing business in your name?" Swamiji replied: "You have seen only one. There are many like her. It is not wrong for her to make a little money for her living. She might have attended my lectures or classes. I may recognize her face but I don't know her name. It is all right that she is making her living in this way." The way Swamiji expressed his compassion and sympathy for that woman made me feel embarrassed for my narrow attitude. Swamiji's catholic feeling is unparalleled; that is why he is so great! . . .

Both of your questions are very difficult. First, the shrāddha ceremony or obsequial rites. You will be able to learn much about it if you read the Shanti Parvan of the Mahabharata. There King Yudhisthira asked questions and Bhishma answered accordingly. There is a distinct sphere called the Pitriloka, the realm of the manes; and the shrāddha ceremony is performed in their honour. As it is enjoined in the scriptures, the relatives of departed ancestors perform this ceremony. They are happy thinking that the departed souls would be happy, although they may or may not be conscious of it. For after their death, a subtle and close relationship becomes established between them and their departed ancestors.

The word *shrāddha* is derived from the word shraddhā. Faith in the other world is verily shraddhā. The souls still exist even after departing from this world, so it is quite natural for their children to pray or perform a ritual for their happiness. The departed souls become pleased — in whatever sphere they may be according to their karma — when their descendants offer food or drink to them. Shraddhā maintains this subtle link. I think this is the purport of the scriptures. You will learn more about it if you read that portion of the Smriti scriptures which deals with the theory of shrāddha.

Your second question concerns the superhuman origin of the Vedas. This means they are not ascribable to any human authorship. Nobody has produced them; therefore, they are eternal. Now everything will be clear if you understand the meaning of the word *Veda*. *Veda* means knowledge. What is knowledge? "Knowledge is twofold: one part arises from the scriptures and the other is revealed by discrimination. Shabda Brahman [Word-Brahman], or the Vedas are the knowledge derived from the scriptures, and the knowledge of Para-Brahman [Supreme Brahman] is revealed by discrimination."

Now if you admit that knowledge is uncreated by man and is eternal, then you will automatically admit that Word-Brahman, or the Vedas, being knowledge due to scriptures, are eternal and not man-made. Certainly they are not books. They are a mass of words — certain symbols used to represent certain ideas. Similarly, a name and the possessor of that name are inseparable. Names can be many, but the possessor of them is one. Similarly the mass of words known as the Vedas is a symbol of the Supreme Brahman and inseparably connected with it. I shall try to clarify this point some other time. This is all for today.

With love and best wishes,
Turiyananda

23

Kankhal
26 October 1912

Dear Sridhar [Swami Nirupamananda],

I have received your postcard dated October 22. . . . I am now answering your questions. Shankara wrote in *Prasnottaramala* [*The Garland of Questions and Answers*]:

Question: Who is the guru?

Answer: He who teaches what is beneficial for the disciple.

Question: Who is the disciple?

Answer: He who is devoted to the guru; in other words, one who obeys the guru's precepts and serves him.

The word "beneficial" refers to spiritual knowledge or the goal supreme; and the opposite of that is *samsara*, or relative existence. He who leads us towards God and helps us to extinguish the world of desire is the guru, and he who obeys and serves such a teacher is a disciple. The relationship between guru and disciple is like that of spiritual father and son. The earthly father begets a son; but the guru saves him from the cycle of birth and death by showing the way to the goal supreme. One can repay the debt to one's father by begetting children [who maintain the lineage] and by performing funeral rites [which carry peace and love to the departed souls]. But the guru takes one across the ocean of maya, so his debt cannot be repaid, even by offering him everything.

The word or name which releases the mind from sense objects and directs it to God is called a *mantram*. The purpose of receiving a mantram is this: If one repeats the mantram one's mind becomes disentangled from sense objects and is established in God. That is the goal of human life. If one accomplishes this goal, his assumption of a human body becomes meaningful and blessed. Otherwise he simply eats, sleeps, and procreates like jackals and dogs. He rotates on the wheel of birth and death indefinitely — sometimes as a human and sometimes as subhuman. This wheel of Mahamaya [the Great Enchantress] is called the world. Therefore, Krishna, out of compassion, said in the Gita, "Having come into this transitory, joyless world, worship me." [IX.33] Otherwise suffering is inevitable. This much for today.

Your well-wisher,
Turiyananda

24

Ramakrishna Advaita Ashrama
Varanasi
27 November 1912

Dear Suresh [Swami Yatiswarananda],

I was pleased to receive your letter after a long time. It is extremely difficult to answer your questions through a letter. It is better to discuss these questions face to face — however, I will try.

Just as in a seed the origin, growth, and blossoming of the future tree is potentially existent, likewise, the word which helps an aspirant to realize the Supreme Reality by releasing the source of all spiritual power is called the "seed mantram." Ramprasad, a mystic saint, sang:

> O mind, you do not know how to farm!
> Fallow lies the field of your life.
> If you had only worked it well,

How rich a harvest you might reap!
Hedge it about with Kali's name
If you would keep your harvest safe;
This is the stoutest hedge of all,
For Death himself cannot come near it.
Sow for your seed the holy name
Of God that your guru has given to you,
Faithfully watering it with love;
And if you should find the task too hard,
Call upon Ramprasad for help.

"Field of your life," "holy name given by the guru," "sowing the seed," "watering with love," and "hedge with Kali's name" — thus performing spiritual practices, one should finally offer oneself fully to God. That is the meaning of the song. The Master used to say, "Call upon Ramprasad for help." This means that even the self-sense, that "I am Ramprasad," should be forgotten.

To be completely merged in God — that is the goal of sadhana. Different gods and goddesses are the manifested forms of the same indivisible Brahman. They are called by different names, and they manifest differently to fulfill the prayers of different devotees, so the seed mantras are also different. You will find this subject described in detail in the Tantric scriptures.

All of Hinduism rests on the Vedas; so no schools of Hinduism — such as Pauranic, Tantric, and others — are non-Vedic. All schools have their basis in the Vedas. The sages have prescribed various methods to facilitate the understanding of various kinds of devotees. That is all. The authors of the scriptures say that their philosophical themes are mentioned in the Vedas. Without studying the whole of the Vedas, if we comment, "That is not in the Vedas," we will undoubtedly be wrong. As all sounds originate from OM, all seed mantras belong to it. Who can deny this fact? I have heard that some people have listened to the anahata [the music of the spheres] sound, and some have seen the seed mantras in golden letters. I do not know whether the seed mantram merges into OM or not; but I do know that the mantram and the deity are identical. The mantram is like the body of the deity. These things cannot be known by questioning. One should practise spiritual disciplines, then by the grace of the guru, one realizes them.

The Master used to say that one does not get intoxicated by merely uttering the word "siddhi," or hemp. One will have to procure it, prepare it, and drink it — only then will one be intoxicated. At that time one dances with joy saying, "Victory to Kali! Victory to Kali!" The scriptures also say that it is not good to reason all the time. Of course, for the sake of understanding, you should ask some questions; but as you go on doing sadhana, gradually your questions will be automatically silenced. It is impossible to stop questioning without sadhana.

As the questions arise within, so their solutions also come from within when one experiences the truth through sadhana. This is called peace or the attainment of complete rest. Only one who is blessed by the Lord knows. No amount of discussion will lead you to that state — this is the conclusion of the scriptures. "The Atman cannot be realized through the study of the Vedas" [Katha Upanishad, I.2.23] — hundreds of such scriptural passages will confirm this truth. Be up and doing. Surely the grace of God will dawn on you. Then you will joyously sing the glory of the Divine Mother and experience the supreme bliss. Enough for today.

With love and best wishes,
Turiyananda

25

Ramakrishna Advaita Ashrama
Varanasi
14 December 1912

Dear Sridhar [Swami Nirupamananda],

I have received your letter dated December 10. . . .

Never cease thinking of God. Whether you get joy or not, continue your meditation daily on a regular basis. If you can practise steadfastly, you will again experience bliss. The great sage Vyasa said: "When there is a disorder of bile secretion, sugar does not taste good in the mouth. But if one goes on taking sugar earnestly every day, he gets cured from the bile disorder and gradually begins to enjoy the taste of sugar." Similarly, one does not taste the joy of spiritual disciplines due to *avidya*, or ignorance. But if one keeps on doing japam and meditation daily with love and zeal, his gloom due to ignorance goes away and the love of God emerges. Therefore, never give up spiritual practices, rather do them wholeheartedly. Eventually you will derive joy from them.

Why do you pay so much attention to the fruits of action? Go on doing your work. In this world an employer pays his employees. Will not God give you anything if you work for him? Do your duty. What will you gain by complaining like this: "I have not achieved anything," or "I am not making any progress"? Rather go on doing your work silently, and the result will ensue by itself. The mystic saint Ramprasad sang:

> Do your work with the steadfastness
> Of a hereditary farmer.
> Make the effort with all of your mind,
> Then you will reap a golden harvest.

That is all. Patience is needed. Does a seed bear fruit as soon as it has been sown? Have patience. One reaps the harvest after so many ordeals — protecting the seeds, watering, weeding, saving them from pests, putting up fences to keep out goats and cattle, and so on. What more shall I say?

Your well-wisher,
Turiyananda

26

Varanasi
29 December 1912

Dear Sridhar [Swami Nirupamananda],

I have received your letter of December 22.

It is avidya, or ignorance, which is the field of lust and anger. Patanjali defines *avidya* as follows: "To regard the noneternal as eternal, the impure as pure, the painful as pleasant, and the non-Atman as the Atman — this is ignorance." [II.5]

In other words, it is ignorance which makes one perceive the unreal world as real, the impure body as pure, happiness in painful sense enjoyments, and to consider wife and children — none of whom is really one's own — as one's own. These false perceptions are caused by ignorance. This avidya is without beginning: there is no way of ascertaining when it originated. It is also without end in the sense that until one attains illumination by the grace of God, it remains and is not destroyed. This ignorance does not allow us to move towards God. So Krishna said in the Gita, "Those who take refuge in me alone shall cross over this maya." [VII.14] Our duty is to take refuge in him and lead a God-centred life.

What Swami Vivekananda said is true: "Devotion to God is dormant in everyone. It manifests itself when the veil of lust and gold is removed." The attempt to remove that veil is called sadhana, or spiritual disciplines; and when this veil disappears, the kundalini awakens. Nothing will be achieved if you scatter your mind in all sorts of things. Hold on firmly to your chosen path and resolve that you will attain liberation and devotion through it; then only will you succeed.

I have told you again and again, yet you won't listen. Now what can I do? You do as you please. You have the choice to select your guru and follow the methods of sadhana. Please don't ask any more questions in this matter. I wrote to you more than once, "He who is full of faith and zeal and has subdued his senses obtains knowledge; having obtained knowledge, he soon attains the supreme peace." [Gita, IV.39] But "The man who is ignorant and without faith and always doubting goes to ruin. Not this world nor the world beyond nor happiness is for the doubting soul." [Ibid., IV.40]

These are the words of God. Now, do as you please.

With love and best wishes,
Turiyananda

27

Varanasi
10 January 1913

Dear Sri [ ],

I see human beings as generally very selfish. They expect that everything should be done for them, and they are unwilling to exert themselves. Especially with regard to spiritual matters, everyone wishes to be perfect instantly. But who is ready to work for it? They do not realize how many bad impressions from their previous lives have accumulated in their minds, which, like a veil, do not allow them to see their own Self. If one can remove those impressions by hard labour, only then does knowledge or devotion manifest. . . .

Your well-wisher,
Turiyananda

28

Ramakrishna Advaita Ashrama
Varanasi
20 February 1913

Dear Suresh [Swami Yatiswarananda],

I have received your letter of February 9. . . .

Man is merely an instrument, and the Lord is the operator. Blessed is he through whom the Lord gets his work done. Everyone has to work in this world, no one can escape from it. But he who works for his own selfish ends — his work, instead of liberating him from the trap of maya, binds him. On the other hand, the wise man, working for the Lord, cuts the fetters of work. "Not I, but the Lord is the doer" — this knowledge severs the bonds. This is a gospel truth. The notion that "I am the doer" is merely a delusion, because it is difficult to trace who this "I" is. If one carefully analyzes this "I," the real "I" dissolves in God. Our identification with the body, mind, intellect, and so on, is simply a delusion created by ignorance. Do they last long? Discrimination puts an end to them all. They all vanish, and there only remains the One Reality — from whom everything evolves, in whom all rest, and wherein they merge at the end. That Reality is the Existence-Knowledge-Bliss Absolute, or Brahman, the witness of the ego-consciousness; and again It is the Omnipresent Lord, who is creating, preserving, and dissolving the universe, and is yet untouched by it all.

This world-machine is based on God and functions through his power. The playful Lord enjoys watching his play. One only knows whom the Lord makes to understand; others cannot understand it even though they hear of it. They get deluded and think themselves separate from God. This is his maya. This maya vanishes if one works while surrendering himself to the Lord. The doer then realizes that he is not the doer, but only an instrument. This is what is called inaction in action. This is realizing oneself as not doing anything — this is *jivan-mukti*, or liberation-in-life. The Atman assumes a human form in order to enjoy the bliss of liberation while living in the body. Otherwise, it is unreasonable for the ever-free Atman to be born merely to desire worldly enjoyments. The supreme goal of human life is to experience the state of bodilessness while still in the body. Attaining this, a person finds fulfillment in his life. I sincerely pray to the Master that we may taste the bliss of jivan-mukti in this life by his grace. May this life be our last birth; in other words, may we not have to be born again for selfish reasons. May we live only for him and for nothing else — let this conviction, faith, and experience be deep-rooted in our lives. May the Master be propitious unto us.

With love to yourself and all,
Turiyananda

29

Kankhal
14 May 1913

Dear Suresh [Swami Yatiswarananda],

I was glad to receive your letter of May 6.

"Let a man be lifted up by his own self; let him not lower himself; for he himself is his friend, and he himself is his enemy." [Gita, VI.5]

Please remind your friend S—: "Father, mother, wife, son, relatives — none of these stays to help you in the hereafter. Only dharma [righteousness] remains." Let him realize it fully. The Lord is your helper. Don't worry. All troubles will pass away. Be firm and devoted to the Master — there is nothing to be afraid of.

With best wishes,
Turiyananda

30

Ramakrishna Sevashrama
Kankhal
23 May 1913

Dear S—,

I was glad to receive your letter of May 17. After coming to Kankhal from Varanasi, I feel a little better; but I don't think there has been any abatement of the disease itself. . . .

Whatever is to happen to us has happened. Now I sincerely wish that you all arise and be blessed in doing the Divine Mother's work. "One should lead life for one's own liberation and for the good of humanity" — let this message of Swami Vivekananda be fulfilled in your life. I am glad to know that your mind is now much better and firm in determination. This is what is wanted. Is there anything greater than giving up one's life for a great ideal? "When death is certain, it is better to sacrifice life for a noble cause." [*Hitopadesha*, ch. 3] Will such teachings be confined to the study of books? Will you not translate them into your life?

You did right. [Most probably S— joined the monastery.] After listening and learning everything, if you had not acted as you did all of your knowledge would have turned into ignorance. Never allow any weakness to come near you. Hold the ideal of the Master and Swamiji in front of you and then move forward without fear. Don't worry: the Divine Mother herself will protect you. If you reflect a little, you will realize that she has always been protecting you. If she had not held and protected you, could you have remained unscathed all this time? Never. The Divine Mother herself has cleared the path for you and then has drawn you to herself; so why should you have any fear? Now intensify your relationship with her. First realize, "I have severed all connections with the world"; then Mother herself will graciously show you that nothing exists but she. "The same Rama sports in every being." Mother dwells in everything. Mother will reveal to you: "Brahmamayi, or the Divine Mother, pervades everywhere, and the Ganga, Gaya, and Kashi are at her feet." When you have had this experience, you have reached the highest. At that time the ego-sense disappears, and one realizes everything as Mother.

Now, as you have said, you will have to find joy by associating with the devotees of God, who will lead you towards him. Stay away from those who will take you away from God. Now all relationships are through the Mother and through none else. Now try to experience this by all means: "In my heart I have known this truth — I belong to the Mother, and Mother is mine." To achieve this, you should be ready to pluck out your heart with your own hand if necessary. You are an intelligent person. What more shall I say? . . .

Your well-wisher,
Turiyananda

31

Kankhal
25 Bhadra [August 1913]

Dear X,

I have received your letter dated 18 Bhadra [August 1913].

You have asked me to write about the quintessence of the Gita. Perhaps you are aware of what Sri Ramakrishna has said about the Gita. The Master used to say: If one repeats the word "Gita" a few times, he will comprehend its meaning. In other words, when you repeat "Gi-ta-Gi-ta-Gi-ta," it sounds like "Ta-gi-Ta-gi-Ta-gi", which means "one who has renounced." So the quintessence of the Gita is renunciation. In fact, after studying the Gita, one understands that "offer everything to God" is the central teaching of the Gita.

Some say that the message of the Gita is: Perform *sva-dharma* [one's duties] in the spirit of nonattachment and offer the fruits of action to God. I say that if one can do this, what more does one need? The Lord himself said in the Gita, "Whatever you do, whatever you eat, whatever you offer in sacrifice, whatever you give away, and whatever you practise in the form of austerities, O son of Kunti — do it as an offering to me." [IX.27] In other words, don't keep anything for yourself. But is this an easy task? One has to make a tremendous effort; it does not happen by itself. But there is no need to be discouraged. The Lord said, "Becoming perfect through many births, a yogi reaches the supreme goal." [Gita, VI.45] If the goal is not attained in this birth, it will be attained in the next; only we must not forget the goal. The practice should be continued, and one day success is bound to come. In his last life a man will be born endowed with divine qualities [daivi-sampat]; all of his *samskaras* [inner tendencies] will be good; and he will definitely realize God.

The sum and substance of the Gita, according to my view, is: Surrender oneself to God and completely efface the ego. To belong entirely to God — and not to depend in the least on oneself or anyone else — this indeed is the main teaching of the Gita. In whatever way one accomplishes this, one's life becomes fulfilled. God is very compassionate; if we can depend on him, he will do whatever is necessary for us. Krishna promised in the Gita, "My devotee never perishes."

[IX.31] There is another pithy teaching of the Gita, "No evil, my son, befalls a man who does good." [VI.40]

With love and best wishes,
Turiyananda

32

Kankhal
27 September 1913

Dear X,

I have received your letter of 4 Aswin [September 1913]. . . .

I am glad to hear that you have enjoyed my comments on the Gita. The import of the verse [IX.27] "Whatever you do or eat, and so on," which you have written, is correct. The idea is to think of oneself as an instrument and God as the doer. There is another idea: He has become everything, and he plays all these games while residing in every being. Like this, there can be so many interpretations. All of these attitudes demand the cessation of this puny "I." Know for certain that this petty ego is the root of all troubles and ignorance.

Self-surrender means: To practise contentment by thinking that wherever the Lord keeps me is for my good; to unify one's will with the will of God; and to practise even-mindedness in happiness and misery, gain and loss, and so on. In other words, one can surrender oneself completely only after liberation. Before that one will have to practise yoga repeatedly. Real resignation to God is liberation. If a person practises this attitude of resignation sincerely and wholeheartedly, he attains liberation by God's grace.

You have mentioned renunciation. In this context, the Master used to say: "A housewife at first does all sorts of toilsome work; but when she becomes pregnant, her mother-in-law gradually curtails her work and does not allow her to do very much. At last when she brings forth a baby, she is released from all work. Her only work then is to stay with the baby and nurse him; and the happiness of the baby becomes her happiness." Now pregnancy means to install God in one's heart, and giving birth to a child means God-realization.

There is another attitude: Stay at the door of the Lord and wait for his grace. If you are sincere, divine grace will be bestowed on you. The Master explained it through the parable of the kitten. It neither desires something different nor attempts to do anything on its own; wherever its mother keeps it, it remains there. To have perfection in any one of these sadhanas — that is the only thing needful. The Lord is omniscient. He knows each and all. "As your faith, so is your attainment."

With love,
Turiyananda

33

Kankhal
1 November 1913

Dear X,

I am glad to know that you have benefitted immensely from my letters, and so I consider my labours fruitful.

In the realm of religion, *shraddha*, or faith, alone is the cause of well-being. In the Gita the Lord says, "He who is full of faith obtains knowledge." [IV.39] In the Katha Upanishad we find that when faith dawned in Nachiketa's mind, he realized the truth. In the Yoga scriptures also, we find great praise for faith. There is a well-known saying, "As one's disposition, so one's fulfillment." Remember that your faith is the cause of your spiritual growth.

Try to practise constant recollectedness of God, and pray to him wholeheartedly so that your mind dwells on him — then he will bestow grace on you. Happiness and misery are inevitable in life. Human life will be fruitful if we have devotion to God; otherwise it is mere suffering.

Yours,
Turiyananda

34

Dehra Dun
14 April 1914

Dear X,

I am sorry to hear that your health is not good. You are having treatments, but with no result — that is quite a matter of frustration.

However, you should continue your sadhana. Whether the body is ill or well, let there be no forgetfulness or negligence in repeating the Lord's name. The Master used to say, "Let the affliction and the body take care of themselves; O my mind, you dwell in bliss." Don't fail to remember the blissful Lord. He who thinks that he will call on God once he has good health will never make it. The great sage Vyasa said, "He who wishes to think of God after solving the problems of his life, is like a fool who wishes to have a bath in the ocean when the waves have subsided." The waves of the ocean will never subside. He alone will have his bath who can plunge into that stormy ocean.

Similarly, he who can practise sadhana in the midst of happiness and unhappiness, sickness and grief, pain and poverty — he attains perfection. On the contrary, he who thinks that when the favourable opportunities come he will practise sadhana, will not be able to make it. Very few people in this world are fortunate enough to get completely favourable conditions. Disease, grief, pain, and anxiety are constant companions in human life. Call on God in whatever circumstances you are, otherwise it is extremely difficult to make any progress in spiritual life. . . .

With best wishes,
Turiyananda

35

Kankhal
14 June 1914

Dear X,

I was glad to receive your letter of June 9. It is natural that all bodies are affected by disease. One achieves perfect health as a result of great virtue. The scripture says, "Disease, bereavement, suffering, bondage, and misfortune — these are the fruits of one's bad karma." [*Hitopadesha*] One can greatly minimize the suffering by taking refuge in God and saying, "Let the afflictions and the body take care of themselves; O my mind, you dwell in bliss." Lamentation or complaint does not help in any way, it only accentuates the suffering and in addition makes one forgetful of God. It is terribly frustrating for a person who has craving for sense-pleasures but has a sick body.

On the other hand, for practising spiritual disciplines one needs a good mind: perfect health may not be so important. One worships God with one's mind. And the mind remains in good condition if one does good works — irrespective of the condition of bodily health. That is why one should be extremely watchful about the purity of one's actions. Every day the body is moving slowly towards destruction — none can stop it. But the mind continues eternally. Body after body will come and go, but the mind will persist and take up bodies again and again until one attains complete illumination. Therefore, the main task is to make an effort to purify the mind.

Dualism or nondualism — whatever you say — both are connected with the mind. When one experiences "I am the Atman," one becomes established in Advaita, or nondualism, automatically. Again when one experiences both body and mind, he is in the dualistic plane. When one realizes oneself as the Atman, the sense of duality at once disappears. Then only does the awareness of undifferentiated consciousness remain. All problems arise because of attributes [*upadhi*]: "I am so and so, son of such a person, of this caste, endowed with these qualifications, and so on" — such ideas increase the sense of duality. "I am not the body, the mind or the intellect; I am the Atman — pure and untainted by sin; I am Existence-Knowledge-Bliss Absolute" — when one feels this, where is duality? It is not enough to recite these words: one has to experience them. You now have full awareness of your name and personality; when that awareness is identified with the Atman, you will have the nondualistic experience. Dualistic worship is needed to attain nondualistic experience because we live in the dualistic plane. This dualistic attitude has to be gradually purified by establishing a close relationship with God through worship. Now our relationship is only with the world. We must sever our attachment to the world and connect it to God. When that is fully accomplished, duality will vanish by itself. Only God, the Supreme Self, will then remain. This puny "I," or ego, will disappear. This is a mode of sadhana through which one reaches nondualism from dualism.

Another way of attaining the nondualistic experience is by the practice of discrimination — "not this, not this." Deny everything this very moment and reflect: "I am not the body, nor the mind, nor the intellect; I am the Atman — Existence-Knowledge-Bliss Absolute. I do not die at the death of the body. Happiness and misery are characteristics of the mind and not of me. I am the Atman — full, one without a second, and beyond mind and speech." When one experiences this, one becomes established in the nondual state. But is it an easy affair? Does it happen simply by talking about it? Certainly not. The Master used to say: "What will happen if you simply close your eyes and say, 'no thorn, no prick; no thorn, no prick?' Whenever you place your hand on the thorn it pricks. . . . What will happen if you simply say, 'I am of the nature of the sky?' Then when you have to pay taxes, you are in agony." Therefore one cannot reach the nondualistic state at one stroke. That is why Krishna said to Arjuna in the Gita, "The ideal of the Unmanifest is hard to attain for those who are embodied." [XII.5]

But, "Those who consecrate all their actions to me, regarding me as the Supreme Goal, and who worship me, meditating on me with single-minded concentration — to them, whose minds are thus absorbed in me, verily I become ere long, O Partha, the saviour from the death-fraught ocean of the world." [XII.6-7]

If one can truly depend on God, one receives help from him. The Lord makes everything favourable for him. Again, is it also so easy? Can each and all do that? Not at all. It is only possible by the grace of God and the association of a great soul, otherwise not. Mere prattling does not help. Learn to explore your mind and see what tendencies are there. Then purify your tendencies and offer them to God. This is also not an easy job. If a person can achieve this full resignation to God, at the cost of his whole life's effort, he becomes blessed. On the whole, spiritual life is not a joking matter.

Dualism or nondualism — whatever you may say — is very difficult to translate into life. Shankara, the great teacher of Vedanta, points out the difference between dualism and nondualism: "The dualist says, 'I am yours'; and the nondualist says, 'I am verily you.' There is a slight distinction between these two attitudes, but their results are the same — cessation of ignorance and suffering." [*Bodhasara*, XXXII.23] So one can adopt one of these two attitudes according to one's temperament.

The main thing is: One should follow one's sadhana sincerely. Otherwise, it is like the pandit in the Master's parable of the milkmaid, who walked over the river chanting God's name. Whereas, the brahmin pandit, while trying to walk over the river, chanted God's name and lifted his cloth and eventually sank due to lack of faith. This kind of double dealing does not work.

If I want to adopt the nondualistic attitude, I will have to deny the body, mind, and intellect. As soon as I say, "I am the Atman," my feelings of happiness and misery must go, and I shall experience myself as "partless, actionless, tranquil, blameless, unattached." [Svetasvatara Upanishad, VI.19] On the other hand, if I say, "I am the child of God, his servant," then I will have to resign myself completely to him with the firm conviction that whatever he does for me and wherever he keeps me is absolutely for my good. Both paths are equally difficult, and both demand spiritual disciplines. But the results of both are the same: the cessation of ignorance and the attainment of supreme bliss. There is no doubt about it. Let one follow the path which is suitable for that person, but one must practise it wholeheartedly. Otherwise, neither path will yield any result.

The Lord Krishna, while instructing Uddhava in the eleventh book of the Bhagavatam, has clearly stated different paths of yoga suitable for different types of persons. I am mentioning this here for your information: "I have spoken of three yogas for the welfare of mankind. They are the yogas of knowledge, action, and devotion. There is no yoga other than these. Those who have dispassion and no yearning for action should follow the path of knowledge. Those who have not developed dispassion and in whom desires persist should follow the path of action. And those who have innate feelings of love and devotion, who take delight in my word, who are neither attracted to the world nor have complete dispassion for it, should follow the yoga of devotion in order to attain perfection." [Bhagavatam, XI.20.6-7]

If you carefully reflect on the above passage, you will easily ascertain who is fit for which kind of yoga. There are not many persons whose minds are completely withdrawn from sense objects. Therefore, the followers of the path of knowledge are very few. Those who are very much attached to worldly things cannot remain without doing any work. Hence, those who are in-between — that is to say, who are not completely dispassionate nor too much attached to the world — those who have faith and devotion to God, if they follow the yoga of devotion they will soon attain knowledge. This yoga of devotion is easy to practise and yields quick results, and it begins with a dualistic attitude. Afterwards, when by the grace of God this attitude has developed, non-dualistic awareness dawns by itself. Enough for today.

Yours,
Turiyananda

36

Kankhal
27 July 1914

Dear X,

I have received your letter of 5 Shravan [July 1914]. . . .

Quoting from the Bhagavatam [XI.20.7], *karmayogastu kaminam* [karma yoga is for those who have desires], you have asked: What kind of karma is this? First we see the word *kaminam,* which means "those who have desires." How can those who have desires perform unmotivated action [nishkama karma]? Their actions are invariably associated with desires [sakam], but that does not mean that they are bad. The desires really become bad when they are against the injunctions of the scriptures or motivated by evil. Those who have strong desires for enjoyment must work to fulfill their desires. Such people cannot grasp the precepts that describe motiveless action. For that reason, the scriptures teach them to perform action to fulfill their desires. The Gita mentioned not only work without attachment to the fruits of action but also work associated with desires, such as, "The Prajapati, in the beginning, created men together with sacrifice, and said: 'By this shall you multiply. Let this be the Cow of Plenty and yield unto you the milk of your desires.'" [Gita, III.10]

The fact is that merely listening to advice does not help. And is advice of one kind only? Different kinds of instructions are used for different kinds of aspirants. A person is attracted to a teaching according to his temperament, and he derives benefit by following it with faith. So Krishna said, "Man attains high perfection by devotion to his duty." [Gita, XVIII.45] In other words, by performing one's own duty one will endow his nature with divine qualities — this is the purport of the scriptures. Persons who have strong desires for enjoyment should fulfill them. Force or mere advice does not stop a person's craving for enjoyment. But along with enjoyment, one should have discrimination between the real and the unreal, for satiety never comes from enjoyment. Instead, desire increases more and more, like fire fed with melted butter. Therefore, along with enjoyment, one should practise discrimination. Then, in the course of time, self-awareness will arise from discrimination — as happened to King Yayati in the Mahabharata.*

Of course selfless work should be the goal, but that ideal cannot be achieved by force. In fact, it is impossible for a person without Self-knowledge to perform desireless action, as such a person cannot be completely desireless. Before Self-knowledge, the performance of desireless action is like *akamo vishnukamo va* — "Desire for God is not considered a desire." [Because the desire for the world binds the soul, and the desire for God releases the soul.] As the Master used to say: "Desire for devotion is not counted as desire; hinche [a kind of spinach] is not to be counted as an ordinary green; sugar candy is not to be counted as a sweet; the sour of lemon is not to be counted as sour." [Hinche, sugar candy, and lemon are said to have medicinal value.] In other words, the desire for devotion does not cause bondage. Thus if a person works for God, his work becomes desireless. Truly desireless actions can be performed only by the illumined souls, for their desires have been destroyed by knowledge. However, as I have already said, actions done with a desire to attain knowledge are also called desireless.

---

*King Yayati was so amorous that he exchanged his old age with the youth of his young son. He enjoyed sensual pleasures for many years and at last realized that the desire for sexual pleasure cannot be satiated by sexual pleasure. It increases more and more, like fire fed with melted butter.

Discrimination about work is very difficult. For that reason Krishna said in the Gita: "Hard to understand is the way of action. . . . Even the wise are perplexed as to what is action and what is inaction." [IV.17,16] So the Master, without going into these complexities, would pray: "Mother, here is thy good karma and here is thy bad karma — take them both and grant me only pure love for thee. Here is thy vice and here is thy virtue — take them both and grant me only pure love for thee," and so on. No one has ever taught such a simple and easy method — suitable to all — for God-realization. "If food is mixed with oil-cake, a cow devours whatever is given to it; similarly, if sprinkled with devotion, all actions are accepted by God" — what a wonderful hint has our Master given! A man finds fulfillment in his life if he can somehow offer everything to God, regard him as his own, and direct all his thoughts and actions towards him. As the Master said this, so did Krishna repeatedly tell Arjuna in the Gita:

> Whatever you do, whatever you eat, whatever you offer in sacrifice, whatever you give away, and whatever you practise in the form of austerities, O son of Kunti — do it as an offering to me. Thus shall you be free from the bondage of actions which bear good or evil results. With your mind firmly set on the yoga of renunciation, you shall become free and come to me. [IX.27-28]

Undoubtedly, it is a matter of great regret that we cannot put into practise such direct and easy instructions. The person whose mind is attached to sense objects must work according to the injunctions of the scriptures and perform his own duty; thus gradually his mind will be purified and he will attain the state of desirelessness. That is why this process is called karma yoga. This also explains why the injunctions of the scriptures are so highly valued: "He who discards the injunctions of the scriptures and acts upon the impulse of desire attains neither perfection nor happiness nor the supreme goal." [Gita, XVI.23] These are the words of God.

However, if one can offer everything to God, one no longer has any worry, anxiety or fear. Such a person does not get confused by the intricacies of the scriptures and can avoid various complexities of life. May the Master give us right understanding, so that by following his path we can attain eternal peace.

With best wishes,
Turiyananda

37

Kankhal
10 September 1914

Dear X,

I have received your letter yesterday. . . .

I am glad to know that you have learned many new ideas about karma yoga from my previous letter [27 July 1914]. It does not matter whether your actions are with desire or without desire, the main thing is: "Whatever you do, whatever you eat, whatever you offer in sacrifice, whatever you give away, and whatever you practise in the form of austerities, O son of Kunti, do it as an offering to me." [Gita, IX.27]

Hold this idea constantly in your mind: "Within me art thou; outside me art thou. I am the machine; thou art the operator. I act according to thy bidding." What more is needed? Can it be achieved by one stroke? Practice is necessary and through repeated practice comes success. God will then truly be the operator of the body. This is a fact: "By some artifice the Divine Mother remains bound by the cord of devotion." She is doing everything. Incapable of understanding this, we think we are the doers and thus get bound by action. Suppose a person is cooking rice in a pot with potatoes and other vegetables. After a while, when the vegetables begin to toss to and fro, children think that the vegetables are jumping. But those who understand say that it appears that way because of the fire below the pot. Take the fire away and everything will be quiet. Likewise, God is doing everything, residing within us as the power of consciousness and the power of action. Unable to understand this, we say we are the doers.

Is there anyone but the Lord in this universe? It is he alone who is manifested in different forms. Because of our ignorance we see many things in place of him. If one can perceive him, one will not see diversity anymore and will not suffer. He is within everyone. He is everything. When one is established in this knowledge, one becomes free.

In the Vyadha-Gita of the Mahabharata, the hunter had attained knowledge in his previous birth, but due to prarabdha karma [the results of past action] he was born as a hunter. He followed his duty according to his caste, but he himself would not kill any animals. He used to buy meat from others and sell it in the market. This is what we find in the Mahabharata.

You have quoted from the Gita: "He who is free from the feeling of I-consciousness and whose understanding is undefiled — though he slays these men, he slays not nor is he bound." [XVIII.17] If you reflect a little you will understand: when a person does not have any ego-sense or think "I am the doer," there cannot be any bondage. It is the sense of "I" that binds. "When shall I be free? When I will cease to be." If there is no "I," where is the bondage? "Not I, not I, but thou, thou." He who has no ego-sense sees God only. So he is not bound.

Yours,
Turiyananda

38

Kankhal
23 September 1914

Dear X,

I have received your letter of 1 Aswin [September]. . . .

Worship of the Divine Mother will bring nothing but good. When she awakens herself in our hearts, we become free from troubles; it is very difficult to achieve anything by self-effort. Her grace does not flow unless a person offers his body and mind to her. Once you realize her, this world and its wiles can do you no harm. Then you can see her presence even in this world. You will clearly perceive: "Thou art action, thou art righteousness, thou art also unrighteousness." You will realize perfectly that she has become everything, and nothing exists but her. Then all troubles cease.

Always pray to the Mother and remember her in the midst of all your activities and daily duties. Why don't you try this wholeheartedly? Then you will find that everything becomes easy. Never stop calling the Mother, whether your health is good or bad. Say, "Let the affliction and the body take care of themselves; O my mind, you dwell in bliss." Only by practising these things, can one get the results.

With love and best wishes,
Turiyananda

39

Kankhal
1 October 1914

Dear X,

I have received your letter of 11 Aswin [September]. . . .

I am sorry to hear that your health is not good. Continue your spiritual practices. By the grace of the Mother all troubles will cease. Whether your health is good or bad, don't stop your sadhana. For a time, practise constantly and hard; your health will surely improve. When the mind becomes pure and calm, the body also becomes free from ailments. Only spiritual practices can make the mind pure. Practise, practise, practise sadhana without selfish motives. One must cultivate love and devotion to God, then automatically the mind will be withdrawn from worldly objects. At that time the thought of the body won't trouble you much; the thought of the Mother will be predominant. And when that happens, one floats in bliss.

With love and best wishes,
Turiyananda

40

Varanasi
6 November 1914

Dear X,

I am glad to receive your letter of November 1, 1914. . . .

Happiness and misery alternate in this world. Have you ever seen anyone completely free from them? It is impossible: this world is made up of the pairs of opposites. By meditating on the Atman one can get rid of them. This does not mean that there will be no happiness or misery, but by God's grace they won't be able to perturb one. So Krishna said in the Gita, "Endure them, O Arjuna." [II.14] Mark, he didn't say that there would be no happiness or misery. Rather he said: "Notions of heat and cold, of pain and pleasure, arise only from the contact of the senses with their objects. They come and go; they are impermanent. So endure them." [II.14] If there were any way other than forbearance, the Lord definitely would have told his dearest friend and disciple Arjuna about it.

Sri Ramakrishna said, "Sha, sha, sa — forbear, forbear, forbear," as though he were swearing that there is no other way than to endure. He further said, "He who forbears, survives; and he who does not, perishes." Therefore we will have to forbear. There is a glory in forbearance. Pain and suffering are inevitable in life, so what good will it do to lament over them? Rather, if one can endure them, one can avoid fruitless moaning. The great saint Tulasidas said: "Suffering is inevitable for all embodied beings. In this respect there is no difference between the wise and the ignorant. But here lies the difference: The wise man endures affliction calmly, knowing full well that it is inevitable and unavoidable; whereas the ignorant man makes himself miserable by constantly weeping and wailing."

Always remember the words of the Master, "Let the affliction and the body take care of themselves; O my mind, you dwell in bliss." This will save you from being overwhelmed by suffering.

Yours,
Turiyananda

41

Varanasi
19 November 1914

Dear Sridhar [Swami Nirupamananda],

I have received your postcard dated 9 November 1914. . . .

Your nature will not allow you to be without work. Therefore, you will be better off if you work with a spirit of dedication to the Lord; in other words, for the welfare of the people. You will undoubtedly derive spiritual benefit from it. Work to the best of your ability and try to get the blessings of the Lord. It is extremely difficult to relinquish all activities and contemplate God continually, and it is not possible for everyone. Calm your mind, and engage yourself in the service of human beings as God. It will do you good. Have the firm conviction that you are an instrument and the Lord is the operator — then there will be no problem.

Always be prayerful. Work with your hands and pray to the Lord with your mind that he always remain in your heart and guide you. This will make you free from fear and anxiety. He is omniscient and all-auspicious. He will do what is good for you. So without holding any doubt in the mind, work for the Lord.

Your well-wisher,
Turiyananda

42

Varanasi
6 January 1915

Dear X,

Let me answer the first part of your question:

> An eternal portion of myself, having become a living soul in a world of living beings, draws to itself the five senses, with the mind for the sixth, which abide in prakriti [nature]. [Gita, XV.7]

Thus Krishna described the real nature of the *jiva* [the individual soul] in the Gita: The jiva is a portion of God and enjoys sense objects while residing in the body. At the time of death, it departs from the body along with the mind and the senses. Later, after experiencing pleasure and pain according to its own karma and knowledge, the jiva assumes a body again to reap the fruits of action. Thus it goes through the rounds of births and deaths until it reaches illumination.

The mind is the ruler of the senses; with its help all the senses function. The prana [vital force] remains awake and sustains the body even when the mind is asleep. Prana is the chief force in the body: when it is absent, the body is declared dead. The jiva, mind, and prana are not the same; they are different from one another.

Cosmology has been explained in the Sankhya philosophy, in many places of the Mahabharata, and also in the Upanishads. If you study the Gita carefully, you will find that cosmology has also been explained there. The sequence of creation is not the same in all philosophical systems, but that does not matter. Basically all concur. In the Yoga Vashistha Ramayana, everything has been clearly explained in detail. If you read it, you will easily understand.

With best wishes,
Turiyananda

43

Varanasi
19 February 1915

Dear D—,

It seems that your mind does not remain in a good state because of your poor health. Mind and health are closely related. But you must continue your effort to have constant recollectedness of God. If you do not look after your own good, no one else can. "Let a man be lifted up by his own self; let him not lower himself. For he himself is his friend, and he himself is his enemy." [Gita, VI.5] "Perception of the evil of birth, death, old age, sickness, and pain; nonattachment, nonidentification of self with children, wife, home, and the rest. . . . " [Gita, XIII.9-10] One is supposed to practise these virtues as they are the means of attaining knowledge.

Dry discussion does no good. One should pray for the grace of God, then one will gain the results. One should pray with heart and soul; this inner prayer is very effective. God is omniscient: he knows all our inmost thoughts. Take refuge in him with all humility. You know all these things, and I have also told you many times. What more is there to say?

In everything there is a time factor. God is very compassionate. One who waits at his door achieves something — either this very moment or in the future. There is no doubt about it. Always pray that you may have devotion to the Lord. If you can love him, all attachment to the world will drop off of itself. Once you taste divine love, everything else will become insipid. You should strive heart and soul for that devotion. Otherwise, can it be attained without any effort? If a man doesn't exert himself, no one else can help him. That is certain.

With love and best wishes,
Turiyananda

44

Varanasi
7 March 1915

Dear X,

. . . Devotion to God develops the divine nature of human beings. Krishna himself said in the Gita, "For those who take refuge in me, O Partha, though they be of low birth . . . even they attain the supreme goal." [IX.32] "So what doubt can there be that those who are of high birth will attain liberation by taking refuge in me?" After saying this, Krishna concluded: "Having come into this transitory, joyless world, worship me." [Gita, IX.33] There is no other way to be saved than by worshipping the Lord.

I could not understand the purport of your letter. You have written, "I find in the Gita 'that work which is performed with much effort is declared to be of the nature of rajas,' the result of which is suffering." After writing this you have requested, "Please let me know if this conclusion is correct." Should I understand from this [passage] that because one has to face hardship to visit Lord Shiva in Varanasi, it is not necessary, because it is rajasic karma and it results in suffering? Is that your conclusion?

You have quoted from the eighteenth chapter of the Gita, where Krishna described to Arjuna how knowledge, action, and doer are of three kinds according to the three gunas [sattva, rajas, and tamas]. You have quoted only half a verse, which is inadequate to get the meaning. After explaining sattvic karma, Krishna mentioned rajasic karma: "The action that is performed with much effort by one who seeks to gratify his desires or who is prompted by a feeling of 'I' — that action is declared to be of the nature of rajas." [XVIII.24] Now, if your conclusion is that there is hardship in sadhana, therefore it is rajas and one should not practise it; then what can I say?

Again, you have written, "For such a long time I have seen and heard so many things, still the mind does not move towards the truth. That is indeed a matter of regret." How long have you really seen and heard? King Yayati, borrowing the youth of his son, enjoyed sensual objects for ten thousand years; and then being unsatisfied, remarked: "Enjoyment cannot be satiated by enjoyment; it increases more and more as fire fed by melted butter." [Vishnu Purana, IV.10.9] Therefore, shun all worldly desires; that only brings joy in life. This is the conclusion according to the scriptures.

Yours,
Turiyananda

45

Varanasi
10 March 1915

Dear Sridhar [Swami Nirupamananda],

I have received your postcard dated March 4, 1915. . . .

I am glad to know that you are well and have resolved to continue your work. Try to make progress in that field. By the grace of the Master you will surely succeed. I asked you to start independent work because I knew that you wanted to work on your own. If one gets work of one's choice one feels at ease, which may not be the case when working for someone else. In the beginning you may feel lonely, but gradually you will get used to it and others will join you. To persist in one's work is important and it is very difficult. But if one sticks to the work under all circumstances, one surely succeeds. This is a tested truth.

Try to do good to others to the best of your ability. Seeing your example, others will learn to do the same. Do not harbour any desire in your mind, except to serve God in human beings. It will do you good. Offer your name and fame and everything to God. Be grateful to the Lord that you are able to serve him with your body and mind, and pray to him sincerely that he may, sitting in your heart, always guide you.

There will be no fear of falling if you look upon all women as manifestations of the Divine Mother and serve them to the best of your ability. Be careful — let no other feeling than that of Mother ever cross your mind. When people know your attitude towards women, none will be displeased — rather they will be pleased.

Your well-wisher,
Turiyananda

46

Varanasi
22 March 1915

Dear X,

It seems that this time also you did not understand the purport of my letter [7 March 1915], so I am writing to you in the light of my understanding. Don't think that I am displeased with you. It is true that the sattva guna is calm, luminous, and free from evil: but not everyone is endowed with it. A tamasic [lazy] person will have to reach sattva through rajas [activity]; and the rajasic person can be sattvic by subjugating the rajas. It is not enough to know that the sattva guna is peaceful, that rajas is strenuous, and that tamas is infatuating. One has to enhance the sattva guna. It is true that if a person overexerts himself practising sadhana, it may cause more harm than good. For that reason, the Gita suggested: "Let a man little by little attain tranquility." [VI.25] "Be temperate in eating and recreation and in exertion at work." [VI.17]

Overwork is not good; and by the same token a wishy-washy attitude is not good either. Sri Ramakrishna used to instruct us to resolve enthusiastically, "I shall be free in this very life." The Master might have said something different to a person with fragile health, but that should not be taken as general advice. It is the opinion of all, not only of Swami Vivekananda, that one should practise spiritual disciplines regularly. What to speak of Buddha? It is he who said, "Let this body dry up; let the skin, bones and flesh of the body fall apart; but I will not leave this seat until I attain that supreme knowledge." [*Lalita Vistara*, ch. 19] Such austerity was practised not only by Buddha but by others also; they did not achieve anything without striving unto death. The great mystic saint Chaitanya said to his disciple, "Sanatan, is it so easy to attain Krishna, the most valuable of all valuables?" Do you know how Haridas and other disciples of Chaitanya practised japam? They were oblivious of the passing of days and nights. If you read a description of Sanatan Goswami's sadhana, you will learn what he did for God-realization. The body is not permanent. One day it will surely pass away. What great fortune if the body is used for spiritual sadhana! And when a person cannot do it, he quotes, "All excess is harmful." [*Chanakya Sloka*, 48]

One should not babble in order to cover up one's inability. I shall repeat this a hundred times: There is nothing greater than sacrificing one's body for spiritual sadhana. Patanjali said in his Yoga Aphorisms [I.30]: "Disease, mental laziness, doubt, lack of interest, sloth, clinging to sense-pleasure, false perception, lack of concentration, and unsteadiness in concentration — these distractions are the obstacles to knowledge."

The great sage Vyasa said: "When there is disorder of bile secretion, sugar does not taste good in the mouth. But if one goes on taking sugar earnestly every day, one gradually begins to enjoy the taste of sugar and the disease goes away. Similarly, the name of God may not appeal to those who are in ignorance. But if one practices spiritual disciplines regularly, ignorance disappears and a taste for the Divine Name is acquired."

Yours,
Turiyananda

47

Almora
24 May 1915

Dear X,

As long as one has a body, one is subject to happiness and misery. The Chandogya Upanishad says, "As long as one is identified with the body, there is no cessation of pleasure and pain." [VIII.12.1] It is not good to spend one's whole life clinging to the body. The same Upanishad says, "But neither pleasure nor pain touches one who is not identified with the body." In this body dwells the bodiless Atman, which is untouched by good and evil. "I am the body" — this attitude makes one a victim of happiness and misery. One should try to go beyond the reach of happiness and misery by cultivating the attitude, "I am not the body; I am the Atman without a body." Undoubtedly, this will reduce a lot of suffering.

In this world, everything is created by thought. As one thinks, so one becomes. It will definitely do good if one occasionally thinks of oneself as the disembodied Atman, instead of harping on the body idea all the time. Lord Jesus said: "He that has, to him shall be given. He that has not, from him shall be taken even what he has." [Mark, 4.25] It is so true. Our Master used to say: "He who always laments, 'I have achieved nothing, I am a sinner,' and so on, he truly achieves nothing and becomes a sinner."

Therefore, don't yield to despair. Instead, try to cultivate this attitude: "I am repeating the name of the Lord. Why should I be afraid? By his grace all my difficulties will disappear." Say, "Victory to the Divine Mother!" and then engage yourself in thinking of her. Thus you will gain strength. If you yield to laziness, your tendency to remain so will continue. If you can use your willpower to get up, your inertia will go away; the very movement of your body will bring more strength. One needs great enthusiasm. The Master did not care for a namby-pamby attitude; he encouraged his disciples to adopt the attitude of a fearless robber. By the same token, Swami Vivekananda untiringly preached, "Arise, awake, and stop not till the goal is reached!" [Katha Upanishad, I.3.14]

Never fear; pray to the Lord. He will make everything favourable. He is not a stranger. Know from the bottom of your heart that he is your very own, then pray to him. Everything will be all right. This body is ephemeral, but the Lord is eternal. You must make him your own.

Never be discouraged. Summon up your mental strength and constantly think of God. He is the refuge of all. Dedicate yourself completely to him and be at rest. All fear and anxiety will leave of themselves, and a new strength will flow into your heart. Victory to the Lord!

With love and best wishes,
Turiyananda

48

Almora
3 June 1915

Dear X,

You have asked me to answer your letter within a couple of lines. Tradition goes that Rupa Goswami, a disciple of Chaitanya, sent a letter to his brother Sanatan through a brahmin which contained four pairs of letters from the Sanskrit alphabet: ya . . . ri, ra . . . la, i . . . ram, na . . . ya.

> Yadupateh kva gata mathurapuri
> Raghupateh kva gatottarakosala.
> Iti vichintya kuru svamanah sthiram
> Na sadidam jagat iti avadharaya.

When deciphered, the letters revealed this meaning:

Where now is that Mathura city, where Krishna lived?
Where now is that Ayodhya, where Rama ruled?
Thinking of this deeply, make your mind firm;
Know for certain: This world is not real.

These hints were enough for Sanatan to realize what his brother wished to convey: because Sanatan had become engrossed in worldly pleasures, he had lost all sense of discrimination. But your case is different. You have known for certain that life in this world is like a child's play: there is no substance in it. God is the only reality. And you have understood through God's grace that worshipping him is man's only duty. So it is needless to tell you, "This world is not real." You are fully aware that Krishna emphatically declared in the Gita, "Having come into this transitory, joyless world, worship me." [IX.33]

I quite understand why you have expressed your regret for not practising fully this teaching of the Gita: "Having cut down this firm-rooted Ashvattha with a strong axe of detachment, then seek the Supreme Goal." [XV.3-4] We learn from the songs of great souls like Ramprasad and Kamalakanta that in past ages many devotees felt like you. But we also find that they said repeatedly, "Wherever the Divine Mother keeps you, it is for your good." They only wanted to remember Mother in all circumstances. The Master used to sing:

In whichever way you may keep me, Mother Kali —
Besmeared with ash or bedecked with gold and jewels,
Residing under a tree or seated on a royal throne —
That is propitious if I do not forget you.

The Master would say, "The mother cat keeps the kitten sometimes on an ash-heap and sometimes on a cushion, but the kitten says nothing but 'mew, mew.'" Again he said, "The Mother knows where it will be good for the kitten to be kept." She is all-auspicious; whatever she does is good for us.

The real devotees do not ask for anything. Even if they were offered five kinds of liberation — such as living in the abode of God, having power similar to God's, and so on — they would not accept anything. [Bhagavatam, III.29.13] On the contrary, they only pray for the privilege of serving the Lord. You know this very well. Our Master could not bear the word *sin*. He emphatically forbade people to consider themselves sinners. Rather he taught them to think: "I am repeating the name of God. Why should I worry? Of whom shall a child of the Mother of the Universe be afraid?"

You said it right: If Mother wishes, in a moment she can dissolve everything and create everything anew. She not only can — she has done it and is still doing it. You have experienced this from the bottom of your heart. This is not the fancy of a madman; this is the truth. Everything belongs to God. He is the ocean of mercy and beyond all "whys." He is the wishfulfilling tree and our past, present, and future. Why should we accept anything but him as ours? "I am the Self, O Gudakesha, seated in the hearts of all creatures. I am the beginning, the middle, and the end of all beings." [Gita, X.20] These words of Krishna are our proof, refuge, and support. Why should we not say —

Thou art all good, O Lord, every moment we find proof of it.
Give us joy, give us sorrow — whatever you please;
But thou art all good.
Whatever thou mayest do, thou wilt not forsake us —
that we know.
Come, Lord, come, reveal thyself within our hearts;
And surely all will be well.

Let us pray: May our minds be fully absorbed in God. If we forget him, may he not forget us. May he endow us with discrimination and dispassion. As the scripture says, "A man with strong discrimination never suffers from the crises of the world."

Yours,
Turiyananda

49

Almora
4 July 1915

Dear D—,

I have received your letter of June 26, 1915. . . .

One gets a human body as a result of great merit in past lives. Once one is born as a human being, the gate to liberation is open. Having a human body, if one fails to strive for liberation, who knows when such an opportunity will come again? Therefore, one must make every effort to attain illumination in this very life. So it is mentioned in the scriptures: "As a result of many acts of virtue you received this body as a boat to cross the ocean of misery. Make proper use of it while yet it is not destroyed."

The Bhagavatam says: "He who after having obtained a human birth, which is like an open door to liberation, becomes attached to home like a bird — the wise ones know him as fallen from a high state." [XI.7.74] Even upon reaching the gate of liberation, a person falls again and again because of his attachment to wealth, relatives, home, or his own body. Therefore, one should shift his attachment from the world to God. Thus the attachment to and love for God make a person free. There is no other way.

God is extremely compassionate. If one takes one step towards God, he comes a hundred steps, nay a thousand steps, towards him. It is absolutely true. It is a matter of doing and not of talking. If someone could say wholeheartedly, with mind and speech united, "Lord, I take refuge in you; I have none else," the Lord will definitely accept him. It cannot be otherwise. One must say and feel:

> Thou art my mother and father;
> Thou art my friend and companion;
> Thou art my wealth and wisdom;
> Thou art my all in all, O Lord. [Prapanna Gita]

Can the Lord keep from accepting a person who prays like this? Now the question is: Who is truly praying and thinking in this way? Lord Chaitanya said:

> So vast is thy mercy, O Lord!
> How huge, then, is my wretchedness
> Who finds, in this empty life and heart,
> No devotion to thy name. [Shikshashtakam, 2]

One needs love and longing, then only will one get the results of spiritual life. Pray: "Master, give me longing for you; give me devotion." The Master answers the sincere prayer. Pray sincerely and wholeheartedly, then the Master will be pleased. When he is pleased, you will attain everything, your heart will be filled with love and devotion, and your life will be blessed. Then you will taste the bliss of this song:

> To him who meditates on Mother,
> The riches of heaven are poor indeed;
> If Shyama casts her glance on him,
> He swims in eternal bliss.

With best wishes,
Turiyananda

50

Almora
7 July 1915

Dear Bihari Babu,

You have inquired about the attainment of peace. Well, you know that real peace belongs to him "who lives completely free from desires, without longing, devoid of the sense of 'I' and 'mine,'" [Gita, II.71] and also, "Not the desirer of desires attains peace, but he into whom all desires enter as the waters enter the ocean, which is full to the brim and grounded in stillness." [Gita, II.70]

You may not have perfect peace, but surely you have some peace. The more you are able to drive away the sense of "I" and "mine" by installing the Lord in your heart, the more you will attain peace, by his grace. It cannot be otherwise. He is doing everything and we are mere instruments in his hand. By his grace, the more we master this attitude, the more our sense of "I" and "mine" will disappear, and tranquility and peace will dawn in our hearts.

The *Panchadashi* is a treatise on Vedanta, which emphasizes the path of knowledge and delineates how to practise sadhana to attain Brahman without qualities. But the Lord says in the Gita: "Fix your mind on me alone, rest your thought on me alone, and in me alone you will live hereafter. Of this there is no doubt." [XII.8] What a succulent, sweet, and joyful message!

You have asked whether a householder can attain samadhi. If it were not true [that a householder can attain samadhi], then how will the Lord's words be true? Krishna says in the Gita:

> Even the most sinful man, if he worships me with unswerving devotion, must be regarded as righteous; for he

> has formed the right resolution. . . . For those who take refuge in me, O Partha, though they be of low birth . . . even they attain the supreme goal. [Gita, IX.30,32]

Can one attain "the supreme goal" without experiencing samadhi?

One can attain samadhi even without practising the limbs of yoga according to the following aphorism of Patanjali: "One attains samadhi by dedicating everything to God." [II.45] It also is clear in this aphorism, "Or by devotion to God." [I.23] The great sage Vyasa has commented on this aphorism: "Being pleased with his devotion, God bestows grace on him. Again, by God's wish, the yogi attains samadhi and its fruits instantaneously." This is the best evidence supporting the view that one can attain samadhi without practising yoga.

In this connection you may remember the description in the tenth book of the Bhagavatam of how some gopis [cowherd girls of Vrindaban] were absorbed in God, leaving their natural bodies. "Indeed, those who constantly cherish lust, wrath, fear, affection, kinship or devotion to God, they attain oneness with him." [X.29.15] Is there any distinction between attaining oneness with God and samadhi? The fact is that there is a difference in the attitude and the means, but the ultimate attainment and its result are the same. Krishna also says in the Gita: "The state reached by men of renunciation is reached by men of action too. He who sees that the way of renunciation and the way of action are one — he truly sees." [V.5]

In the twelfth chapter of the Gita, Krishna described both worship of God with attributes and without attributes, and then concluded that the worship of God with attributes is easy and joyful. And he clearly stated that he himself saves the devotee. Therefore, I don't understand why we should forsake such a compassionate Lord and take refuge in someone else.

With love and best wishes,
Turiyananda

51

Almora
11 July 1915

Dear Girija,

I was pleased to receive your letter the day before yesterday.

You are doing well. Continue in this manner. Never forget this adage of Swami Vivekananda: "Make your own fair — whether you have a companion or not." To whom else should you look for help? The Master used to say, "I am and my Mother is." That is all. Whom else do you want? The main thing is to adhere to the ideal with patience. If you can do that, gradually everything will be favourable. Hold on to the Master; you will be surprised at the result that will follow. The Master used to say, "An imitation custard-apple reminds one of the real fruit." Similarly, the Master's photograph will remind you of the Master. Feel his presence in his photograph and devote yourself to his service and worship. You will surely be imbued with his spirit.

Just make up your mind to engage yourself in the Lord's work. Let others go wherever they please; you calmly stay in your place with your beloved Master. Let your body and mind be absorbed in him. What will you gain by running around? Days are passing by, never to return. Don't forget your main task. Make the Master your very own. Then everything will follow by itself. Those who are devoted to the

Master and want to practise sadhana, please allow them to stay with you. There is nothing wrong with that if the monks live on alms.

Atul rightly said that in the beginning there was so much insistence on getting a house, and now that you have it, there is no one to live in it. And again, it may so happen that your place will be overcrowded and you won't be able to accommodate all. Every undertaking passes through different stages. One needs infinite patience. If one perseveres, then after a while everything becomes favourable. Man cannot accomplish anything because of impatience. Success is inevitable for one who continues on with patience.

At present I have no plan to go to Kankhal, but that does not mean I have no sympathy for you. I support you fully. Continue your spiritual disciplines fearlessly and wholeheartedly. Whatever others say about you, don't pay any attention to it. Never deviate from your spiritual path. You will succeed, I am confident of it. Victory to the Lord! Gird your loins and plunge into the task.

With love and best wishes,
Turiyananda

52

Almora
21 July 1915

Dear X,

I have received your letter of July 14, 1915. I am glad to know that you are keeping well. When the body is fit, spiritual disciplines, recollectedness of God, and meditation become easy. So one can realize the truth of this Sanskrit saying, "The body is indeed the first requisite for spiritual life." I am extremely delighted to know that, by God's grace, you are having deep meditation. What more is needed than to think of him? Everything of this world will be left behind. If you can make the Lord your own, it will be a true accomplishment here and hereafter. His relationship with us is eternal — not only for ten or twenty years.

You want to know the characteristics of a person who is trying to live in this world while taking refuge in God. This is a good question. But it is more important to resign oneself to God than to know the signs of it, because the signs will manifest themselves. Yet it is not a bad idea to know the signs of a person of self-surrender.

The characteristics are generally of two kinds. First, *sva-samvedya* — that which is known intuitionally by oneself. This is the best method. Second, *para-samvedya* — that which is known by others. Seeing the external signs of a person, people understand that he has attained knowledge. But there is the possibility of a mistake in this second method, because the external signs may not be genuine. They may appear from some cause other than knowledge. So this method is not flawless. On the other hand, there is no chance of error in what is tested by and realized through one's own experience. Therefore that [sva-samvedya] is true. Only the eater himself knows whether his stomach is full or not.

For instance, others may think that a person is angry if they see that his face is flushed. This is para-samvedya, or the signs known by others. But this knowledge can be wrong, because without being angry, the signs of anger may manifest on someone's face for some reason other than anger. Just by feigning anger, one may manifest these signs. Only an angry person knows undoubtedly whether his anger is genuine or not. This is sva-samvedya, or his own experience. He may not even show the signs of anger [and yet be angry]. Therefore, one's own experience alone is real and flawless.

However, the signs you have mentioned in your letter are wonderful. Once you take refuge in God, there is no more dependence on any other person; and the feeling of fearlessness spontaneously arises from within. For then one feels God's grace and realizes that the Lord is protecting him. All bad thoughts leave his mind; good tendencies always manifest in his heart; and a great tranquility reigns supreme within him. All these are signs of sva-samvedya, or he who knows by himself. Others see him free from worry, calm, loving towards all, and always content, cheerful, and so on. These are the signs that become apparent to others. There are other characteristics too. What more is there to write.

Yours,
Turiyananda

53

Almora
24 July 1915

Dear Bihari Babu,

Very little happens through my will — "It is God's will that always prevails." I am greatly pleased that you prayed for my recovery. Please accept my heartfelt thanks for it. Your desire to realize God is praiseworthy. The Kena Upanishad says: "If a man knows the Atman here, he then attains the true goal of life. If he does not know It here, a great destruction awaits him." [II.5] He who longs for God surely attains him. "The Atman is attained by him alone whom It chooses." [Katha Upanishad, I.2.23] "I search and seek but cannot find him. He, who is chosen by him, finds him." One can realize God very easily. He is extremely kind. But who wants him? That is the question. God has promised, "I will reveal myself instantly if anybody seeks me genuinely." But who seeks him? Such is the play of Mahamaya — the Great Enchantress! The Divine Mother keeps us busy with various things, and we do not feel inclined to seek her.

In this connection, Sri Ramakrishna told a parable: The grain merchant keeps puffed rice and sweetened rice on a winnowing fan at the entrance of the warehouse. Attracted by its smell, mice come and eat it sumptuously. They are completely unaware of the huge quantity of rice in the warehouse, although it is there. In the same way, man is happy in the company of his wife and children. He does not endeavour to have divine bliss, although God dwells within his very heart. Such is the play of Mahamaya! There is a song:

When such delusion veils the world, through
 Mahamaya's spell,
That Brahma is bereft of sense,
And Vishnu loses consciousness,
What hope is left for men?
The narrow channel first is made, and there the trap is set;
But open though the passage lies,
The fish, once safely through the gate,
Do not come out again.
The silkworm patiently prepares its closely spun cocoon;
Yet even though a way leads forth,
Encased within its own cocoon,
The worm remains to die.

Such is the delusion of Mahamaya! But there is a message of hope and fearlessness:

> Those who take refuge in me alone, shall cross over this maya. . . . Take refuge in him alone with all your soul, O Bharata. By his grace will you gain supreme peace and the everlasting abode. [Gita, VII.14, XVIII.62]

One needs faith [shraddha]. By God's grace, when faith dawns in the heart one becomes fearless. "He who is full of faith and zeal and has subdued his senses obtains knowledge; having obtained knowledge, he soon attains the supreme peace." [Gita, IV.39] It does not matter what other people say — one realizes this peace oneself; one feels it within. It is called *sva-samvedya*, or one's own experience, and others' opinions do not change it. The heart of a realized soul remains full of bliss; "He neither grieves nor desires." [Gita, XVIII.54] It is not at all impossible to realize this state through the grace of the Lord. A room covered with darkness for a thousand years becomes lighted in a moment by striking a single match.

The Master used to say, "All jackals howl alike." That is to say, all people have the same experience when they attain the supreme knowledge. And no contradictions exist in their utterances. They are all the children of the Divine Mother. Opinions differ, paths differ, but they all reach the same goal. "As all rivers flow into the same ocean, so people following different paths — straight or crooked — according to their temperaments, will reach the same goal." [Shiva-mahimnah Stotram, 7]

"Uncle moon is everybody's uncle" — is there any error in it? Why do you consider yourself weak-minded? You are the child of the Divine Mother — endowed with infinite strength. "He whose mother is the Divine Mother, how can he be afraid of anybody?"

The great saint Ramprasad sang:

> Safe do I stand by drawing round me the magic circle
>   of Kali's name.
> If you speak harshly to me, O Death,
> And I report it to the Mother, you will be punished.

> Shyama, the Destroyer of death, is a madcap woman.
> Listen, O Death, to what I say: I am not a weakling
> That I will obey you meekly.
> This is not a sweetmeat in a child's hand
> That you will cajole it away and eat it.

Does the Mother's child lack any strength? By her grace you possess infinite power. The Master used to say, "She is not a Mother in name only; she is one's own real Mother." "The Divine Mother is the embodiment of Brahman and dwells in all beings, and pervades all places, such as, Gaya, Ganga, and Kashi."

> O Mother, you are the power of Vishnu and the origin of infinite energy. You are the primeval maya and the source of this cosmos. O Goddess, you have enchanted the whole world by your deluding charms. If you become gracious, you bestow liberation on human beings. [Chandi, XI.5]

This Power of Brahman [Brahmamayi] is our Mother. What fear could we have? Why should we be weak? He who thinks himself weak becomes weak. You are Mother's child. How can you be weak? You are all-powerful. By her grace, what can you not accomplish? How long does it take to get rid of the sense of "I and mine"? Mother, out of mercy, can illumine the heart in a moment — and truly she does.

Yours,
Turiyananda

54

Almora
27 July 1915

Dear Suresh [Swami Yatiswarananda],

Very glad to have received your letter the day before yesterday after a long time. . . . May the Lord have his work done through you, and may you all carry out that work with your heart and soul and be blessed! What more is there to covet?

I could not understand why you lamented in your letter: "So far I have not experienced anything; I am passing my days in sorrow." If you really feel sad for not having God-realization, rest assured that your auspicious moment is at hand. The more intensely you feel like that, know that the Lord's grace is approaching. But if any other desire lurking in the mind creates this sort of depressed mood, try to remove it immediately. Do not neglect this, because such a mood is the greatest obstacle in the path of spiritual life. Always try to become competent for your spiritual journey, then the Lord will be pleased and make you the recipient of all bliss.

"Remain in the house of your guru like a cow, without murmur" — this is what Swamiji learned from a celebrated saint [Pavhari Baba of Gazipur] and used to repeat to us. Another most beneficent teaching the saint gave was, "Look upon your brother disciples as you do your guru."

Our main duty is to wait with all humility at the Lord's door. If you can do that, his mercy is bound to come; and sadness will be replaced by great joy. "It is God's immense grace that he has allowed me to remain at his door" — he who realizes this undoubtedly receives his full grace without delay. Try to love God with all your heart and soul. Why do you care so much about joy and sorrow? Surrender to him, and know that wherever he keeps you is good for you. Pray wholeheartedly that the attitude of self-surrender may be firmly established in your mind. Then everything will be fine.

Your well-wisher,
Turiyananda

55

Almora
14 August 1915

Dear Bihari Babu,

This is the nature of the body: Time consumes childhood and gives way to youth, and youth to old age. The body is decaying day by day. "The human body is not everlasting." "He who is born, must die. Who is or ever was immortal?" He is really fortunate who is not afflicted along with the affliction of the body. It is not a small matter to know oneself as separate from the body. Such a person enjoys supreme bliss by God's grace.

Why are you anxious about your wife and children? What I said was: Surrendering everything to God, be at peace. Your wife, son, and all belong to him; and your responsibility is to take care of them. As the Master said: "A maidservant in the house of a rich man brings up her master's children as if they were her own. But in her own mind she knows very well that they do not belong to her at all, and her home is somewhere else." You should have inner renunciation. Be unattached and know that your family belongs to the Lord. There are no obstacles for devotees like you; obstacles arise for those who try to know God through discussion. For people like you, Krishna said: "Solely out of compassion for them, I, dwelling in their hearts, dispel with the shining lamp of wisdom the darkness born of ignorance. . . . To them, whose minds are absorbed in me, verily I become ere long, O Partha, the saviour from the death-fraught ocean of the world. . . . I will deliver you from all sins." [Gita, X.11,XII.7, XVIII.66]

The Lord himself has taken all responsibility for you. There is a saying, "God bears the burden of a fortunate person." You are all fortunate people. The verses you have quoted are meant for the followers of knowledge, who are afraid to be reborn. But the devotees of the Lord pray: "O Krishna, even though I be born among insects, birds, beasts, reptiles, demons, ghouls, or men or wheresoever, still through your grace may I have unshakable and unwavering devotion to you." [Prapanna Gita]

The Master told me: "Those who seek nirvana are selfish and small-minded. They are full of fear. They are like those parcheesi players who are always eager to reach home. An amateur player, once he sends his piece home, doesn't like to bring it out again. Such players are unskilled. But an adept player is never afraid of coming out again, if by doing so he gets the opportunity to capture an opponent. Then he rolls the right number and returns home once more. It seems that whenever he rolls the dice, the right number comes up for him. So do not fear. Play without any fear."

I asked, "Does it actually happen?" The Master replied: "Of course it happens. By Mother's grace everything takes place. Mother likes people to play. Take the game of hide-and-seek. [*There is a granny, there is a thief who is blindfolded, and there are children trying to escape being caught by the thief.*] The granny likes to have the children run about and make the game go on. She may extend her hand to help a child so he will not be caught by the thief, if she thinks it necessary. Similarly, the Divine Mother is not really pleased with those who seek nirvana, for they want to retire from the game. She wants the game to continue. That is why devotees do not seek nirvana. They say, 'O mind, it is not good to become sugar. I want to eat sugar.'"

The Master told me many times: "What is there in the scriptures? They are like sheets of paper with a shopping list on them. The list is useful only to check off the items once purchased. When you have done that, the list is thrown away. So you should check your knowledge and your devotion, then consult the scriptures to see whether they agree. It is said, 'When you have the knowledge of the Absolute, the scriptures are worth only a straw.'" The Divine Mother had shown Sri Ramakrishna what was in the scriptures, the Puranas, and the Tantric literature. So, though he was an unlettered person, he was able to lower the pride of the pandits. He used to say, "If you get a tiny ray of light from the Divine Mother, it makes all learning pale into insignificance."

You are struggling your utmost to attain the treasure of wisdom. By gathering the treasure of devotion, you enjoy Divine Bliss. That very treasure [Sri Ramakrishna] — either because of our good fortune or his unconditional grace — has manifested himself before us. Therefore, all that we need to do is to love him with all our heart and soul, then all else will come about of its own accord. If one can love him, one will forget the world. And through his grace body-consciousness also goes away. As regards success through austerities or reasoning — those who believe in such, let them be — we are disappointed in that respect, so we have taken refuge in the Master. Now we are waiting at his door, thinking, "let him do what he likes." I know he is also your refuge, so there is nothing to fear.

With love and best wishes,
Turiyananda

56

Almora
12 September 1915

Dear Bihari Babu,

You have written a very long letter, but what purpose does it serve? It reminds me of the Master's saying with reference to "squeezing the almanac": "The almanac predicts that there will be a great flood during the year. But if you squeeze the book, you won't get one drop of water." In the scriptures many things are written about the various states of God-realization, such as *jivan-mukta* [liberated-in-life], *paramahamsa* [an adept who enjoys enlightenment], and so on. But what good is this if these states are not realized or manifested in our lives? There is a verse which says: "The learning which is confined in books and the wealth which is in the hands of another man serve no purpose when the need for them arises." [*Chanakya Sloka*]

This much I have understood — that nothing can be achieved through self-will. It seems to me absolutely true that without his grace, nobody can attain God or any high spiritual states.

O foolish mind, think of Rama always;
What is the good of hundreds of other thoughts?
O tongue, chant unceasingly the name of Rama;
What gain is there in vain meaningless talk?
O ears, hear the story of Rama;
What benefit do you get by listening to secular music?
O eyes, behold everything as full of Rama;
And give up all else besides Rama.

This is the real truth. If we can practise this recollectedness of God, we will be saved. Otherwise there is no escape from suffering and the rounds of birth and death.

"Uncle moon is everybody's uncle." "I search and seek but can't find him. One who is chosen by him, finds him." Everyone has the right to worship God. She is everybody's real mother, not a "godmother." None has come to this world without purpose. Why do you consider yourself an animal? You are a true child of the Mother. Mother's children have no fear; therefore, neither you nor I have any fear. As she keeps us, so we shall remain — this much I know. Because my puny intellect is limited, I do not understand what is good and what is bad. "Thou art beyond good and evil, take me also beyond them" — this is my heartfelt prayer. "I don't know how and in what way you will lead me beyond, Lord, but I have the conviction that you will." The Master said: "None will remain unfed. Everybody will get food, but some will get it in the morning, some at noon, and some in the evening." Let thy will be done! That is all.

The state of a knower of Brahman is a lofty one. I don't care to know these high-flown things. I told you once that my main support is this saying of the Gita: "Verily I become ere long their saviour from the death-fraught ocean of the world." [XII.7] "For the ideal of the Unmanifest is hard to attain for those who are embodied." [Gita, XII.5] I am unfortunate because still I cannot transcend the body-consciousness. Therefore, it is very difficult for me to attain that imperishable absolute Brahman. This does not mean that we are helpless without the knowledge of Brahman. I became convinced of this, it seems, as a result of the Master's words. Let me tell you an incident.

One day when I went to see Sri Ramakrishna, there were many other visitors. Among them was a great Vedantic scholar. The Master said to him, "Let us hear some Vedanta from you." The scholar with great deference expounded on Vedanta for more than an hour. Sri Ramakrishna was very pleased. The people around were surprised at this, but after eulogizing the scholar, the Master said: "As far as I am concerned, I do not like all those details. There is nothing but my Mother and I. To you, knowledge, knower, and known — the one who meditates, meditation, and the object of meditation — this sort of triple division is very good. But for me, 'Mother and I' — that is all and nothing else." These words, "Mother and I," were said in such a way that it made a very deep impression on all present. At that moment all ideas of Vedanta paled into insignificance. The Master's "Mother and I" seemed easier, simpler, and more pleasing to the mind than the three divisions of Vedanta. I realized then that "Mother and I" was the ideal attitude to be adopted.

It is true that meditation, japam, and austerity are mental activities; but spiritual experience is also a mental activity. Meditation is not possible with a worldly mind. Meditation is the activity of the pure mind when it has been purified by japam and austerity. "The goal of spiritual practices is to realize the Atman" — this means that the mind must be purified, and then one experiences the Atman. Attainment of the Atman does not mean that It is to be brought from somewhere else. It is always present, but covered. This covering exists in man's mind and must be removed. Nothing can veil the Atman. It is self-luminous and eternal.

For example, a woman was searching for her necklace here and there, forgetting that it was around her neck, but covered by her sweater. She finds it later when she becomes aware of its presence [under the sweater]. Similarly, the Atman always exists, although the knowledge of the Atman is absent. When this knowledge dawns, it is said to be the attainment of the Atman. Otherwise, It is ever-attained. The Atman can only be known by the pure mind. Thus the mind becomes pure: "When the mind is attached to sense objects, it becomes impure. When it is detached from sense objects, it becomes pure." The same mind, when it is shifted from sense objects to God, becomes pure.

When a pet cat goes to the forest, it becomes a wild cat. One's imagination (of the truth) ripens into realization. Today's imagination becomes tomorrow's realization. But one should hold onto the truth firmly. If one imagines in the beginning then realization may follow, otherwise it will not. The Atman is first to be heard of, then reflected on, and finally meditated upon. Afterwards, when It is experienced, that is known as realization.

Yours,
Turiyananda

57

Almora
29 September 1915

Dear Bihari Babu,

I am glad to receive your letter of September 21. . . .

I have not thrown Vedanta overboard. Is it a thing to be thrown away? Vedanta indeed is our life. But the question is: What is Vedanta? You have given a wonderful exposition; I don't find anything more to say about it. However, I want to point out that no worshipper worships mere matter: the embodiment of Satchidananda [Existence-Knowledge-Bliss] is the Chosen Deity and the object of worship to all worshippers. People who have desires pray for heaven and other objects of enjoyment. Krishna says in the Gita: "Having enjoyed the vast heavenly world, they come back to the world of mortals when their merit is exhausted. Thus abiding by the injunctions of the three Vedas and desiring desires, they are subject to death and rebirth." [IX.21]

This is for the ritualists who perform Vedic sacrifices for heaven; heaven is neither the goal of the devotees nor the jnanis [the followers of knowledge].

Now the topic of discussion is the Atman: The Atman is Existence-Knowledge-Bliss Absolute, and consciousness itself. The devotees, according to their temperaments, look upon the same Atman, or Brahman, as an object of worship in different ways. Some look upon him as the whole, and they are his parts; some consider themselves identified with him; and again, some consider him as the Lord and regard themselves as separate from him. But even they [the dualists] do not regard themselves as matter; on the contrary, they also consider themselves to be consciousness. So we see, nowhere is it said that the worshipper is matter. Both the worshipper and the worshipped are consciousness; only the attitudes of the worshippers are different according to their temperaments.

I think it will not be out of context if I mention a delightful story of Rama and his devotee Hanuman. Once Rama was seated in an assembly of saints and sages and saw Hanuman in the audience. To satisfy all of his devotees, Rama asked Hanuman, "How do you look upon me?" Hanuman, who was the "wisest among the wise," thought within himself: "The Lord knows our inmost thoughts. Still, as he has asked this question, there must be some deep significance behind it." Thinking thus, Hanuman said: "O Lord, when I identify myself with the body I am your servant. When I consider myself as an individual soul, I am part of you. And when I look upon myself as the Atman, I am one with you — this is my firm conviction."

By this statement Hanuman expressed the feelings of all classes of devotees. This is the conclusion of all schools of Vedanta. No one has been neglected. On the contrary, everyone has been given his due place. He who has not transcended the body-consciousness, for him is the servant attitude: "Lord, you are my master and I am your servant." He who thinks of himself as an individual soul [jiva] and has transcended body consciousness to some extent, but not fully, for him is the attitude of the whole-and-part: "Lord, you are the whole and I am part of you." And he who has realized the Atman, for him is the attitude of nondifference: "You and I are one." There is no sense of separateness in that feeling.

These views represent three schools of Vedanta: Dualism, Qualified Nondualism, and Nondualism. Rama, in order to satisfy all the devotees assembled before him, expressed these three aspects of truth through the lips of Hanuman, the greatest of all devotees. This is the best exposition of the truth of Vedanta.

Nobody has to be disappointed. In whatever circumstances people may be placed, all are worshipping the same God and all are connected with him only. Krishna says in the Gita:

> I am seated in the hearts of all; from me are memory and knowledge, and their loss as well. It is I alone who am to be known through all the Vedas; I am indeed the author of Vedanta and knower of the Vedas. [XV.15]

That one Supreme Being, the embodiment of all-pervading consciousness, envelops all — within and without. He is the object of knowledge of all the Vedas; he is the creator of Vedanta; and he is also the knower of the Vedas. One who knows this, knows Vedanta. If one does not perceive this, truly one has not understood anything about Vedanta, although he might have studied all the books. This is what I have understood. "I am and my Mother is" — I have understood the meaning of the Master's saying thus: he did not refer to matter and consciousness. He only talked about consciousness: "The worshipped is conscious and so is the worshipper. The child's attitude is that he knows none besides mother. This is called one-pointed devotion."

The Lord is everything. Krishna says in the Gita: "What need is there of your acquiring this detailed knowledge, O Arjuna? With a single fragment of myself I stand supporting the whole universe." [X.42] It is also mentioned in the Rig Veda: "All beings and the universe are only one quarter of him; the remaining three quarters dwell in the immortal heaven." [X.90.3] Thus Brahman has been described.

Now about the individual soul, or jiva: the jiva evolves from the dualistic experience to the qualified nondualistic and at last ends in the nondualistic experience. This is the unanimous truth of Vedanta. Brahman indeed is all. He is the proof, the provable, and the prover. He is the Atman, the jiva, and the universe. There is nothing apart from Brahman. One who says that there is something besides Brahman remains deluded. This person is like someone who speaks while asleep but is not aware of it.

The unmanifested Brahman appears to be manifested through the process of superimposition and de-superimposition. In this context, the Taittiriya Upanishad referred to creation: "From the Atman [Brahman] was born* akasa [space], from space, air," and so on. [II.1.3] It does not indicate real creation. "There is neither dissolution nor creation, none in bondage and none practising disciplines. There is none seek-

*From the standpoint of Brahman, Brahman alone exists. It is changeless, nondual, neither a cause nor an effect. Therefore it cannot be maintained that anything is really born of Brahman. From the standpoint of Brahman one cannot speak of creation. We speak of creation only from the standpoint of the relative world, which is conjured up by avidya or ignorance. Therefore avidya alone, which inheres in Brahman as Its creative power, is the cause of creation.

ing liberation and none liberated. This is the absolute truth." [Mandukya Karika, II.32] This is the conclusion of Vedanta.

You know that the Lord has declared in the Bhagavatam [III.29.13] that a true devotee is desireless and would not accept even heaven and liberation if offered; he only prays for the privilege of serving the Lord. Nobody says that scriptural study, japam, austerities, meditation, concentration, or samadhi are the ultimate goal. "Only by knowing God does one pass over death; there is no other way to the supreme goal." [Svetasvatara Upanishad, III.8] This is the declaration of Vedanta.

Furthermore, Krishna says in the Gita:

> The dwellers in all the worlds, from the realm of Brahma downward, are subject to rebirth, O Arjuna; but for those who reach me, O son of Kunti, there is no further return to embodiment. . . . I am the Self, O Gudakesha, seated in the hearts of all creatures. I am the beginning, the middle, and the end of all beings. . . . I am the goal and the support; the Lord and the witness; the abode, the refuge, and the friend. I am the origin and the dissolution; the ground, the storehouse, and the imperishable seed." [VIII.16, X.20, IX.18]

Therefore it is no longer necessary to elaborate that God is our all-in-all. Having come to the mango garden, it is best to eat mangoes. What is the use of counting leaves? Those who are entrusted by the Lord as teachers, they will consider others' problems and guide them in their spiritual pursuits. We will be blessed if we can eat mangoes. May the Master introduce you to the owner of the mango garden [God] — that is my earnest prayer to him.

Yours,
Turiyananda

58

Dear Sachin,

I was glad to receive your letter. May such zeal and longing never leave you. Everyone should have great earnestness in order to improve this life and to cultivate purity of heart. Thus one attains devotion to God and makes his life blessed. I am delighted to know that you have such longing. May the Master bestow strength on you — that is my fervent prayer.

It is extremely difficult to control the senses, but there is no other way. You have asked which sense organ should be controlled first. Regarding this, Krishna said in the Gita: "The yogi restrains them all and remains intent on me. His wisdom is steady whose senses are under control." [II.61] Manu said: "If even a single one of the senses is uncontrolled, all knowledge leaves a person just as water drains from a leaking water vessel." [Manu Samhita, II.99]

Therefore all the senses should be brought under control. Although all senses are turbulent, the tongue and sex organ are undoubtedly the prominent ones. It is mentioned in the Bhagavatam: "Even if a person has gained mastery over all the other senses, he cannot be called conqueror of the senses until he has subdued the tongue. If the tongue is conquered, all the other senses are as good as conquered." [XI.8.21] Therefore control of the tongue is the first duty. But the Lord has said from another standpoint: "The objects of the senses fall away from a man practising abstinence, but not the taste for them. But even the taste falls away when the Supreme is seen." [Gita, II.59]

Our Master used to say, "He who has tasted syrup made from sugar candy regards a drink made from treacle as a mere trifle." In other words, if one has developed love for God, one does not care for human love. One should have love for God, then sense objects will become distasteful. Everything becomes worthless in comparison. As "the more you go towards the east, the farther you will be from the west"; likewise, the more you go towards the Lord, the more you will leave sense attractions behind. One need not make any special attempt to get rid of them. That is the secret. The essential thing is to worship God. If you do that, you will not have to strive to control the tongue and other senses — they will be controlled automatically.

To worship God means to dedicate one's heart, soul, and everything to him. He will then become the dearest of all, and all of one's longing will be directed towards him. If one cries to see God and to love him, God bestows devotion on the heart of that person. His grace is needed; without it nothing can be achieved. But the Master used to say: "If a person takes one step towards God, God comes a hundred steps towards him. He is very compassionate." This is our lasting hope.

Try to love the Lord with your heart and soul. Then you will see how compassionate he is. It does not matter much what you eat or wear. There is no harm in fulfilling some of your small desires, but this should be done with discrimination. You must watch carefully so that you may not be attracted to anything else besides God. Holy company, studying holy books which speak of God, and avoiding evil company — these are needed for the cultivation of devotion. Thus try to proceed towards the Lord, then there will be no fear at all. He who takes refuge in the Lord becomes free from anxiety and troubles. Krishna says in the Gita, "By his grace will you gain supreme peace and the everlasting abode." [XVIII.62] What more shall I write? Take refuge in him alone; you will attain uninterrupted bliss.

With love and best wishes,
Turiyananda

59

Almora
23 October 1915

Dear B—,

I received your letter yesterday after a long time. I am happy to know that you are keeping well and carrying on with your work. Only the Lord knows what his will is. It is beyond the reach of the human intellect. But what we understand from the scriptures and the great saints is this: He is all good. He brings out the good even in what seems terrible and incongruous to us. If one has firm faith in this idea, one will have peace; otherwise, one will undergo inevitable unrest and suffering. Krishna says in the Gita, "Having known me, who am the dispenser of all sacrifices and austerities, the great Lord of all worlds, the friend of all beings, one attains peace." [V.29]

We were saddened to read the description you have given about the suffering of the people. But one thing comes to my mind: This is a great opportunity to serve the Lord to your heart's content. I hope you remember the words of Swamiji:

> These are His manifold forms before thee,
> Rejecting them, where seekest thou for God?
> [*To a Friend*, a poem]

If you can properly serve those famine stricken people, you will thereby undoubtedly serve the Lord. Blessed are you all! The Lord has given you this wonderful opportunity to serve him. Take the fullest advantage of it and make your lives blessed. What more shall I say? Your mental condition also will be good if you can serve with the right attitude. Try it and you will see the result. Without actual practice, how will you understand? Your problem with lust will disappear.

Lust is nothing but weakness of the mind. Just as a fire dies out if you do not add fuel to it, similarly, lust leaves you if you don't supply it with enjoyment. When you feel lust, pray intensely to the Lord and cry for his help. Then you will find that lust will not arise again.

Practise japam and meditation regularly as much as you can. And don't consider your work as mere secular work, rather regard it as worshiping the Lord. "Whatever work I shall do will be my worship of thee, O Lord!" [Shiva-manasa-puja Stotram, 4] "Yoga is skill in action." [Gita, II.50] Ordinary work, done in a spirit of dedication to the Lord and thus transformed into worship, becomes yoga. Such performance is a great feat! That work really becomes worship when it is done by effacing one's ego and resigning oneself to God. It is enough if you can remember this. If you don't succeed all at once, practise this again and again.

With best wishes,
Turiyananda

60

Almora
25 October 1915

Dear Priyanath,

I am extremely pained at learning about the distressed condition of the Bankura people. X. also wrote a heartrending description in his letter. You are now supposed to serve the famine stricken people to your utmost and make your life blessed. Instead, you have expressed your lack of understanding. Reading your letter, I was surprised and very sad. You have asked for my blessings so that you may be released from that work. But when you are released from it, what work will you do? Worshipping the Lord? "Who loves all beings without distinction, he indeed is worshipping best his God." [*To a Friend*, a poem] Have you forgotten this message of Swamiji?

Swamiji has left you all such an easy method for attaining liberation. Have you forgotten it in such a short time?

These are His manifold forms before thee,
Rejecting them, where seekest thou for God? [*To a Friend*]

Krishna says in the Gita, "Not by merely abstaining from action does a man reach the state of actionlessness." [III.4] Without action, how will you make yourself free from action? Harbouring such wrong ideas, don't indulge in idleness and consequently fall victim to tamas, or inertia. Rather work wholeheartedly. But why call it work? It is worship. Do this real worship and make your life blessed. Know for certain that such an opportunity does not come often.

Yours,
Turiyananda

61

Almora
26 October 1915

Dear X,

I was pleased to receive your letter on the occasion of Vijaya [Durga Puja]; and you also accept my blessings. I am glad to know that there was Durga worship in your village and that many poor people were served in that connection. It is good that you took part in the service of the poor people. The more you try to do good to others, the more it is good for you.

I am happy to hear of your spiritual experiences. You have witnessed for yourself how you have benefitted from your vision and other experiences. It is needless to raise any question in this regard. If one prays from the bottom of one's heart, God undoubtedly listens.

What you have experienced is beautiful. Both God with form and God without form are true. The snake is a snake whether it is coiled up motionless or wriggling along. The ocean is the ocean whether it is calm or full of waves. Therefore, Brahman is always the same whether It is with form or without form. People, according to their aptitudes, love Brahman, or God, differently. But there is no difference in the object of love — the same Satchidananda — without beginning, without end, all-pervading consciousness.

Practise your meditation regularly. Don't yield to any slackness in your spiritual disciplines. By the grace of the Lord, the cloud of ignorance will go away. Why do you consider philanthropic work as work? Do it as worship. "Who loves all beings without distinction, he indeed is worshipping best his God" — maintain this attitude. Then the work will not be distasteful to you. . . .

With love and best wishes,
Turiyananda

62

Almora
31 October 1915

Dear Bihari Babu,

I am glad to receive your letter of May 27 enclosed with two rough sketches [of the six centres of the kundalini]. Previously I have seen a similar diagram of the kundalini published by the Theosophical Society and also some drawings by others. This human body is the ultimate machine where even Brahma and Vishnu are caught and gasping for breath. That is why the Master used to sing:

O Mother, what a machine [the human body] is this that thou has made!
What pranks thou playest with this toy
Three and a half cubits high!
Hiding thyself within, thou holdest the guiding string;
But the machine, not knowing it,
Still believes it moves by itself.
Whoever finds the Mother remains a machine no more;
Yet some machines have even bound
The Mother herself with the string of love.

The Divine Mother is hidden within this body-machine; only by knowing her alone can one escape from it. Otherwise, one will have to remain in this machine, rotating endlessly through birth and death, pleasure and pain. So the mystic saint Ramprasad sang, "Oh Mother, remove the blindfold from my eyes, and let me see thy form that banishes fear."

May the Mother be gracious and take away this blindfold from our eyes — this is my earnest prayer to her.

Yours,
Turiyananda

63

Almora
3 November 1915

Dear Priyanath,

I am really sad to learn about the terrible famine in that place [Bankura]. The Lord alone knows what his will is; but you, for your part, should try to help the people to your utmost capacity. Let there be no negligence of your duty.

I don't like your arguments — they are good for nothing. You know this proverb, "Cut the coat according to the cloth."

Distribute the relief commodities according to the supply. What else can you do? But it is entirely up to you whether or not this charity is given with love and respect. And there is the test of your spirit of service. You are not anybody's servant working as an official on duty — rather, work in the spirit of religious service. Of course your superiors, who are directing the relief operation, are bound to spend according to their collection. What else can they do if they don't have sufficient funds? You too should spend according to what you receive — that is no problem. The problem lies in the lack of right attitude. Whatever you have, consider that to be Mother Annapurna's [the goddess of food] store and use it; therein lies the success of the work. Otherwise, what is the use of talking about things which you don't have?

Perhaps you have read the story of a general whose son complained that he couldn't fight his enemies because his sword was too short. The general replied, "Add a step to it." That is very sensible advice. He who blames others proves his own inadequacy. Here are some Bengali proverbs: "The child wants that which is not found in the country." "A bad dancer blames the stage." "Those who really know how to play, will play under any condition."

It is out of love and not out of hunger that Krishna ate broken rice-grain from the great devotee Vidura and banana peel instead of banana from Vidura's wife. These beautiful stories are well-known, and everybody talks about them. The important thing is: what is your attitude? If you put your mind one hundred percent on the work, success is bound to come. You need not see what others are doing; you watch yourself and see what you are doing. To the good, everything is good — this is so true!

Yours,
Turiyananda

64

Almora
19 November 1915

Dear X,

I was delighted to receive your postcard dated November 15. Quite often I get news of you and think of your welfare. Saint Tulasidas said nicely: "The lily dwells in the water and the moon in the sky, but that does not affect their friendship. [The lily blooms at night to show its beauty to its beloved moon.] Similarly, he who dwells in another's heart dwells very close to him." My heart is with you. Although I am residing on this remote Himalayan mountain, I indeed feel you are near to me.

Only the will of the Lord comes to pass. What more can I say? I am extremely happy to learn that you are well and serving people as a form of worship. Once Swami Vivekananda complained that Sri Ramakrishna had too much affection for him, and quoted the mythical story of King Jada Bharata who was born as a deer because of his attachment for the deer. Then Sri Ramakrishna replied that there was no such danger as long as one saw God in the person loved. Therefore I don't find any cause for your fear of having affection for others. You are worshipping God — the other things you do are only external. You know very well that book-learning does not really save our lives. Krishna says in the Gita, "No evil, my son, befalls a man who does good." [VI.40] Given this, where is room for your misapprehension?

With love and best wishes,
Turiyananda

65

Almora
20 November 1915

My dear Baburam Maharaj [Swami Premananda],

I was very happy to receive your loving letter the day before yesterday. . . . The memory of all past associations with you gives me great joy. And why shouldn't it be so? You are so full of the Master [Sri Ramakrishna] that there is no room within you for anything else. This reminds me of an incident which took place at the Alambazar Monastery. As you spoke that day, you invoked the memory of the Master in all visible things. At that time, I observed in you the truth of this saying, "Wherever the eyes fall, there the Lord manifests." You did not see anything that did not remind you of the Master. I don't know whether you remember it or not, but it is indelibly imprinted on my mind. That day I realized what it is to be merged in God. The Master, through his grace, showed me that; so your attempts to hide anything from me are futile.

Your household belongs to the Master's household;* it is not the home of terrible maya. In your household even a bull-calf can stay, but there is no room for lust and gold. Your household is made of love. . . . Everything is possible through love. Swamiji used to say, "Love is omnipotent." Can there be more than one Swamiji? He was one without a second — like the moon. He was his own peer, and none else. . . .

With love and salutations,
Turiyananda

---

*Baburam Maharaj, or Swami Premananda, was the manager of the Belur Monastery.

66

Almora
25 November 1915

Dear Bihari Babu,

I was pleased to receive your letter of November 18, 1915....

It is good to be born in a brahmin family, provided one obtains steadfast devotion to God. However, a brahmin without devotion is worse than a pariah. If there is devotion for God, then "even shudras attain the supreme goal." This statement of the Gita [IX.32] is confirmed by the scriptures. We have also learned the same truth from the Master. I am not willing to admit that Brahman is a sealed book to you just because you were not born in a brahmin family. Rather it seems to me that those who hold the view that none except brahmins will realize God do not know the spirit of the scriptures.

I am extremely glad to know that you do not care for anything except holy company. This is good, even if it may be construed as pride. Because Shankara glorified holy company as "a ferry boat that helps one to cross the ocean of maya." [Moha-mudgara, 5] We have learned from the scriptures that if you put all spiritual practices on one side of a scale and the result of a moment's holy company on the other, the latter will be heavier.

Why should you think that the capacity of your brain to assimilate has declined? Rather, your capacity to discriminate between good and bad has increased, and so you are not inclined to accept what is bad. Your humility is undoubtedly praiseworthy; but I don't think you are right in saying that you are still the same as you were twenty years ago. Of course, if you say this with reference to the Atman, then it is true, for the Atman is changeless.

Although a holy man has to deal with spiritual and material things, material things do not add to his stature. Only a sattvic [serene] nature befits a holy man. Your feeling of impatience will not last long; it will go away as soon as you become a little more indrawn. Spiritual practices should be increased slowly and gradually. You are on the right path. The Master used to say: "Thinking of the Lord while living in the world is like fighting from within the fort. There are many advantages to it. In the case of the others [monks], it is a fight in the open. And that is not for all." The main thing is to keep the mind on God by whatever means. Only then will the purpose of life be fulfilled.

One has to give attention to food and clothing — that is necessary "as long as the body lasts." [Narada Bhakti-sutra, I.14] But Ramprasad says, "While eating, think that you are offering libations to the Divine Mother." One should listen to these saints; only then will one be able to develop devotion to God. Ramprasad sang this song:

O mind, I tell you this:
Worship Kali in any fashion you please,
Repeating day and night the mantram given you
  by your guru.
Consider lying down as prostration;
And sleeping as meditation on the Mother.
While eating, think that you are offering libations to her.
Whatever you hear with your ears, all that is
  the mantram of the Mother.
Kali embodies the fifty letters [of the Sanskrit alphabet]
  assuming names letter by letter.
Ramprasad is happy to proclaim that the Mother
  pervades all beings.
As you go about the city, think that you are going round
  the Mother.

Is there any realization higher than this? This is called the experience of Brahman everywhere, in every action, in all beings, and in all respects. This experience of cosmic consciousness has been mentioned not only in the Yajnavalkya Smriti, but also in other scriptures such as Dharmashastra, Yoga-sutras, Purana, and Tantra. The *Mahanirvana Tantra* is an authoritative text for householders to attain the knowledge of Brahman. Raja Rammohan Roy founded the Adi Brahmo Samaj based on this book. God alone is the guru, and he provides according to the needs of the devotees. You tell him what is in your mind, and he will do what is necessary.

You are right when you say that without the grace of the Lord spiritual practice is of no avail. But if someone sincerely practises sadhana, God's grace dawns on him. The Lord is omniscient. If one prays to God wholeheartedly, he fulfills every desire. As longing for him increases, his grace is felt more and more. May you have intense yearning for God, that is my prayer to him.

With love and best wishes,
Turiyananda

67

Almora
10 December 1915

Dear L—,

I was glad to receive your letter of December 3. . . .

It is very difficult all at once to feel the presence of God in every being; it is not entirely possible unless one attains illumination. But God is all-pervading and dwells in all beings — knowing this, if a person serves human beings, he is serving God also. If one can serve in this spirit wholeheartedly and without desiring the fruits of one's action, through the grace of the Lord one will realize in time that service to man is worship of God. For the Lord is present in every being: truly, he alone exists.

Purity and impurity are nothing but differences in one's attitude. Attachment to sense objects is impurity, and attachment to God is purity. That which is real in human beings is God. Without God, man is nothing but a cage of flesh and bones. The consciousness in man is a part of God, and that is pure: everything else is impure. The good tendencies in man lead him towards God, and the bad tendencies keep him away from God. One can understand this gradually, but in the beginning of sadhana one should hear about it.

It is only through the grace of God that one is drawn to having a good character. God is the source of all goodness. Therefore, realizing God, one gets rid of restlessness and becomes blessed by attaining supreme peace. What is needed is that you steadfastly keep waiting at his door, and the Lord will reveal everything to you. Always maintain good tendencies in your heart. God is goodness itself. If you can keep him in your heart, you will lack nothing whatsoever. God is our mother and father, friend and companion, wealth and wisdom — he is our all in all. Thus if you can make him your own, your life will be blissful.

You have asked too many questions; it is not possible to answer all of them. And even if I did answer them, I don't think you would be able to understand. But this is certain: The more you move towards him, the more your understanding will be clarified, and thus all of your problems will be solved. Without having a spiritual mood within, one cannot understand spiritual ideas.

Always try to see the Lord within your heart. When you need to know anything, ask him with utmost sincerity. From within he will make you know everything; he always does that for everybody. If God does not reveal himself, with all one's efforts one can neither understand nor help another to understand. What seems to you now a great mystery will become clear very easily through his grace, and you will see the truth. It takes time; don't be impatient. Call on God with all your heart and soul, and try to make him your own. Pray to the Lord from the depth of your being. He is omniscient. Knowing our intentions, he arranges everything accordingly. There is no doubt about it.

With love and best wishes,
Turiyananda

68

Almora
12 December 1915

Dear Baburam Maharaj [Swami Premananda],

I was extremely delighted to receive your letter of December 1, 1915. . . .

Love is a great power — there is no doubt about it. To pray for the welfare of others, to wish that they may have peace, that they may reach the source of joy — if these desires are a cause of bondage then that bondage is of divine love. It will break the bondage of the world, lead one to immortality and make one blessed. Please bless us that we may have the privilege of getting even a particle of that love. . . .

With love and salutations,
Turiyananda

69

Almora
19 December 1915

Dear Baburam Maharaj [Swami Premananda],

. . . The sweet memory of Swamiji at Meerut [a place between Hardwar and Delhi] is still vivid in my mind. He was very sick at Rishikesh, then he was brought to Meerut for treatment, and we stayed with him for six months [six to eight weeks] until he recovered. I can't describe how blessed were those days! Swamiji taught us everything — from mending shoes to studying the scriptures. On the one hand, he would read and explain to us Vedanta scriptures, Upanishads, Sanskrit dramas; and on the other, he taught us how to cook and many other things.

During this period an incident happened that left an everlasting impression on my mind. One day he cooked pilao and some other fancy dishes for us. It was so delicious that I can't express it to you. While we praised his tasty cooking, he served everything on our plates and he himself did not take even a bite. When we objected, he said: "I have eaten these things many times. It is a great joy for me to feed you. Please eat everything."

Just imagine his attitude! It was an insignificant incident, but it is imprinted on our minds forever. How great were his love and care for us! We talked together; we walked together — the memory of those experiences is still vivid in my mind. From Meerut Swamiji began his journey alone. In Delhi we met Swamiji again and stayed with him for a month. Later, just before his departure for America, Maharaj [Swami Brahmananda] and I met him briefly in Bombay. We were virtually out of touch with him for eight years, until he returned to the Alambazar Monastery as a world figure. Now he is with the

Master. But the immortal memory of our association with him is our lifelong companion. That is the subject of our meditation, our conversation, and our spiritual practice. . . .

With love and salutations,
Turiyananda

70

Almora
19 December 1915

Dear Bihari Babu,

I have received your letter of December 12, 1915. . . .

I feel very happy to know of your spiritual longing. The Master used to say, "The more longing for God increases, the more his grace will be felt." All that is needed is to have faith, love, and devotion for God. A real devotee does not pray for anything else but the vision of God; again, that vision depends on God's will.

Arjuna first said to Krishna, "O Supreme Purusha, I do desire to see your Ishwara-form [divine form]." [Gita, XI.3] But the next moment, as if in embarrassment, he said, "If, O Lord, you think me able to behold it, then, O Master of yogis, reveal to me your immutable Self." [XI.4]

Indeed, this is the truth. If the Lord wills, he reveals himself — even then, it is extremely hard to bear that vision for long. When Krishna showed his universal form to Arjuna, the latter piteously cried, "I don't want to see this form anymore." Then again he plaintively prayed, "Lord, please show me your usual human form." Afterwards Arjuna said, "Looking at this gentle form of yours, O Krishna, I now feel composed in mind; I am myself again." [Gita, XI.51]

Therefore, a real devotee does not covet the mystic vision, rather, he prays only for faith, love, and devotion. When one attains these, he lacks nothing. Krishna says in the Gita, "He who does my work and looks on me as the supreme goal, who is devoted to me, who is without attachment and without hatred for any creature — he comes to me, O Arjuna." [XI.55]

Only one thing is needful: to have love for God. That alone accomplishes everything. It is not that we do not know how to love; we are accustomed to loving our wives, children, relatives, friends, wealth; and now we will have to shift this love to God. Because apart from him, nothing is permanent in this world. Nothing but God should be the object of love, because all else changes and becomes old and distasteful. Only the love of God is ever expanding and infinite. "Divine love is beautiful, sweet, and ever new." Enjoyment of everything else is followed by tiredness and boredom.

So Prahlada, a real devotee of Vishnu, prayed, "That deathless love which the ignorant have for the fleeting objects of the senses — as I keep remembering you, may that love not slip away from my heart." [Vishnu Purana, I.20.23] When a devotee develops this kind of one-pointed love, he does not have to wait for a vision. If needed, the Lord reveals himself to him even from a stone pillar. [The allusion here is to the story of Prahlada. Lord Vishnu broke open a pillar and appeared to Prahlada to protect him from the torture of his demonic father. (Vide, Bhagavatam, VII.1.10)]

The vision of the "transcendent and immanent" Brahman, which breaks all the fetters of the heart, is not possible with physical eyes. The Upanishads say: "He is revealed by the negative [*neti*, or not this] teachings of Vedanta, discriminative wisdom, and the knowledge of unity based upon reflection. They who know him become immortal." [Svetasvatara Upanishad, IV.17] "O my good friend, he who knows this Brahman cuts asunder even here the knot of ignorance." [Mundaka Upanishad, II.1.10]

However, it is not that he does not reveal himself if somebody prays to him earnestly. The Upanishad says: "His form is not an object of vision; no one beholds him with the eyes. They who, through pure intellect and the knowledge of unity based upon reflection, realize him as abiding in the heart, become immortal." [Svetasvatara Upanishad, IV.20]

This is a matter of the heart. The more one's heart dwells in God, the more he too dwells in one's heart. "He is the friend of a sincere heart." God is always residing in our hearts, but we are not anxious to see him. Our attention is fixed on other things. Otherwise, it does not take long to see him. Kabir, a saintly poet, said:

Where do you search for me? I am very close to you.
If you really seek me, you shall find me quickly.
I am neither in temples, nor in mosques,
Nor in sacred places like Varanasi, Dwaraka, or Ayodhya.
I can be seen if you search where faith dwells.

The Lord is constantly with us. We don't have to venture anywhere to seek him. "I search and seek but can't find him. One who is chosen by him, finds him." If one seeks God earnestly for a moment, he appears before that person. But who seeks him? We only babble: our prayers come from our lips and not from our hearts. The Lord is omniscient and knows what is in our hearts. We read this in the scriptures, but we don't really believe it. Krishna says in the Gita, "I am seated in the hearts of all." [XV.15] "An eternal portion of myself has become a living soul in a world of living beings." [XV.7] Are these statements untrue? They are true, but they appear to us to be untrue. Why? Because we only read these things, and neither do we believe them nor do we search for God. That is why we are in this pitiable condition!

The Master used to say, "One got the grace of the guru, the Lord, and the devotee; but for want of the grace of one, the man went to rack and ruin." In other words, even though one is blessed with the grace of everybody else, one should have the grace of one's own mind. "He himself is his friend, and he himself is his enemy. . . . To him who has not conquered himself, his own self is hostile, like an external enemy." [Gita, VI.5-6] That is why if one does not exert oneself, outside help is of little avail. As you have focused on your spiritual unfoldment, the Lord will definitely bless you. Create more hunger for God. May the Lord fulfill your wish — that is my prayer to him.

Yours,
Turiyananda

71

Almora
22 January 1916

Dear Bihari Babu,

I received your letter yesterday after a long time. I heard about your father's passing away from Swami Shivananda's letter. . . .

I am astonished to hear of your wonderful vision. It seems to me that the beautiful "luminous form" would have been a divine being who was kindly waiting to let you know that your departed father had gone through the highest course. It is mentioned in the Vedanta scriptures that an incorporeal being appears at the time of death of a virtuous man and accompanies his soul to a high realm. Or it may have been your father's subtle body. Whatever it was, you are undoubtedly a fortunate person to have had this wonderful vision.

Swamiji used to say that if a person sees a ghost his spiritual experience is greater than that of a scholar or an ordinary spiritual aspirant. Because the seer of a ghost undoubtedly has knowledge about the afterworld, whereas the knowledge of a scholar or an aspirant is limited to books. Such is the characteristic of a supernatural vision, what to speak of your divine vision! Only the gods have luminous forms. Know for certain, this vision will not be in vain.

I see that the old grief for your lost son has again arisen in your mind after the death of your father. What an inscrutable power of Mahamaya! You are well-versed in the scriptures and a man of discrimination and wisdom, still momentarily you are overwhelmed with grief. Referring to the grief for a lost son, the Master used to say: "Lakshmana went to Ravana when the latter fell dead on the battlefield, and exclaimed: 'O Rama, glory be to your arrows! There is no spot on Ravana's body that they have not pierced!' 'Brother,' replied Rama, 'the holes you see in his bones are not from my arrows. Grief for his sons has pierced them through and through.'" However, you have taken refuge in the Lord. He will protect you.

"Proclaim it boldly, O son of Kunti, that my devotee never perishes," [Gita, IX.31] — these words are not a poet's imagination, nor a slogan, but the words of God. A devotee is not afraid of prarabdha [the results of past action]. As we have heard from the Master, "Because of his karma, a man was supposed to be pierced by a pike; but by God's grace, his foot was pricked by a thorn instead."

The more the mind becomes pure, the more a person realizes that there is nothing outside, and that everything is within himself. The only barrier to the vision of God is the impurity of the mind.

There is a saying, "If I could give up hypocrisy, I would attain Krishna." The Master used to say: "God is near to that person who is simple. A man becomes simple due to the accumulation of a great deal of spiritual discipline in previous births." The spiritual path becomes clear to a simple soul. And again, the more a person is crooked, the more he has problems, and the farther he is away from God. "He is far beyond what is far, and yet here very near at hand." [Mundaka Upanishad, III.1.7]

Everything depends on the difference between simplicity and hypocrisy. Ethics alone do not help if the heart is not guileless. If we do not directly understand the term *ethics*, then it will be construed with so many meanings, interpretations, and opinions. You said the right thing: One must be "absolutely pure and calm." This happens when a person shuns hypocrisy. There is a saying among women, "Every wife knows her husband's name, but does not utter it out of bashfulness." [It is an old custom in India that the wife does not utter her husband's name, out of love and respect, because "expression killeth."] This saying is absolutely true. Do we not know what has held us back and is not allowing us to realize God? We know it very well — if not always, at least from time to time. Again, what good is this knowledge? Our attachment for the world is so strong that we are hypnotized by maya; it is as if we are sleeping while awake. We don't really want complete awakening.

There is a beautiful story. Once a king suddenly declared in his court that he would give half of his kingdom to the person who could make him understand how to prepare puffed rice. Afterwards, when the king came to the inner apartment, the queen said to him: "Today you have made a great mistake. Someone will take away half of your kingdom." The king said: "My sweetheart, don't worry. You will see what will take place." The next day several people explained to the king how to prepare puffed rice, but the king said, "No, I don't understand." Then someone brought rice, a stove, a pan and other accessories and demonstrated how to make puffed rice in front of the king. But the king repeated the same thing, "No, I don't understand." What does this mean? It means if the king had said, "I have understood," then he would have lost half his kingdom. So he pretended. Our condition is also the same.

God is real and the world is unreal — if we were fully convinced of this, we would renounce the unreal for the real; but we are reluctant to sever our attachments. That is why we are sleeping while awake. You have said the right thing: "There is no other way than to hold onto God in the crisis of life." Krishna says in the Gita, "Come to me alone for shelter." [XVIII.66] This is the only way.

With love and best wishes,
Turiyananda

72

Almora
4 February 1916

Dear D—,

It seems your mental condition is much better now. This is as it should be. "Let the suffering and the body take care of themselves; O my mind, you dwell in bliss" — if one can practise this teaching of the Master, one will be free from worry. To direct the thoughts always towards the Supreme Reality — that is what is meant by "dwell in bliss." Suffering is inevitable in human life; but that does not mean you will have to forget God. Suffering is not eternal — it comes and goes. But the Lord is the help and support all the time. Let the body experience happiness and misery, but the mind should be detached from them. The wise thing to do is to keep the mind in the thought of the blissful Atman.

You have said rightly that without deep faith it is extremely difficult to keep the mind on God. But one can derive great help from holy company, holy thoughts, and the reading of scriptures; then gradually through this process the mind attains steadiness. The best and the easiest way is to wait, surrendering oneself to God. . . .

With love and best wishes,
Turiyananda

73

Almora
10 February 1916

Dear B—,

This morning I received your registered letter. May the Master keep you all happy. It is the Master's grace that all three of you have similar temperaments and are living happily together.

All other things may be obtained in the world, but devotion to God is extremely rare. And without devotion, all possessions in life become worthless and serve no real purpose. Everyone knows this fact and understands it. Devotion to God makes life sweet and joyful, otherwise life is merely a burden. The Master has bestowed on you all the treasure of devotion. That makes me very happy. One's life becomes blessed if one can spend one's time keeping the mind on God, having the company of his devotees and serving them. By

God's grace you have that kind of mentality — it is no small fortune. The great devotee Tulasidas has said, "Even a sinner may have wealth, power, and friends; but only a truly fortunate person attains devotion to God and the company of the holy." . . .

Your well-wisher,
Turiyananda

74

Almora
16 February 1916

Dear B—,

I have received your letter of February 5. I cannot express adequately how happy I am to know that you had the opportunity to serve so many people on the occasion of Swamiji's birthday.

There is a proverb: "Blessed is that hand which gives something to others." This is a great truth and should not be forgotten. You are blessed to have had the privilege of feeding the people. . . . If you can have the conviction through such work that nothing is impossible in the Lord's name, then your labour will not be in vain; rather, it will be fruitful. Great works create great ideas in the mind, and that makes a person great. So the saying goes: "Even the dustbin of a great soul is ennobling." Now you must have joy and strength, performing this great task in such an orderly manner. You will see in the future, this experience will be of great help to you. . . .

With best wishes,
Turiyananda

75

Almora
4 March 1916

Dear D—,

I have received the news that Maharaj [Swami Brahmananda] has returned to Belur Math and that all are doing well. I cannot adequately express how happy I am to know that you have gotten immense joy and benefit from your association with the Master's disciples. Without good fortune, one cannot have the association of such great souls. Now try to have their grace more and more. I earnestly request that you strive to make the result of the holy company permanent, in other words, continue to think of God constantly. This is the great advantage of holy company, that it directs the mind from transitory things to the Goal Supreme. He is a real holy man whose association awakens divine feelings. This is the best way to recognize a holy man. The great saint Tulasidas said, "Have the company of the holy, for it cures worldly disease [ignorance]; while the company of an evil person gives trouble all the time."

With love and best wishes,
Turiyananda

76

Almora
14 March 1916

Dear Baburam Maharaj [Swami Premananda],

I was extremely happy to receive your loving letter yesterday. . . . I also got some glowing reports about your Dhaka visit. It is needless to say that wherever you go,, by the Master's grace, a current of bliss flows there. "Those who carry the all-auspicious Lord in their hearts, they enjoy festivity all the time and always attain prosperity and perfection." [Pandava Gita] The Master dwells in your heart, so it is no wonder that you create an atmosphere of joy and festivity everywhere. Those who have not experienced this, let them say whatever they like. It does not matter. Pity them — they are objects of pity. Swamiji used to say: "Some people try to be prominent by any means — by breaking down the monastery, tearing up works of art, or climbing mountain peaks." But what is the result? Without God's grace, all their efforts are in vain and they cannot be famous.

Some people in Dhaka say that you are dogmatic. What does it matter? Now the veil around you has been removed, and the people have come to see that you know only God. A devotee has written, "It is impossible to remain a stranger when one goes to Baburam Maharaj; he makes people his own in no time." Therefore why bother about criticism? The tendency to criticize others is a part of human nature. It does not help. All problems cease when a person resolves to hold the truth and pays no attention to the criticism of others. Such people, I have seen, have truly attained peace, inspiration, and have made progress towards God. Criticism does not change anyone. God can do wonderful things even through a straw, and now he is working through you. Is there any doubt about it? There is no mistake that your earthly existence is for the purpose of spreading the Master's message. God indeed does his work, still he chooses particular instruments to accomplish it. . . .

With love and salutations,
Turiyananda

77

Dear X,

What a great joy it would be if we knew how to become instruments in the hands of God! Believe that if anybody prays to him wholeheartedly, he fulfills that prayer. It is also absolutely true that without God's grace one cannot pray properly. We learn from the Gita, and from the company of the holy, that he who takes refuge in God, all his troubles cease and the Lord carries all of his responsibilities. As you have taken refuge in the Lord, you have nothing to worry about. The Lord promised in the Gita, "Proclaim it boldly, O son of Kunti, that my devotee never perishes." [IX.31]

You will experience the truth of the Lord's words when you watch your own mind. You will see how the Lord is slowly guiding you towards him and how your spiritual thoughts are replacing worldly thoughts. When you reflect on this truth, your mind will automatically be filled with strength, zeal, faith, and devotion. As you have done so much sadhana, undoubtedly you will continue to do more. There is no other way than to depend on his grace. In time he will fulfill all your wishes.

Yours,
Turiyananda

78

Almora
21 April 1916

Dear Suresh [Swami Yatiswarananda],

After a long time I received your letter yesterday. . . .

I am glad to know that A— has taken monastic vows. I pray, may the Master endow him with strength to observe the monastic vows rightly and make his life blessed. Otherwise it is not enough to receive formal sannyasa [monastic vows]. Sannyasa is a very difficult undertaking. The Master used to say, "They are only fit for sannyasa who have the courage to jump from the top of a tree in the name of the Lord." It is not easy. It is not possible without complete resignation to God. . . .

With love and best wishes,
Turiyananda

79

Almora
3 May 1916

Dear Nirmal [Swami Madhavananda],

I was pleased to receive your postcard. I had learned about your arrival in Varanasi, and I prayed to the Master to fulfill your noble aspiration. The goal of human life is to realize God. And God-realization is only possible in human life, so it is the best life. Sense enjoyments can be had in other lives, but God-realization is possible exclusively in human life. Metaphysically speaking, the goal of human life is the cessation of all misery and the attainment of supreme bliss.

Truth is one, although it is expressed in different ways. What is called God by the devotees is named Paramatman by the yogis and Brahman by the knowers of Truth. Therefore, God-realization, Self-knowledge, and liberation — all denote the same thing; and undoubtedly that is the goal of every human being. You are learned and intelligent, therefore it is natural and reasonable that you intend to achieve that state.

It is the law of nature that one gets what one wants. The desired object is obtained if one has sincere earnestness and yearning. You have heard that one realizes God when one has such longing that life without God is unbearable. If you can develop that longing in this life, you will succeed. One's inmost self must abide in God. The Master used to say, "Be merged with him." Krishna said in the Gita, "He who does my work and looks on me as the supreme goal, who is devoted to me, who is without attachment and without hatred for any creature — he comes to me, O Pandava." [XI.55]

There is no doubt that one should practise japam and meditation. But there is no guarantee that by doing so one will attain God. His grace is the only means to realize him, and nothing else. Swamiji used to say: "Is God like fish or vegetables that you can purchase for a price? Can anybody put a price tag on God that one can have him for a certain number of japam or after so much austerity?" He can be attained only through his grace. And his grace dawns on that person who waits patiently at his door. Don't think that I am discouraging you; please practise spiritual disciplines more, but remember that you will succeed when you surrender yourself fully to him. Offer everything to him and be at rest — that is what I want to tell you. Move towards him as much as you can, then he will help you do the rest.

If one can wait at the Lord's door, at the right time he will fulfill all one's wishes. He becomes extremely pleased when a devotee waits without expectation. Swamiji prayed thus: "My only desire is to know thee, O Lord. Free me even from this." [*A Song I Sing to Thee* — a poem]

With love and best wishes,
Turiyananda

80

Almora
6 May 1916

Dear X,

I have received your letter of April 29. I am very happy to know that you are feeling much better after reading my letter. One needs enthusiasm. The more you know that the Lord is your own and experience his close presence, the more worldly suffering will disappear and you will feel great joy and comfort. The Master used to say, "The more you go towards the east, the farther you will be from the west." If you can advance towards God, this world of maya will automatically go away from you.

The Lord is always present in the heart; we must keep our attention on him. God is the Soul of our souls, the Life of our lives; it is through his grace that we are alive and functioning in this world. Therefore he is truly the first object of our love. Without knowing this, we undergo endless suffering. When we realize this fact, all of our troubles cease to exist. May the Master always keep this awareness awake in your heart. Then your life will be blessed.

The Lord said in the Gita, as if he were swearing an oath: "Having come into this transitory, joyless world, worship me. Fix your mind on me, be devoted to me, sacrifice to me, bow down to me. Having thus disciplined yourself, and regarding me as the supreme goal, you will come to me." [IX.33-34] In spite of this encouraging and positive message of the Lord, we still do not turn towards him. What else can be more unfortunate and regrettable than this?

Happiness and misery — none of them are permanent in this world. So the Lord has advised us to go beyond both. That is possible if we can fix our minds completely on him, and by no other means. Therefore always keep him in your heart, and he will do the rest.

O foolish mind, think of Rama always;
What is the good of hundreds of other thoughts?
O tongue, chant unceasingly the name of Rama;
What gain is there in vain meaningless talk?
O ears, hear the story of Rama;
What benefit do you get by listening to secular music?
O eyes, behold everything as full of Rama;
And give up all else besides Rama.

With best wishes,
Turiyananda

81

Almora
20 May 1916

Dear Bihari Babu,

I have received your letter of May 13, 1916. After reading it I was both happy and sad. Happy — because I find you have so much dispassion for worldly pleasures and so much sincerity in discharging your duties. And sad — because I find your depressed mood, low self-esteem, and lack of spirit without any valid cause. Vanity is not good; on the other hand, it is not good either to harbour negative thoughts, such as, "My life is worthless" and "I have achieved nothing." The Master did not care for self-conceit, nor could he bear self-pity or self-abasement. Rather he instructed us to be proud of being related to God and to repeat emphatically: "I am the child of God, what fear have I? Through his grace I will easily cross this ocean of maya."

We find similar ideas in the songs of the mystic saint Ramprasad: "Whom shall he fear who has the Divine Mother as his mother?" Ramprasad wouldn't even hesitate to quarrel with the Divine Mother. Like a petulant child, he sang, "I shall never call you 'Mother, Mother.'" The Master taught us this attitude emphatically. Therefore you must get rid of this depressed mood. Are you an insignificant person? Even while engaged in great activities you make time to talk about God, and you devote your leisure hours to his contemplation. All time belongs to the Lord — what to speak of noon and evening? One's entire life belongs to him. Besides, one should have faith that if one takes refuge in God wholeheartedly even for a moment, one's life will be pure and blessed and all imperfections will disappear.

I read *Veda-stuti* [Bhagavatam, X.87] long ago. I don't remember it much, except that its language was difficult. It is very true that one cannot enter the realm of spirituality without developing devotion to God and the guru. But God always dwells in our hearts; if he did not, there would be no hope of meeting him anywhere else. God is also the guru. "My lord is the Lord of the universe; my guru is the Guru of the world." [Guru Gita, 75] If this were not true, what would be the necessity of such a God or guru? God and guru are always within us. If not, how could we live? Who would always protect us? He is bestowing grace on everyone. Those who seek him, find him.

The domestic cat becomes a wild cat when it goes into the forest. These ordinary eyes, hands, and skin become transformed into the divine when one realizes God. It is fruitless to learn only words. But words become fruitful when one realizes that God is in the beginning, middle, and end of all words. The word gains its value when it tries to express the Lord. Sridhar Swami expressed this great truth. The Master also used to say, "All jackals in the world howl in the same way."

"Those who are free from attachments, know Brahman, and constantly remember Narayana, the guru of all gods; they, through meditation, get rid of all pains which originate from sins, and they will never be born again." [Prapanna Gita] God purifies every being and pervades everything. "His one foot is this universe and all beings."* We are always living at his feet. Whom shall we worship other than him? And we have every right to worship him. He is our "Life of life and the Eye of the eye." [Kena Upanishad, I.2] Whether we know it or not, undoubtedly he is our all-in-all. Therefore may we offer ourselves to him and fully abide in him. May we not see anything else but him. Om.

With love and best wishes,
Turiyananda

82

Almora
21 May 1916

Dear D—,

This morning I have received your letter of Jaishtha 3 [May 1916]. I am glad to know that nowadays you feel much better. "A cloudy day is not considered to be a bad day; that day is really bad when we do not drink the nectar that springs from talk about God." [*Shabdartha-chintamani*] Days pass through happiness and misery, good and bad. But if the day goes by without worshipping God, it is a great waste.

---

*"One foot or quarter of the Cosmic Being constitutes the universe and all beings. Three quarters are transcendental in heaven." Rig Veda, X.90.3

I cannot adequately express my joy, knowing that your mind is now steady in your spiritual disciplines and that you are experiencing bliss. Practise more and get absorbed in him, only then will your life be blessed. Do only that much work which is necessary to maintain the body. And it is better to do that work calmly, rather than with disgust.

Remain wherever God keeps you, and pray to him to your heart's content. One place or another does not make much difference, but it is good to have a place where it is convenient to practise spiritual disciplines. If your home is a convenient place, what is the necessity of going somewhere else? Try to do your worldly duties with the utmost detachment. You can accomplish this through practice. Surrendering yourself to God, try to be at rest. He is doing everything. Man is deluded and thinks he is the doer; consequently he becomes bound. Never forget this great mantram: "*Naham naham, tuhu tuhu* — Not I, not I; but thou, O Lord." Always think of him, then you will find that all worldly thoughts will dissipate. Physical ailments are obstacles to the recollectedness of God, therefore you should try to keep the body fit and free from disease. You should take care of the body not for the sake of the body, but for the sake of spiritual practice.

I am pleased to see your enthusiasm and earnestness. This is very laudable. It helps a person make progress in spiritual life. On the other hand, despair and sluggishness make a person more and more depressed. He who takes refuge in God has no fear or anxiety. God gives all help and attracts his devotee towards him.

It is common to have ups and downs in the mind. Sometimes one tastes the joy of spiritual practices and the mind is easily drawn towards God; at other times, one experiences no joy, the mind does not feel inclined to do spiritual disciplines, and the heart remains overcast with great gloom. But he who continues his spiritual practices under both good and bad conditions and does not neglect his sadhana, gradually his mental fluctuations go away and one blissful current flows in his mind. Then the mind is constantly engaged in the recollectedness of God, and joy and sorrow cannot perturb him anymore. He continues his sadhana under all circumstances and experiences great joy within. By God's grace, when a person attains this state, he becomes blessed.

Your well-wisher,
Turiyananda

83

Almora
1 June 1916

Dear Prajnananda,

Now the question of spiritual practice: Meditation and concentration, japam and austerity, worship and study of the scriptures, yoga and Vedic ritual — all these actions or sadhanas are only meant for purification of the mind. And the purpose of purifying the mind is Self-realization or Self-knowledge. The mind becomes impure when it is swarming with desires and becomes pure when it is free from desires. Now the main task is to make the mind unselfish by any means — whether it is through meditation, or service, or discrimination, or devotion. Everyone has his own choice. But everybody will have to destroy the ego. And when this "little ego" dissolves, one experiences the manifestation of the "Cosmic Ego," or Brahman. This is called jivan-mukti, or freedom while living in the body.

The grace of the Lord is always there; it is never absent. When the mind is purified, one experiences and tastes fully that divine grace. Self-knowledge is ever-existent; it has no past or future. The sun appears when the cloud is blown away. Similarly, when ignorance is removed, the self-luminous, ever-present Self manifests. People do so many things to attain this Self-knowledge, but *shraddha*, or unswerving faith, is the most important prerequisite. The Gita says, "He who is full of faith and zeal and has subdued his senses obtains knowledge." [IV.39]

Your well-wisher,
Turiyananda

84

Almora
7 June 1916

Dear Bihari Babu,

The day before yesterday I received your letter of May 31. . . . I am happy to learn about your resolution to drive away the feeling of despondency. The more you give up the feeling of hopelessness, the more you will see the light of hope. I always pray to the Lord for your welfare. You also pray to him; he will answer. . . .

I have read the translation of your book *Veda-stuti.* [Bhagavatam, X.87] It seems to me that it is well done. The translation of the commentary is elaborate and the suggestions are beautiful. What shall I say about the subject matter? It is the conclusion of all scriptures. "God is glorified in the beginning, the middle, and the end of the Vedas, Puranas, Ramayana, Mahabharata and other scriptures." There is no refuge other than God, because he alone is true and eternal. Everything else is impermanent — it exists this moment and disappears the next. It is therefore meaningless to depend on impermanent objects; furthermore, this inevitably causes misery. But God's maya is so powerful that it does not allow us to understand this simple truth. Therefore the Lord tells us the secret, "Those who take refuge in me alone shall cross over this maya." [Gita, VII.14]

With love and best wishes,
Turiyananda

85

Almora
12 June 1916

Dear Prajnananda,

... In this world no place, or person, or thing is flawless. So the Gita says, "All undertakings are beset with imperfections, as fire with smoke." [XVII.48] Thus all works are also defective. Still the Lord says, "One ought not to give up the work to which one is born, O son of Kunti, though it has its imperfections." [XVIII.48] And again he says, "Practising steadiness of mind, fix your heart, O Arjuna, constantly on me." [XVII.57] When this is done, all troubles cease.

This state of God-consciousness can be achieved through repetition of practice. Patanjali says, "One becomes established in God-consciousness when practice has been cultivated for a long time, uninterruptedly, with faith and devotion." [Yoga-sutra, I.14] Nothing happens in a trice. Steadfastness in practice is the secret. "Stick to God; gradually, you will be divine." One should learn how to be united with God; and through practice, when it becomes one's second nature, one attains the goal. Then one perceives the presence of the Lord within and without, and consequently the changing circumstances of the world cannot perturb one anymore. It is not that disturbing elements do not arise, they do; but they come and go away without having any effect. "Suffering is inevitable for all embodied beings. The wise man endures affliction calmly, knowing it is unavoidable; whereas the ignorant man makes himself miserable by constantly weeping and wailing." [Saint Tulasidas] This is the difference.

The Master will make everything favourable for you. Those who have surrendered themselves to him have no fear.

With love and best wishes,
Turiyananda

86

Almora
18 June 1916

Dear D—,

You have asked me about eating fish and meat in spiritual life. There is a variety of opinions in this respect. Food habits vary according to the country, and moreover there are differences in human nature. Nonvegetarian food is beneficial for some people, and for others the reverse is true. It becomes a different issue when it is considered as a patient's diet. Medical science prescribes a nonvegetarian diet; again, it sometimes prohibits this. Prescriptions for diet differ according to different cases.

It has been seen that what is sattvic [good] food to one person may be the opposite to another person. Milk is such an excellent food; it nourishes the body with health and beauty. Again, when this same milk becomes a snake's food, that increases its poison. There is a saying, "When a snake drinks milk, it emits deadly poison."

About food, the Master's advice is excellent: "That food is the best which helps a person to fix the mind steadily on

God." This is the way one can judge whether food is sattvic or not; because the sattvic nature turns the mind towards God. Swamiji discussed food elaborately in his *Bhakti Yoga*. You should eat that food which keeps your body and mind healthy. The mind should remain in God — that is the main objective. Rules and regulations about food are meant for those whose aim is to make their bodies vigorous for sense enjoyments. It seems that rules and regulations are ineffective for those whose goal is to worship the Lord. If the body is in good condition, one can meditate on God. Therefore it is advisable to eat that food which keeps the body healthy and helps one to practise spiritual disciplines.

With love and best wishes,
Turiyananda

87

Almora
8 July 1916

Dear Bihari Babu,

. . . I was so happy reading your letter, and again I became sad noticing your old self-deprecating mood. You are a child of the Divine Mother. Why do you consider yourself so worthless? Please shun this negative feeling completely. The Master taught us to repeat, "I chant God's name. Why should I worry?" Truly, I feel pain when I hear your self-reproaching attitude. We have heard from the Master that this is an obstacle to spiritual progress. Knowing your strong relationship with God, you have to move towards him. Never forget that you are his child. Human relationships are casual and momentary, but the relationship with the Lord is eternal.

"The ever-free Atman takes a human birth in order to taste the bliss of liberation-in-life and not for the fulfillment of any worldly desires." I can hardly convey to you what a wonderful joy and light dawned on me when I first read this verse of Shankara [actually Narahari]. Then the purpose of life shined forth before me, and all problems were solved automatically. I realized that the purpose of human birth is nothing but tasting the bliss of jivan-mukti or freedom while living. Truly there is no reason for the ever-free Atman to assume a human body, except that It likes to enjoy freedom while in the body.

You are that ever-free Atman; your expression of self-pity does not befit you. No doubt it is difficult to look directly into the sun, but it is easy to look at the reflected sun. Likewise, it may be difficult to realize the Existence-Knowledge-Bliss Absolute as "I am Brahman"; but one can definitely identify oneself with him as "I am his child or part." One should not think oneself separate from God: it is not beneficial.

Whatever I may be, I belong to him and to none else. A son may be unworthy, but he is still a son. There is a song of Ramprasad: "Good or bad — whatever I may be, thou knowest everything. But does a mother discard her son because he is bad?" Whether you are good or bad, you are the child of the Divine Mother. There is no doubt about it.

With love and best wishes,
Turiyananda

88

Almora
19 July 1916

Dear D—,

Yesterday I received your letter of Ashar 19 [July 1916]. I am pleased to learn that you are well and practising your spiritual disciplines satisfactorily.

Discrimination about the right or wrong food is for beginners in spiritual life. Those whose minds are absorbed in God are not affected by anything. The main thing is to fix the mind on him. Perhaps you have read in the works of Swamiji where he said: "Is God a nervous fool like you that the flow of his river of mercy would be dammed up by [eating] a piece of meat? If such be he, his value is not a pie [penny]!" [*The Complete Works of Swami Vivekananda* (1966) Vol. IV, p. 359] In other words, food is not the main issue in spiritual life: it is the purification of thoughts that is important. If a person thinks of God, although he eats pork, his food becomes equal to the purest food, such as boiled vegetables, rice, and clarified butter. On the contrary, if a person eats the purest food but harbours jealousy, hatred, lust, and greed in his mind, what good is that food? "I am a vegetarian" — this kind of religious conceit will drag him downward.

This, however, does not mean that there is no need for discrimination about food. What I mean is, don't put your whole mind on this food business. Try to focus your whole mind on God, and everything else will come afterwards. Do not "tie the knot of your cloth and leave the gold." It is for the sake of gold that one ties the knot. What good is that knot if there is no gold inside the cloth? Similarly, all rules, regulations, and spiritual practices are meant for God-realization. All these mechanical rules and routines are meaningless if one's mind is not focused on God. This reminds me of a song:

Holding what treasure shall I live in this world?
O Lord, you are my only treasure, the priceless treasure
of my heart.
Renouncing all, it is better to live with you in a hut,
When, O beloved Lord, you illumine my heart.
Forgetting all miseries, I pray, "Don't leave me, beloved."

Leaving you, how shall I live engrossed in this world?
What shall I do with wealth and honour?
They will not go with me.
You are mine, I am yours: You are mine forever.

"You are mine forever" — this is the right attitude. Everything in this world is very transient, lasting only a few days. Nothing is permanent except the Lord. Therefore, in whatever circumstances we find ourselves, if we can live a God-centred life, no miseries can touch us. Even in the great calamities of life if one can feel God's presence in the heart one experiences infinite joy. So we need him. Once we attain him, we have everything: we require nothing else.

"If you seek One [God], you will get everything. If you seek many, you will get nothing. If you water a tree at the root, the tree will bear flowers and fruits. But if you water the tree anywhere else, no result whatsoever will be achieved." [Saint Tulasidas]

Therefore, those who have realized God through his grace say: "What shall we long for except you, O Lord? You are the only treasure, the priceless treasure of my heart." This is to be understood with firm conviction.

With love and best wishes,
Turiyananda

89

Almora
27 July 1916

Dear Bihari Babu,

What a wonderful letter you have written! It contains many lofty ideas, although they are disjointed. It does not matter. If the main theme is right, everything else falls into its proper place. How nicely you have written: Holy company is the best means of God-realization. Bravo! Is there anything to add to it? God is Existence-Knowledge-Bliss Absolute. To be in the company of the holy is as good as being in the company of the Lord. . . . You have also mentioned that the proof of the existence of God is God himself. What a great truth!

Arjuna says in the Gita, "You alone know yourself through yourself, O Supreme Person." [X.15] And again Krishna says, "Neither the hosts of gods nor the great sages know my origin; for in all respects I am the source of the gods and the sages." [X.2]

Who can know God? It is possible only if he reveals himself out of his grace. One day the Master made me cry when he sang this song:

> O Kusa and Lava, why are you so proud?
> If I had not let myself be captured,
> Could you have captured me?

I was deeply moved. That very day the Master deeply imprinted on my mind the fact that one cannot attain God through self-effort, by performing spiritual practices. It is only possible to attain God if he reveals himself. "The non-dual Atman, though never stirring, is swifter than the mind. The devas [the senses] cannot reach It, for It moves ever in front." [Isha Upanishad, 4] "The Atman is attained by him alone whom It chooses." [Katha Upanishad, I.2.23]

I am overwhelmed with joy to see that the attitude of self-surrender is infused in every line of your letter. I believe that the Master will listen to your prayer and lead you, holding your hand. Please accept my love.

Your well-wisher,
Turiyananda

90

Dear X,

. . . Varanasi does not appeal to you, so you are thinking of going somewhere else. Where will you go? The mind is restless by nature. Will it be calm if you change your location? You are supposed to quiet the mind within and must rise above circumstances. If you are a slave to circumstances, they will follow wherever you go. But if you have full control over the circumstances, they cannot create any more trouble.

Your well-wisher,
Turiyananda

91

Almora
5 August 1916

Dear D—,

I am delighted to know that you are keeping well and practising spiritual disciplines to your heart's content. It is no wonder that one attains peace of mind by recollectedness of God. . . . "Our will is God's will" — this conviction does not arise when one is in ignorance. God's will is established in truth, but man's will often becomes falsified. For this reason, one cannot say that man's will is the same as God's will. If one's heart is purified through the grace of God, one gets right understanding about everything.

Your well-wisher,
Turiyananda

92

Almora
11 August 1916

Dear Bihari Babu,

Yesterday I received your letter of August 5. I pray to the Master that you may continue to practise sadhana with a healthy body and a tranquil mind. "Sing his name as long as there is life in the body" — this is the essential thing. There is no better prayer than this: "O Beloved, I will soothe the pangs of my heart by singing your name."

"Love is the best form of spiritual practice." What else is spiritual practice? Love towards all beings. Swamiji said, "It [love] is the only boat that ferries people across the ocean of ignorance." This he translated fully in his life. The great sage Narada defined *bhakti*, or love: "The real nature of supreme love is inexpressible. It is like a dumb man trying to express his experience of a delightful taste." [Narada Bhakti-sutra, 51-52] Then he said, "Nevertheless, it manifests to some fortunate souls." [*Ibid.*, 53] Narada also indicated the means of attaining divine love, "When God's name is sung, he reveals himself without delay and makes the devotee experience that love." [*Ibid.*, 80]

Therefore there is no better means than the singing of his name. It is said: "In this Kali Yuga, chanting the Lord's name is the only way to attain realization."*

So the Master used to sing: "O Mother Shyama, my only hope is your name. What do I care for rituals and social niceties?" "In this age chanting the Lord's name is the means of perfection" — this is the truth.

With love and best wishes,
Turiyananda

---

*Harernama harernama harernamaiva kevalam, Kalau nastyeva nastyeva nastyeva gatiranyatha. *Brihat Naradiya Purana*, XXXVIII.126

93

Ramakrishna Kutir
Almora
14 August 1916

Dear Nirmal [Swami Madhavananda],

I received your postcard the day before yesterday. . . . Know for certain that I always pray to the Lord for the welfare of all. Those who have taken refuge in him are very dear to us. "He who is devoted to Chaitanya is verily my life and soul" — this is the innermost feeling of every devotee of the Lord.

I am happy to learn that you are practising spiritual disciplines at Advaita Ashrama. One finds abiding peace if only he can put his whole mind on God. It is very difficult to do so; but if one makes an attempt, the Lord draws that person to himself. The Master used to say, "If a man takes ten steps towards God, God comes a hundred steps towards him." If this were not true, who could realize him? Is it possible to attain him through human efforts? Swamiji once told me: "Brother Hari, is God like fish or vegetables that you can purchase for a price? Can anybody put a price tag on God that one can have him for a certain number of japam or so many austerities? Only his grace is required to realize him."

The Katha Upanishad says: "The Atman is attained by him alone whom It chooses. To such a one the Atman reveals Its own form." [I.2.23] Does this mean that you will not have to practise japam and meditation? Of course you must do so to your heart's content, to your utmost capacity. But you should know that God will not reveal himself to you simply because you are practising spiritual disciplines. The all-compassionate God, out of mercy, will bestow his grace on you. I practise japam and meditation because I can't help doing so. These spiritual practices should be as spontaneous as breathing. This is the only way one can soothe one's heart.

The realization of God depends on his grace and not on my spiritual practices — one should have this strong conviction in his mind. Practising spiritual disciplines is only to "make the wings tired." When the wings of the bird are tired, it wants to rest somewhere. If it finds no other resting place, it is forced to perch on the mast of the boat. Until one is deeply convinced that there is no other resting place but God, one cannot wholly surrender oneself to him. Therefore, one should practise japam and meditation with one's utmost capacity, and later one will come to the conclusion that these disciplines are futile. The mystic poet Kamalakanta sang, "My rosary and other accessories are hanging in my shrine." Then he continued: "If it is your nature to help struggling souls out of your infinite compassion, reveal yourself, O Lord, to Kamalakanta. The hope of realizing you through japam is as false as the marriage of ghosts." The wedding of a ghost has never occurred and will never occur; similarly, nobody has ever attained God by sadhana and no one ever will. Only if God bestows his grace out of his infinite compassion, can a devotee achieve something. Otherwise, why did Ramprasad say:

> Why do you cry for the Mother, O mind?
> You will no longer see her.
> She is dead, otherwise she would have
> Revealed herself to me.

But this is not a cry of despair. Although the poet knew that "God-realization is as impossible as swimming across the ocean," yet he said, "My mind understands this, but my heart does not; and so it expects the impossible — just like the dwarf trying to reach the moon."

God is the Life of our lives, the Soul of our souls. How can we live in this world without him? We must have him. But "God is an object of passionate love; and without it how can one attain him?" He uplifts the devotee to that state. When one calls on him with heart and soul, he reveals himself in the heart and imparts true knowledge. Only then does one see "the face of the Divine Mother."

May the Master soon bless you with that experience — that is my sincere prayer to him.

Your well-wisher,
Turiyananda

94

Almora
7 September 1916

Dear Bihari Babu,

. . . The Lord's will always becomes fulfilled — it cannot be otherwise. He is all good and does everything for our good. We do not feel this because of our selfish nature. There is no motive in his action except doing good to humanity. "I belong to God" — when a person realizes this, his life becomes blessed. Then it does not matter in what circumstances God places us. After having Self-awareness, wherever you live is of little or no import.

By God's grace many of you have a great deal of spiritual awareness, so the world of maya won't be able to do any harm to you. Now it is a matter of spending the last few days of life in contentment, with full resignation to the Lord's will. He is our all-in-all — here and hereafter. Fix your mind only on him and await his grace.

I am sorry to learn that your health is not good, and moreover, you had to do so much work. But in spite of that you keep your mind on God; undoubtedly this is his special grace on you. The life which passes with ease, without focusing on God is not considered to be a good life. Blessed is he who thinks of God in the midst of hard work.

"He who seeks happiness should control his desires and be content, because contentment is the basis of happiness, whereas dissatisfaction brings misery."

[Due to the law of past karma, a virtuous person may suffer and an evil person may prosper.] So seeing present suffering or happiness, one should not judge the result of action. This will not give one any peace. Peace comes only from experiencing the words of God that he is the ocean of mercy and the protector of the universe. "He has duly allotted to the eternal World Creators [Brahma, Vishnu and Shiva] their respective duties." [Isha Upanishad, 8] Krishna says in the Gita: "Having known me, who am the dispenser of all sacrifices and austerities, the Great Lord of all worlds, the friend of all beings, he attains peace." [V.29]

God is the benefactor of all beings and takes care of each and all — this knowledge leads to peace.

With love and best wishes,
Turiyananda

95

Dear X,

"Why do you forget the name of Mother Durga? Always take her name, O my mind. Never leave the Mother, in life as well as in death."

Whatever God does is good for us — let our hearts be impregnated with this faith.

Practise your sadhana intensely. Circumstances are not always favourable in everybody's case. Therefore, in whatever condition the Lord keeps you, you must continue your sadhana. There is no other way to blessedness than to remember him constantly and to depend on him fully. The fullest degree of benefit comes from the fullest degree of dedication to God — this is the truth. Reason supports this truth, and all great souls are also unanimous on this point. The wise man remembers God amidst unfavorable circumstances and thus transcends them all.

In this world a person has no resort except the grace of God. The more one is able to realize this, the more one will be at peace. Never think that you are away from us because you are living in a distant place. Far and near are all in the mind. One may live far away yet still be very close, and vice versa. You are always close to us. . . .

The Lord only knows where he will take me. Wherever he takes me, may I have devotion to him — that is my earnest prayer. Whatever the Lord wills, happens, and it is undoubtedly for our good. But the problem is that we neither understand it, nor have we any patience. Indeed, there is no better way to peace than if we could only believe that whatever the Lord does is good for us. If one does not have this understanding, one cannot have peace of mind. Happiness and misery, disease and grief — these are all inevitable as long as one lives in the body. But it is not right to think that what gives me happiness is good and what causes me pain is bad. This is sheer selfishness. May the Lord always keep us unperturbed, in happiness as well as sorrow, in disease and in grief. May we never be devoid of right understanding in every situation. That is my sincere prayer to the Lord. . . .

What sort of a monk are you? Why are you so concerned about the body? The nature of the body is to grow, to decay, and to die. But there is One inside the body who neither grows nor decays. Try to see him.

You have dedicated yourself to the Lord; therefore, all responsibility is now his. He will get everything done through you. Be an instrument in his hand, and follow the path which he has selected for you — then you will be relieved of fear and worry. Those who have taken refuge in God have nothing to fear. "O brother, always stick to God, gradually you will be divine."

Everything will turn out all right in time. Don't worry. Don't be impatient. The Lord does his own work and he *is* doing it. Blessed are they whom he makes his instruments. You are capable of working as an instrument of God — that gives me joy beyond words. May the Lord imbue your heart with this idea:

> O Lord, O thou the inmost Self of all, I tell thee the truth: I do not cherish any worldly desire in my heart. Do thou grant me intense devotion unto thee. Do thou also free my mind from passions and other impurities. [Tulasidas: Ramayana, V.2]

This very prayer brings the hope of perfect peace to my heart. If one can experience this prayer, one's attainment of perfection becomes imminent.

It is hard to understand the ways of the Divine Mother: "She, the Great Enchantress, veils the understanding even of wise men and forcibly subjects them to delusion." [Chandi, I.55] If that is the case, what to speak of ordinary people? He alone is safe who always remains prayerful to the Divine Mother. You have written rightly; "In this world people do not realize this fact: 'When the dried cowdung cake burns, the cowdung laughs without knowing that it will also be burnt one day.'" "Mother, if you do not protect us from maya, there is no deliverance" — this is the truth. The Lord's will be done. If one can be absorbed in the thought of the

Divine, one need not worry about external things. In this respect, his compassion is one's mainstay.

Always be prayerful. You should constantly speak to the Lord about the needs of your heart. He alone is our own — if this feeling is established deeply within you, you will be free from fear and anxiety. Gradually, the Lord will make everything known to you.

Your well-wisher,
Turiyananda

96

Dear X,

. . . Whatever the Lord wills, happens. Whether we understand it or not, whatever the all-auspicious God does is undoubtedly good for us. If we could understand this, there would be no end to our joy.

I am delighted to see that the Master has granted you right understanding and a good attitude in all conditions of life. This happens when the luminous intellect [sattvic buddhi] manifests. It does not allow any bad thought to enter the mind. Whether conditions are good or bad, the man of luminous intellect always sees the good. It is only through God's special grace that a person develops such an attitude. When he is perfected in it, all his miseries cease forever. Blessed is the grace of the Master!

The more we talk about the Lord and rejoice in his glory, the better it is for us. In this world God is the only essential thing — this is what the Master taught us again and again.

A poet [Surendranath Majumdar, a Bengali poet] has said:

All happiness is in imagination;
All suffering is in fear;

> Things do not happen as you think.
> Needlessly does a man suffer from worry.

This is the gospel truth. We become upset only because we worry; otherwise, everything can be endured.

The Master used to say: "As the water of a dam comes from one direction and goes to the other, likewise, those who spend their money for holy causes, they never get bound. Even handling money in this world of maya, they remain like free souls." Swamiji used to say, "If the door of a room is kept open, the inside air cannot be befouled; similarly, those who spend their money for good purposes, no evil can touch them."

In whatever condition the Lord keeps us, that is best for us. If through his grace our thoughts are fixed on him, external circumstances count very little. During his terminal illness, I heard the Master saying, "Let the affliction and the body take care of themselves; O my mind, you dwell in bliss." As long as the mind dwells in bliss or God, what does it matter if the body suffers pain? It is the suffering of the mind that is really unbearable. If God, out of compassion, keeps our minds absorbed in him, then pain won't be felt as such.

It is good news that Holy Mother [Sri Sarada Devi, the spiritual consort of Sri Ramakrishna] is coming to Calcutta soon. So many people will come to see her and find peace thereby. Blessed is the grace of the Mother, and how great is her forbearance! Nothing ever disturbs her. People are constantly flowing towards her, and she does good to them without any reservation. It is wonderful that you are planning to go to Calcutta with your son when the Mother is there. It will be like "the gopis who would finish two errands — selling the milk and meeting Krishna — in one trip." [Saint Suradas] What a beautiful attitude! The gopis did everything for Krishna. The Lord first, and all else afterwards. Their steadfast love for Krishna is unparalleled. The more the mind becomes pure, the more one understands this. The grace of the Lord is upon you. Gradually, you will realize everything. If the Lord is gracious, one does not suffer from any wants.

> Janaka's might was unsurpassed;
> What did he lack of the world or the Spirit?
> Holding to one as well as the other,
> He drank his milk from a brimming cup!

Singing these lines of a song, the Master inspired his householder devotees to be like King Janaka, who was a householder as well as an illumined soul. The main thing is that one must be absorbed in the thought of God — whether one is at home or in the forest. Without realizing God, what good is a life of renunciation in the forest? Again, if your mind is fixed on God, it does not matter where you live. We need God. We must think of him while we are sitting or standing, eating or lying. Through his grace, all will take place in time.

The Master used to say, "The monk and the snake never build homes; they live in others' homes." This is a wonderful idea. I am now experiencing how difficult it is to build a house. [*Swami Turiyananda was then supervising the building of a cottage for the monks in Almora, Himalayas.*]

A devotee of God has no fear or anxiety. I mentioned this to you when I quoted from the Gita where Krishna said to Arjuna, "Proclaim it boldly, O son of Kunti, that my devotee never perishes." [IX.31]

Pure devotion is rare even amongst gods. Is it so easy to attain that supreme love which puts God at the beck and call of the devotees? The Master used to sing with intense feeling [this song of Krishna]:

> Though I am never loathe to grant salvation,
> I hesitate indeed to grant pure love.

Ramprasad said: "The source of spiritual life is devotion, and liberation is only a byproduct." Truly if one can develop love for God, one achieves everything.

It is the duty of a householder to talk about religious matters with his wife. As you and your wife are studying *The Gospel of Sri Ramakrishna* together, it will definitely do you good. If both of you are of one mind and one goal, you will be happy in every respect. What could be a better goal for you than becoming ideal householder devotees of the Lord? The Master quite often used to sing this line: "A devotee of Mother Kali is jivan-mukta [liberated-in-life], and ever blissful." Gold always remains gold, whether it is in a box or in a garbage can; similarly, wherever God's devotee lives, he belongs to God.

Your well-wisher,
Turiyananda

97

Almora
24 September 1916

Dear X,

Have the conviction that you are working for the Lord, and then don't worry anymore. Why do you allow your mind to become disturbed? "Whatever work I do, O Lord, all that is your worship." [Shiva-manasa-puja Stotram, 4] He is in everything and he is everything — reflecting and meditating thus one attains realization. Imagination will become reality — that is how it happens. At first one has to imagine; afterwards it becomes real.

Yours,
Turiyananda

98

Almora
12 October 1916

Dear D—,

I was pleased to receive your letter on the occasion of Vijaya [Durga Puja], and to learn that you are physically and mentally well. It is really good news that your sadhana is continuing smoothly.

The human body is subject to disease and grief; he who steadfastly worships the Lord in spite of that, transcends the pairs of opposites and delusion. Lord Krishna indicated this in the Gita, "The men of virtuous deeds, whose sins are ended, are free from the delusion of the pairs and worship me with firm resolve." [VII.28]

The Master used to say, "Let the affliction and the body take care of themselves; O my mind, you dwell in bliss." It is wonderful that you have understood the implication of the Master's saying. The main thing in life is to worship the Lord. Wherever you are, if you can hold the Lord in your heart and stay at his door with patience, his blessing and compassion will dawn on you. . . .

God is all-auspicious — this faith brings peace and happiness. If you try to explain the world through intellectual reasoning, you will be in trouble. That is why the Master advised us to realize God first and then try to understand the world. Hold onto the Lord, then all good will attend you.

With love and best wishes,
Turiyananda

99

Almora
26 November 1916

Dear Bihari Babu,

I have received your letter of November 20. I am very sorry to learn about your family troubles, but I don't know what to say. "Only if you are extremely expert should you ride on a horse" — this proverb is very true. It seems that your troubles are due to the fact that you cannot behave as necessary in leading a householder's life.

And again I wonder — those who are worldly-wise, are they happy? It does not appear to be so. There is a saying, "The depth of a river varies from place to place, but the average is always the same." So the long and short of it is: No one is really happy in this world. For that reason, Krishna said in the Gita, "Having come into this transitory, joyless world, worship me." [IX.33] There is no happiness in this world. We think we could have been happy if we had been able to act this way or that; but this is a vain thought. This world itself is "*asukham*" [joyless]; so the Lord says, "*imam prapya bhajasva mam*" [living in such a world, worship me].

The main thing in life is to worship the Lord. He reminds us: "Let happiness or misery come, you go on worshipping me. Nothing is permanent in this transitory world. Happiness and unhappiness — both will pass. I alone am eternal. If you worship me, you will inherit my eternal treasure. Therefore, *bhajasva mam* — worship me." And you are doing that.

Your involvement in translating the *Veda-stuti* [Bhagavatam, X.87] is giving you wonderful spiritual intoxication. Blessed are you! There is rarely any person in this world who is without some kind of intoxication. But undoubtedly, it is rare that a person finds joy in the *Veda-stuti*.

As you have mentioned, your life is passing through happiness and misery. You know that the world is not everlasting. Just spend the remaining few days of life in his thought and in divine inebriation. What else is there in this world?

This worldly life is not for you. Those who have a worldly nature, let them do as they please. You try to spend the remaining days of your life in repeating the name of the Lord and praying to him that you may do so. After reading your letter, I first thought of advising you to take legal action; but later I realized that that was not for you. You are a man of a different nature. You would rather endure the financial difficulties than get involved in that horrible legal battle. It is neither your mistake nor any mental weakness. You are a householder — but not an ordinary one. If you were, you would not be afraid to sue that person.

Don't you see what people are doing to make money? They have no sense of right or wrong; they make money by hook or by crook. And you? You are reluctant to enforce your legitimate demand lest it create a hardship for the other person. So how can I say that you are a so-called ordinary householder?

As I said: endure whatever happens to you. Holding the Lord, pass the remaining days of your life. "He who endures, survives; and he who cannot, perishes" — remembering these words of the Master, pass your days through both happiness and misery and eventually you will attain supreme peace.

Your well-wisher,
Turiyananda

100

Ramakrishna Advaita Ashrama
Varanasi
3 January 1917

Dear Bihari Babu,

. . . Liberated souls do not acknowledge the results of past karma in their lives, although outwardly these do seem to exist. This is because the effects of karma in past lives arise from body consciousness. "Prarabdha karma [the results of actions that were begun in former lives and are now working themselves out in the present one] can be maintained as long as one lives identified with the body. But no one claims that an illumined soul ever identifies himself with the body. Hence prarabdha karma should be rejected in his case." [Viveka-chudamani, verse 460] This is the conclusion. Devotees abide by the will of God, so they do not use the word prarabdha. Those who follow the path of karma yoga, generally they use the word prarabdha.

Your well-wisher,
Turiyananda

101

Belur Math
4 April 1917

Dear D—,

I was pleased to receive your letter on April 1. It is indeed good news that you are keeping well and that your mind is not depressed anymore. It is really a good sign that you are having spiritual thoughts most of the time and have a great longing for holy company. It is good and desirable that you don't care for mundane talk and the association of worldly people.

God alone is the way and the goal of all. Always meditate on him in your heart. Don't worry. He will set everything right. Wherever the Lord keeps you, always pray so that your mind dwells on him; and however he may keep you, that is for your own good. The Sufi poet Hafiz said: "If my beloved loves to see me wallow in the dust of poverty, and if I turn my gaze towards the lake in heaven, then I am short-sighted indeed." It is always good to be content wherever the Lord places you. He is all-good and omniscient; he knows what is best for each person and arranges accordingly. But we demand something from him according to our liking and create a mess.

"Those who have worldly desires suffer from restlessness even in the solitude of the forest. Those who have disciplined their senses, they practise austerities even while living in a crowded home." [Hitopadesha, ch. 4] This is the real truth. There is no harm in praying thus: "O Lord, wherever I may be, may I never forget you. May I have the company of your devotees. Please keep me away from worldly people." Call on him wholeheartedly and he will do what is good for you.

As long as the Lord keeps you at home, serve your mother as the manifestation of the Divine Mother. It will do you good. Whatever path the Lord has earmarked for you, follow it without any doubt. Your duty, my duty, and everyone's duty is to tread the path of God. There is no other duty.

Worship the Lord with heart and soul. He is the adorable one and the Chosen Deity. If he is worshipped, all duties end. If the root is watered, the entire tree gets nourishment and produces flowers and fruits.

Your well-wisher,
Turiyananda

102

Belur Math
17 April 1917

Dear D—,

I have received your letter of 31 Chaitra [April 1917].

"The Lord dwells in the hearts of all beings, O Arjuna, and by his maya causes them to revolve as though mounted on a machine." [Gita, XVIII.61] These words of the Lord remind us that he is guiding us.

"In whatever way men approach me, even so do I reward them; for it is my path, O Partha, that men follow in all things." [Gita, IV.11] These words of the Lord prove that we all are following his path.

Now we have to obey his command: "Take refuge in him alone with all your soul, O Bharata. By his grace will you gain supreme peace and the everlasting abode." [Gita, XVII.62]

You have mentioned in your letter, "Our duty is to try to think of God and nothing else." Then where is room for any confusion? I was pleased reading your line of thought. You have reasoned very well. Thus move towards him and wait for his grace. In due course you will receive his grace and your life will be blessed. Even now your life is blessed, as you are able to think of God. What else do you want?

With love and best wishes,
Turiyananda

103

Belur Math
5 May 1917

Dear Ramesh,

I have received your long letter of May 3. Don't worry. More or less, everyone experiences that kind of feeling.

Never discontinue your meditation even if it is distasteful. Again in the course of time, the mind will change its mood. You will feel love for God and the world will seem beautiful and joyful. Don't be depressed. Pray to the Master from the bottom of your heart. Then strength will come and you will be able to make all situations favourable.

When the cyclone blows, people become perturbed; but at that time one should try to be calm. Likewise, a storm also arises in the mind. At that time if one can hold onto the Lord firmly, the storm can do nothing. Take refuge in him wholeheartedly. The storm is not eternal. Good thoughts will come again to the mind and you will experience peace. Never give up the Lord who is the embodiment of peace. Now this is your duty.

Be calm and steady and do your duty by surrendering yourself to God. Know for certain that your body and mind will improve again. Never deviate from the path of blessedness. At last all good will attend you. There is a saying, "Call on God when you are in trouble." Therefore, call on him. All troubles will go away. Don't fear. Suppressing all other thoughts, try to think only of God and nothing else. Undoubtedly you will succeed.

Your well-wisher,
Turiyananda

104

Belur Math
11 May 1917

Dear D—,

I have received your letter of May 6. I can clearly see from your letter that your love of God and reliance on him are growing more and more. It is evidence of the Lord's special grace to you. May the Lord give you more devotion, faith, and inner strength; may you gradually advance towards him, dedicate your life and soul to him, and be freed from the clutches of all trivial and useless thoughts; and may you take refuge in him alone, knowing him to be the mainstay of your life. When that happens, all pain and suffering, all want and imperfection will disappear, and you will attain supreme peace.

The more you move towards the east, the farther you will be from the west. The more you are able to fill your heart with thoughts of the Lord, the more worldly thoughts and worries will move away. You will not have to make any extra effort to drive them away. One should cultivate the recollectedness of God in one's heart with love and care constantly over a long period; only then will it become permanent.

It is necessary that one should always be prayerful. If one supplicates his inner feelings to the Lord again and again, the Lord listens to them.

I was pleased to notice the mode of your prayer. One should pray to him for love, faith, and devotion. These are rare things, and once you have them you lack nothing. Then the heart becomes full of bliss, and under all circumstances one experiences perfect peace. One should wait at the door of the Lord with patience, then everything turns out all right. He makes everything favourable.

The nature of the body is that sometimes it is good, sometimes it is bad, and all the while it is moving towards destruction. The body is not eternal — sooner or later it will perish. So what more shall I say about it? If the mind is absorbed in God, then the purpose of assuming the body is fulfilled.

Be at rest, surrendering yourself completely to God. There is no higher blessedness than this.

Your well-wisher,
Turiyananda

105

Shashi Niketan
Puri
10 July 1917

Dear D—,

I was pleased to receive your letter of July 7. Your prayers to the Lord are all very nice. Thus one should supplicate one's inner feelings to God. He is omniscient, and he listens to our prayers and undoubtedly fulfills them if they are one with our hearts. Try to fix your mind on God; he will surely help you.

Doubt prevails when the mind becomes impure. Be watchful so that no selfishness finds a place in your mind. Surrender yourself completely to God, and after doing so, you will not have to seek him anymore. "I have sold my body in the marketplace of the world and bought Mother Durga's name" — if one can apply this attitude wholeheartedly in one's life, one will never encounter fear or anxiety. This happens gradually.

O mind, be absorbed at the feet of the Divine Mother,
Be absorbed fully, only then will you escape suffering.
This world is not real, so why do you travel aimlessly here?
Meditate on kundalini, the power of Brahman in your heart.
Kamalakanta says, sing the glory of Mother Shyama;
Then life will be a river of bliss,
And then row your boat slowly.

First know that life is a river of bliss, and then row your boat slowly. Do not hurry. We must go on calling the Mother. What else do we need? One should consider oneself blessed if one can call on Mother. If there is any desire other than this, then it is a worldly desire, which breeds misgiving, doubt, and restlessness. Therefore, be careful; let there be no desire in your heart other than the desire for Mother. Worldly desires are troublesome. Gradually the Mother will make you understand everything. Pray to her so that she may give you strength to fulfill your right intention. If the mind and speech are united, you will accomplish everything.

Your well-wisher,
Turiyananda

106

Shashi Niketan
Puri
21 July 1917

Dear D—,

I am pleased to receive your letter of Shravan 1 [July 1917]. I was extremely delighted to learn from your letter that the Lord is inspiring you with good thoughts, and that your mind is becoming purer and purer. May he bless you more — that is my sincere prayer to him.

Truly, it is not easy to get rid of all desires; but if the mind is endowed with discrimination, then desires cannot overpower it. The sage Vashishtha told Ramachandra, "If one has discrimination, then even in a great crisis one is unperturbed." Indeed the power of delusion cannot overwhelm if one can keep the discriminative faculty ever steady. What harm can desire do to that person who always thinks that everything is transitory? There is nothing to fear from trifling desires. That desire is really harmful which takes the mind away from God. If the mind is fixed on God, cravings cannot mislead a person even if he is in family life. Pray to God and open your heart to him; he will set everything right.

There is a beautiful story in the Yoga Vashishtha Ramayana about renunciation. A brahmachari [young monk], considering himself a man of renunciation, gave up everything except a piece of loincloth, an asana [carpet for meditation], and a water pot. In order to give him right understanding, his guru said to him: "What have you renounced? I see that you have renounced nothing." The brahmachari thought: "I have nothing except this loincloth, asana, and water pot. Does my guru want me to give up these things?" Deliberating thus, he kindled a fire and one by one threw those possessions into it. He then felt that he had achieved true renunciation. The guru said: "What have you renounced? A piece of cloth? It is made of cotton. Your asana and water pot are also made with different materials. All of these materials belong to nature. What have you renounced of your own?" Then the brahmachari pondered: "What else do I have? Of course, I have my own body. Well, I shall sacrifice this body into the fire." When the brahmachari was about to throw himself into the flames, the guru said: "Wait a minute. What are you doing? Just reason it out: Does this body belong to you? This body was made by your parents with their semen and blood, and later it grew from the nourishment of food. What has it to do with you?" Then the brahmachari finally came to his senses. Through the grace of the guru he realized that his ego was the root of all evil. Real renunciation is the renunciation of ego; otherwise, renunciation of external things, even one's own body, is not considered to be renunciation.

Therefore, taking or giving up — these pairs of opposites are futile because they are in the domain of maya. The essential thing in life is to take refuge in God. One should pray for one-pointed devotion, love of his devotees, and a taste for his name.

Your well-wisher,
Turiyananda

107

Shashi Niketan
Puri
31 July 1917

Dear D—,

I was pleased to receive your letter of Shravan 10 [July 1917]. . . . I was also glad to hear about Krishna's swing festival [*jhulan-yatra*] in your home. In the Bhagavatam, Krishna said to Uddhava that, "observance of my festival" is one of the forms of practising devotion. [IX.11.36] Here in Puri also the festival of Lord Jagannath is being celebrated and everyone is happy.

If the Lord is pleased, everyone is pleased. Therefore, never forget to serve the Lord first. But generally it becomes the reverse. Instead of serving the Lord, we enjoy ourselves during the time of festivity. This is one of the greatest drawbacks to the religion of service. One is protected from this if one is careful, mindful, prayerful, and dispassionate.

In the immature state, every religious path is attended with the fear of falling and failure. There is no fear, however, if the love of God deepens. But this intense love does not arise unless one is free from selfishness. Whatever path you follow, spirituality cannot be fully manifested unless egoism, selfishness, and craving for sense-enjoyment are eliminated.

A devotee of God has nothing to fear because the Lord protects his devotee if he has the right attitude. Sincerity is the only thing needed. To unite the mind and speech is the supreme sadhana. Although it cannot be accomplished all at once, there is no doubt that it can be done by gradual practice. The Lord himself helps one to do this. Without his grace everyone is helpless.

"Solely out of compassion for them, I, dwelling in their hearts, dispel with the shining lamp of wisdom the darkness born of ignorance." [Gita, X.11] These words of the Lord are our only hope and support.

Your well-wisher,
Turiyananda

108

Shashi Niketan
Puri
31 August 1917

Dear D—,

I can see from your letter that you are in good spirits. It is undoubtedly the Lord's great grace to you. Continue to practise recollectedness of God and pray to him intensely and sincerely. He is omniscient and very compassionate. He fulfills the heart's earnest prayer.

Restlessness is the nature of the mind. It becomes calm through prayer and meditation. There is no other method. As a result of spiritual disciplines and by the grace of God, one's mind becomes tranquil.

"Undisturbed calmness of mind is attained by cultivating friendliness towards the happy, compassion for the unhappy, delight in the virtuous, and indifference towards the wicked." — this is the advice given by Patanjali in his Yoga-sutra. [I.33]

God dwells in all beings, so everyone is an object of love. By cultivating this attitude one can also quiet the mind.

Your well-wisher,
Turiyananda

109

Shashi Niketan
Puri
7 September 1917

Dear Nirmal [Swami Madhavananda],

I have received your letter of August 28. . . .

In the beginning one has to understand the Truth through discrimination. Afterwards, when that discrimination becomes firm and free from doubt, realization takes place immediately. Whenever there is a cessation of doubt, misgiving, and contrary notions with regard to Truth, the mind becomes firmly settled on the Self. This is called the realization of Truth. Through the grace of the Lord "one attains it within himself in course of time." [Gita, IV.38]

Today I have received a postcard from M. Tell him that one cannot get rid of egoism simply by not doing anything. The way to do this lies through work. If you want to fry something, you must use fire to heat the oil. To refine sugar you have to remove a lot of scum by boiling it. Likewise, if you want to purify your mind, you will have to perform action without seeking its results. It [purification] cannot be achieved by drawing in one's hands and feet like a tortoise. "I won't work because it may cause pride" — this attitude springs from sheer selfishness. It is a sign of a dreadful tamasic [sluggish] nature. One must convert tamas into rajas [activity] through work, and then gradually it will be transformed into sattva [calm] through spiritual disciplines — thus will the ego be driven out.

One who has no sense of ego is not the doer, although he may be engaged in work. One who harbours a feeling of pride will be proud even when he is idle. And one who is humble and calm does not feel that he is doing anything, although he does many things.

With love and best wishes,
Turiyananda

110

Shashi Niketan
Puri
19 September 1917

Dear D—,

. . . I am pleased to observe your power of discrimination. You wanted to know about my early life, but I don't like to talk about it. However, you also wanted to know how I first met Sri Ramakrishna. That I am answering in brief:

I first saw Sri Ramakrishna at Dinanath Basu's house in Baghbazar. That was long, long ago. In those days the Master would frequently go into samadhi. About that time Keshab Chandra Sen had become acquainted with him. Kalinath Basu, Dinanath's brother, was a follower of Keshab Sen. He happened to see Sri Ramakrishna and was deeply impressed, so he asked his brother Dinanath to bring Sri Ramakrishna to their house. That is how the Master came to visit Baghbazar. We were all young, about thirteen or fourteen years old. People referred to Sri Ramakrishna as the Paramahamsa, so they were all talking about the Paramahamsa's visit. Some other boys and I were curious, and we went to see him. We saw a carriage with two men in it stop in front of Dinanath's house. Immediately people around began to say, "The Paramahamsa has come, the Paramahamsa has come," and began moving towards the carriage. First, one of the men in the carriage got down. [*This was Hridayram Mukhopadhyay, Sri Ramakrishna's nephew.*] He was well-built; and there was a large vermilion mark on his forehead and a golden amulet tied around his right arm. Looking at him, one felt that he was a strong and very active person. He stood close to the carriage and helped the other person alight.

The other man appeared very thin. He had a shirt on, and his cloth was securely tied around his waist. One of his feet was on the step of the carriage, and the other was inside. He was in a semi-conscious state, and it seemed as if someone quite drunk were being taken out of the carriage. But when he got down, what a wonderful sight! There was an indescribable radiance over his face. I thought: "I have heard from the scriptures about the great sage Shukadeva. Is he the same Shukadeva?" By that time many others had joined them, and they were taken to the second floor of the house. I followed them. When the Paramahamsa became a little conscious of the outer world, he opened his eyes and saw a large picture of Mother Kali on the wall. Immediately he saluted her and started to sing in a soul-bewitching manner. It stirred a wave of devotion in all who had gathered there. The song expressed the idea that Kali and Krishna are identical: "O Mother, for Yashoda thou wouldst dance, when she called thee her precious Blue Jewel. . . . " It is impossible to describe the extraordinary feeling this song aroused in everybody. Two or three years later I went to Dakshineswar and saw Sri Ramakrishna in his room. This much for today.

Your well-wisher,
Turiyananda

111

57 Ramkanta Bose Street
Calcutta
25 November 1918

Dear Nirmal [Swami Madhavananda],

Glad to receive your letter of November 19. . . .

I was delighted to learn that you have derived joy from studying Swamiji's *Jnana Yoga*. There is tremendous power in those lectures in *Jnana Yoga* because he spoke from his own experience. That is the difference between speaking from personal experience and speaking from hearsay.

Why did you express so much despondency? If the ego does not go, remember what the Master said, "Whose ego is this?" This ego belongs to God — knowing this, be at rest. The Master taught that if the ego does not leave, one should follow these attitudes: "I am a servant of God"; "I am a child of God." If one can establish a relationship with him, then there is no more fear or anxiety.

Stay wherever the Lord has placed you and fix your mind on him, then you will find joy everywhere. In fact, far and near are in the mind. So the Upanishad says: "The Atman is far and likewise near. It is inside all this and It is outside all this." [Isha Upanishad, 5] May the Lord fulfill your prayer — that is my sincere prayer to him.

Your well-wisher,
Turiyananda

112

57 Ramkanta Bose Street
Calcutta
4 December 1918

Dear Ramesh,

I received your letter a few days ago. I was very happy to learn of your noble resolve. It is very rare and unlikely that a man will not make any mistake; but by realizing one's fault and desisting from repeating it, one manifests one's manliness. Without brooding over past deeds, if one is cautious about the present and the future, one derives immense benefit. It is very important that one should try to keep the body and mind strong, healthy, and pure; otherwise one is not fit for any noble work.

Before practising meditation, one should acquire the requisite qualifications. It is extremely difficult to be absorbed in meditation all at once. At first, one should try to withdraw the mind from all sense objects and direct it to one particular thought. This is called *pratyahara*. After practising pratyahara, one focuses the mind on a particular part of the body — such as on the tip of the nose, or between the eyebrows, or on the heart, whichever is convenient — that is called *dharana* [concentration]. When one has mastered this practice, one should attempt meditation.

If one can make the flow of thought on a particular object or idea as steady as the unbroken flow of oil, it is called *dhyana* [meditation]. The illustration of the flow of oil is given because there is no interruption in that flow. In meditation, the thought flows continuously towards the object of meditation. Through long spiritual practice, one acquires the power of concentrating the mind and thus becomes fit for meditation.

At first one should practise meditation on a concrete form such as the image of a deity. As it is not easy to meditate on the complete image right in the beginning, one should try to meditate on a particular part of the body, such as the face or the feet. When one becomes adept in this practice, one will find it easier to meditate on the full form. Then, gradually, meditation with form leads to meditation on the subtle, formless aspect of God. But in this stage of meditation one should be extremely careful, because various obstacles arise at this time, such as sleep or inertia, distractions, torpidity, and so on. One should be aware of these things.

You have written that the mind becomes concentrated while thinking about the solution of some problems — this is also an aspect of meditation. "If I strive, I shall be able to be very meditative" — this faith of yours is undoubtedly extremely good. In the sixth chapter of the Gita, Krishna has given specific instructions on meditation, beginning from "In a clean spot having fixed his seat" [verse 11] to "attains the peace abiding in me — the peace that culminates in nirvana" [verse 15]. If one reads the Gita daily, one's heart will be purified.

Fix your mind on God and move towards him; then you will not have to be afraid of worldly maya. God will protect you and make you his own. If there is no theft in the chamber of your heart and if your mind and speech are united, then the omniscient Lord will grant what is right for you. Know this to be the undisputed teaching of all scriptures and great souls. Stay away from evil company and be always prayerful. If you can do that, the Lord will guide you while sitting in your heart. What more shall I write?

Your well-wisher,
Turiyananda

113

57 Ramkanta Bose Street
Calcutta
16 December 1918

Dear Phani,

Some days ago I received your letter. I am glad to learn that you are well. . . .

Now I shall try to answer your questions:

1. The word *nirodha* means "to control completely." Not allowing the mind to dwell on external objects is called *chitta-nirodha* in Yoga terminology. It is a state in which the mind is drawn inward.

2. You have rightly mentioned, "That state is called nirodha, when the mind becomes completely devoid of thought-waves." As soon as the mind stops thinking, the Atman, who exists as the witness, is established in its own nature.

3. "Concentration" means making the mind one-pointed, just as the end of a piece of thread has to be pointed before it can pass through the eye of a needle. The Master used to say, "A thread cannot pass through the eye of a needle if the tiniest fibre sticks out." Likewise, if the mind is even slightly disturbed, one cannot meditate. Concentration, or one-pointedness, means to make the mind still.

4. "Control of the thought-waves of the mind" comes from concentration. The previous state of nirodha, or complete control, is one-pointedness.

5. Thought-waves are controlled by practice and detachment. Practice means to hold one idea in the mind again and again. Generally the mind jumps from one idea to another, and it never remains still. To fix the mind on one object without allowing it to wander is called practice. In this connection Krishna said in the Gita, "Let him withdraw the fickle

and unquiet mind from whatever causes it to wander away, and restore it to the control of the Atman alone." [VI.26]

6. You have asked, "Can the thought-waves be fully controlled through discrimination, practice, and dispassion without practising concentration and meditation?" From discrimination comes the result of meditation — complete control over the changes in the mind. In other words, it is possible to control the mind's changes either through meditation or through discrimination. Through the practice of discrimination between the real and the unreal, the mind becomes controlled and ultimately reaches the goal. In that superconscious state, one experiences the Atman, absolute existence. And through the practice of concentration and meditation, the mind also becomes controlled and attains the superconscious state, thus, being unmodified, it experiences the Atman. Discrimination is the path of Self-knowledge. Concentration and meditation are the paths of yoga. Although the paths are different, the goal is the same. Followers of both paths realize the Atman and go beyond all misery. A devotee, however, without going through such arduous and difficult methods, dedicates his heart and soul to God. The devotee becomes blessed by attaining God through intense love. This is the easiest path for the devotee.

Your well-wisher,
Turiyananda

114

57 Ramkanta Bose Street
Calcutta
6 January 1919

Dear Phani,

I received your letter yesterday. . . .

Now I shall answer your questions:

1. According to the Yoga Aphorisms of Patanjali, "Yoga is the control of the thought-waves in the mind." [I.2] In the Gita, the word *yoga* has been defined in many ways, such as, "Even-mindedness in success and failure is called yoga" [II.48]; "Skill in action is called yoga." [II.50] Please remember, all these definitions are meant for restraining the changes of the mind.

2. Therefore, yoga as "control of the thought-waves in the mind" and yoga as "even-mindedness in success and failure" — both refer to the same state and not to different things.

3. Equanimity of the mind is attained when the thought-waves are completely stopped, otherwise equanimity is not possible.

4. I did not see whether there was any mark of a wheel on the soles of the Master's feet, nor have I heard about this from anyone else. If somebody has seen that sign in a dream, I can't say whether that is true or false. But it is undoubtedly auspicious to see the Master in a dream.

5. "Skill in action is called yoga." This means that the same action, when it is done ordinarily, becomes the source of bondage; and when this action is done in the proper spirit, it purifies the mind and eventually destroys bondage. Thus it becomes yoga. For instance, work done with attachment leads to bondage; and when the same work is done with nonattachment, it becomes the cause of liberation. This attitude of nonattachment springs from yoga. Therefore, this very skill is called yoga.

Your well-wisher,
Turiyananda

115

Varanasi
18 April 1919

Dear Sharvananda,

I received your letter some time ago, but I could not write to you until now because I was ill. Though the subject [*What is Sri Ramakrishna's Philosophy*] is extremely difficult, with the Lord's grace, I will try my best to answer your questions.

It is not so easy to speak about Sri Ramakrishna's philosophy. It seems to me that to encourage the followers of all religions, he declared, "As many faiths, so many paths." He made this statement after he himself had practised the disciplines of various religious paths and experienced that their paths lead to the same Truth.

The ultimate Truth is one and nondual. It is called by various names: Brahman, Paramatman, Bhagavan [Lord], God, and so on. Whoever has realized that Truth has tried to express it according to his own temperament and understanding by giving it a particular name. But nobody has been able to express the *whole* truth. "What he is, he is" — that is the final conclusion of those who have realized him.

From different standpoints, Gaudapada's doctrine of no creation, Shankara's doctrine of superimposition, Ramanuja's doctrine of transformation, and [Sri Kantha's] doctrine of Shivadvaita — each one of these is true. Again, apart from all these doctrines, God is beyond all human expression and beyond the cognition of the mind. The founders of all these philosophical systems practised austerities, and having received God's grace, they preached the various doctrines at his command. God is the subject from which these doctrines evolved, but he himself is beyond them. The philosophy of Sri Ramakrishna is to express this truth. That is what I think.

Hanuman said to Rama: "O Lord, when I identify myself with the body, I am your servant. When I consider myself as an individual soul, I am a part of you. And when I look upon myself as the Atman, I am one with you — this is my firm conviction." Sri Ramakrishna referred to this statement as the best conclusion of different phases of spiritual experience.

Why should it not be possible to see the worship vessels as Brahman, saturated with consciousness? [*This is a reference to Sri Ramakrishna's vision in the Kali Temple, where it was revealed to him that everything is Pure Spirit.*] "Throughout the universe he exists, pervading every being and every thing, animate and inanimate." There is nothing but God. God verily is all. Because we cannot see him, we see objects instead; but the fact is that God is everything. Names and forms originate from him and remain in him. The waves, the foam, the bubbles — they are all nothing but water. Who cares if your doctrine of superimposition stands or falls! He who has known this truth [that Brahman is all] cannot be content with a lesser viewpoint.

The Master used to experience a state beyond all thoughts and ideas. That state transcends name and form, words and mind. There exists only One without a second, beyond the realm of prakriti [that is, beyond relativity]. Where is the doctrine of superimposition or the doctrine of no creation in that realm of Oneness? And yet again, all doctrines — whether of superimposition, or of no creation, or of transformation, etc. — originate from the Lord.

He alone is the Reality, the Truth. And again he is the source of all individual beings and of the universe. This manifestation is also true if he is not forgotten. Name and form become unreal if we forget God because they cannot exist without him. [*Sri Ramakrishna said: "Zeros added together amount to zero. Place the digit one before them, and they add in value." The digit one is God.*] But if he dwells in our thoughts, only then can we understand the truth that "the pith belongs to the sheaths and the sheaths belong to the pith." [*A reference to Sri Ramakrishna's saying that as long as the plantain tree contains sheaths, it also contains pith. He was illustrating the point that while God keeps the "ego of a devotee" in a person, the Relative (the sheaths) is real and so is the Absolute (the pith).*] At that time one can understand these sayings of the Gita: "All things in this universe are pervaded by Me" [IX.4]; "All is strung on Me as a row of gems on a thread." [VII.7]

The *main thing* is we must see God. When we see the Lord, everything else disappears. One experiences God as everything. Before we see him we have doubts and confusion and all sorts of theories and controversies. But these cease to exist as soon as we see him. Then one experiences uninterrupted peace and bliss.

Therefore, Sri Ramakrishna's philosophy is: In whatever way and at any cost we must attain God. The Master said, "Tie the nondual knowledge in the corner of your cloth and then do as you please." This means: Once you attain God, it does not matter which doctrine your temperament bids you to uphold. Liberation is assured when you know him. Then there is no more bondage. After death, whether you take another body or not depends upon your wish.

The seekers of nirvana [final liberation] consider this world a dream. They merge their minds in the impersonal aspect of Brahman and become one with It. The devotees who are attached to the Personal God consider this world a manifestation of God's power. They attach themselves to the Lord, who is Existence-Knowledge-Bliss Absolute. They are not afraid to be born again and again. They consider themselves to be playmates of God, and they come to the world to join his divine play. They delight in the Atman and at the same time remain devoted to God. They covet nothing in this world. They even refuse to accept nirvana if it is offered to them. That is enough for today.

Turiyananda

116

Varanasi
11 June 1919

Dear X,

I have received your letter of Jaishtha 21 [June 1919]. Quite often you come to my mind. I see that you are still the same as you were before. Why don't you try to settle yourself? You may not call on God or have faith in him, but why don't you try to love yourself? Does anybody disbelieve oneself? You exist all the time. Then why don't you make an effort to do good to yourself? Why do you think trashy things? Don't you understand that there is something called "progress"? Why don't you try for that? Others' efforts are useless, unless you find the way through self-effort.

Who has advised you to repeat, "I am a sinner, I am worthless"? By all means raise yourself from inertia. A person can help you to lift the heavy luggage from your head, but your hunger will not be satiated if someone eats for you. Eat for yourself if you do not want to suffer from hunger. Never be disheartened. Make an effort and you will succeed. Mere lamentation does not bear any result; rather, it does harm to a person. Try to practise concentration of the mind, and don't allow it to be scattered.

With love and best wishes,
Turiyananda

117

Varanasi
18 June 1919

Dear Ramesh,

A few days ago I received your undated letter, which was redirected from Calcutta. . . .

I am very happy to know that you have been blessed by Holy Mother. Through her grace you will be able to know everything. She herself will make you realize that the guru and the Chosen Deity are identical. The guru is realized as the Chosen Deity; in other words, the Chosen Deity is perceived in the guru. As power, both are the same — this becomes revealed to one through spiritual disciplines. "Guru is Brahma, Guru is Vishnu, Guru is the Lord Shiva; Guru is the Supreme Brahman. Therefore my salutations to that guru." From this verse of the Guru Gita you will grasp the implication. Try to develop pure devotion for her [Holy Mother]; then all of your bonds will be cut asunder.

Your well-wisher,
Turiyananda

118

Varanasi
16 July 1919

Dear X,

This morning I have received your long letter. It seems to me that your mind is in turmoil because you have discontinued your sadhana [spiritual practices]. You might have gotten some peace if you could have continued your sadhana some days more. However, nothing is lost. It will definitely turn into good if you can vigourously start again with a one-pointed mind. But once you give up it is extremely difficult to start again — especially if you have had a worldly experience. It seems that by the grace of the Master you did not have that.

The body does not remain the same all through life. If one does not have discrimination, dispassion, and intense love for sadhana, one feels uncomfortable living on alms; and his mind rushes towards physical comforts. Then one seeks good food, gathers devotees, and contemplates saving money. Thus he slackens his sadhana, and gradually his scattered mind ruins his meditation. During this time, it is very beneficial to have the association of a great soul who has self-control and renunciation.

However, you should start your sadhana again with might and main. If it is hard to live on alms, then from time to time cook some meals for yourself. Watch your health so that you may not fall sick. It is difficult to start an ashrama. As you have mentioned, some say they are doing it for others, but actually they do it for themselves. Therefore they experience misery rather than happiness. There is good and bad in everything. It is easy to say that one will give up the bad aspects and take up the good, but this is difficult to practise. It is better not to make any plan in this respect; but it is a different matter if it happens to you by the Lord's will. Then all works will be accomplished smoothly without making any special effort. The doer does not even know how the work has been done. It will be well and good if you can give up all plans and engage yourself wholly in the worship of God.

If you wish to go somewhere else, find a peaceful place where alms are easily available and live alone. Over and above this, try to engage yourself constantly in spiritual disciplines, have the company of the holy, and study the holy scriptures. If you can continue this way for some days, you will get peace by his grace and your mind will taste the joy of sadhana again. If long meditation is too tiring for you, then repeat the mantram for some time; again, if japam becomes tiring, then read or sing some songs and hymns. Thus whatever way it may be, try to engage your mind in the Lord.

Never put your mind on saving money. Money begets various kinds of evils. Maya is of two kinds — kama and kanchana [lust and gold]. Meditation is possible when you stay away from these two. However, by the grace of God, if you have self-awareness then there is no fear. But it is not a small thing to have that awareness. One has to work laboriously. Worship the Lord and don't put your mind on anything else. You will see that the Lord will shower his mercy again and everything will be favourable for you.

Your well-wisher,
Turiyananda

119

Varanasi
1 August 1919

Dear X,

I have received your letters of July 3 and 28. . . .

Why do you sing the song of despair all the time? This is not at all good. You have done it for a long time. Have you gotten any benefit from it? Why don't you change your tune once and see what happens. Why don't you try to have faith in God, love for human beings, firmness in your own action and life, and faith in the words of the scriptures and holy men? You will not lose anything. Follow this mode of life for some time. Why do you torture yourself unnecessarily, harbouring doubt and weakness? You are no longer a child who needs constant guidance. Now you will have to do everything for yourself. Enthusiasm, courage, strength — all these things are within you. Eventually they will manifest more and push you forward. Now gird up your loins and make a move towards the goal. What more shall I say?

Your well-wisher,
Turiyananda

120

Varanasi
8 December 1919

Dear X,

I received your letter yesterday. I am sorry to learn that you are not feeling well.

Why do you unnecessarily make your mind restless? It is not good to be worried; it does not help, rather, it hampers the work. When a person exerts himself to the utmost capacity with self-confidence and then surrenders to God — that is true resignation. Otherwise, he who without making any effort verbally surrenders himself to God, is harbouring nothing but laziness. Those who are enthusiastic and active, only they get help from God and not lazy people.

I am glad to know that you are practising japam. Learn its method from Maharaj [Swami Brahmananda]. Every action should be done with attention. Give up your misgivings. Whatever you practise with one-pointedness, that is best; otherwise, practising spiritual disciplines mechanically does not seem to produce any result. But there is a necessity of steadfast devotion. Don't pay too much attention to time. It creates distraction. The main thing is to keep the mind on God. If you have any questions, please ask Maharaj. It is good to be guided by a good teacher.

Your well-wisher,
Turiyananda

121

Varanasi
15 January 1920

Dear X,

I have received your letter of January 13. I am glad to know that you are working hard for your examination. The work which you have undertaken should be done wholeheartedly, and that leads to success. This is the truth.

I am delighted to see your earnestness for God-realization. One may boldly say, "God does not exist" —but that does not make God nonexistent. God remains as he is. It only makes the intellect of the nonbeliever more clouded. The Katha Upanishad says: "He is to be realized first as Existence limited by adjuncts [upadhis] and then in his true transcendental nature. Of these two aspects, Atman realized as Existence leads the knower to the realization of his true nature." [II.3.13]

The very existence of everything is God. Existence cannot be nonexistence. The Gita says, "The unreal never is. The Real never ceases to be." [II.16] This is a gospel truth. There is no reason that one cannot realize God. It is possible if one has intense longing, right efforts, perseverance, and a true guru. "He who desires, receives." "Ask and it shall be given." [Matthew, 7.7]

I asked you to pass the examination because I wanted to check your steadfastness and power of action. One can test the greatness of a person by observing his small actions or behaviour. A straw best shows how the wind blows. This much for today!

Your well-wisher,
Turiyananda

122

Varanasi
16 January 1920

Dear Ramesh,

Yesterday I received your letter of January 12. . . . It would have been better if you had written this letter to Swami Saradananda instead of to me, as he is the author of *Sri Ramakrishna, the Great Master* [*Sri Ramakrishna Lilaprasanga*]. He could have clearly answered your question pertaining to that book. However, I shall try my best to explain the point of your question.

Sri Ramakrishna used to say that for him there was no mukti [liberation]. I heard this from his own lips. Mukti here means *nirvana-mukti* — that is, upon attaining this liberation, one does not have to be reborn in the world. The *jivakotis* [ordinary souls], sorely afflicted by the miseries of the world, do not want to be reborn. They seek to escape from these miseries once and for all. That is why they strive for liberation. Nirvana means: nir=not, vana=body. Nirvana-mukti means that person will never again have a body.

He who has to come again and again to the world, impelled by the compassion to do good, how can he have absolute nirvana? This is why Sri Ramakrishna said to Swami Vivekananda, "He who was Rama and Krishna is now Ramakrishna in this body, but not from the standpoint of your Vedanta." The point stressed here is that the Advaita school of Vedanta holds jiva and Brahman to be one. Some take this to mean that everyone is equal to Rama and Krishna, and that they [Rama and Krishna] have no distinctive qualities. Lest Swamiji misunderstand the saying, "He who was Rama and Krishna is now Ramakrishna in this body," Sri Ramakrishna qualified this statement with the words, "not from the standpoint of your Vedanta." That is to say, the consciousness of Sri Ramakrishna was the consciousness of Ishvara [God] and not of the jiva. According to Advaita Vedanta, the jiva can attain the knowledge of his identity with Brahman by removing his ignorance through spiritual practices culminating in samadhi. Yet, despite all imaginable efforts, the jiva can never become Ishvara. He who is Ishvara is eternally the Ishvara. Even when he assumes a human body and appears like a jiva, he remains the same Ishvara and does not become the jiva.

As Krishna said in the Gita: "Many a birth have I passed through, O Arjuna, and so have you. I know them all, but you know them not, O scorcher of foes. Though I am unborn and eternal by nature, and though I am the Lord of all beings, yet, subjugating my prakriti [nature] I accept birth through my own maya." [IV.5-6] Likewise, the Master said, "Not from the standpoint of your Vedanta." He said the same thing as Krishna did. . . .

Your well-wisher,
Turiyananda

123

Varanasi
13 February 1920

Dear S—,

I was glad to receive your letter of December 18. . . . I could not follow your questions clearly. However, I will try to answer them according to my understanding.

Vedanta is expounded by three schools of philosophy — dualistic, qualified nondualistic, and nondualistic. According to the dualistic and qualified nondualistic systems, this world is not considered to be unreal; rather, it is real. In other words, prakriti [the world], jiva [the individual soul], and God — these three are eternal and real. But the world and individual souls sometimes remain manifested and at other times unmanifested; they are not absolutely unreal. These schools believe in various kinds of liberation, such as *sayujya* [union with God], *samipya* [living near God], and so on. There is no nirvana-mukti [final absorption with Brahman and no more birth] in these systems. Instead of saying that, it is better to say that the followers of these schools do not aspire to nirvana.

Both dualists and qualified nondualists admit that the world is full of misery, but they say that it can be joyful by the grace of God. On the other hand, the nondualists know that the world is full of misery; so, with a view to getting rid of it, they sever all connections with the world and aspire for nirvana, or final liberation. They live in this world experiencing nondual knowledge, and after death they merge into Brahman and leave the world forever. In their opinion, this world is unreal. Referring to these liberated souls, the Chandogya Upanishad says, "He does not return anymore." [VIII.15.1] Once our Master also gave such instructions to Swami Abhedananda about attaining nondualistic knowledge.

This subject will be more clear if we study side by side what Krishna said to Arjuna in the Gita and what he taught to Uddhava in the Bhagavatam. In the Gita, Krishna said about himself, "It is I alone who am to be known through all the Vedas; I am indeed the author of Vedanta and the knower of the Vedas." [XV.15] In the Bhagavatam, Krishna says:

> I have proclaimed three kinds of yoga for the spiritual enlightenment of human beings. These are jnana yoga [path of knowledge], karma yoga [path of action], and

bhakti yoga [path of devotion]. There is no other way besides these three. The path of knowledge is for those who are disgusted with work, and as a result, have renounced it. The path of karma is for those who have desires and are therefore not yet disgusted with work and its fruits. The path of devotion is very effective for that person who by some good fortune has developed faith in my divine life and message, but has neither extreme renunciation nor excessive attachment for the world. [XI.20.6-8]

From these scriptural passages we understand that jnana yoga is meant for those whose minds have been withdrawn from sense objects. Its results are renunciation of the world, cessation of birth, and attainment of nirvana. According to this nondualistic school, "Brahman alone is real and the world is unreal." It cannot be otherwise. But those who have some attachment for the world, how can they say that the world is unreal? They consider this world as the divine manifestation of God, so they do not say it is unreal. They discard its *avidya* [ignorance] aspect and accept the *vidya* [knowledge] aspect, and do not try to attain nirvana. This is the general rule.

But there are special rules also. For example, some, even after attaining knowledge and becoming recipients of nirvana, do not accept it. Rather, they assume human births by embracing spontaneous divine love. They have been referred to in the Bhagavatam this way, "The sages whose only pleasure is in the Self, and from whom all fetters have fallen off, even they love the Supreme Lord with motiveless devotion." [I.7.10] They do not have any desire for worldly life. They are the companions of the Lord's divine play. Swamiji has mentioned many times in his lectures about these kinds of souls, who are liberated-in-life [jivan-mukta]; and he expressed his eagerness to be born again and again, relinquishing his personal liberation, for the good of mankind.

For the attainment of liberation-in-life, the Master gave many examples, such as: "In the hide and seek game, if you touch the granny you are safe." "Holding a pole, if you whirl around you will not fall." "Be gold after touching the philosopher's stone." "Churning the milk, make butter; then place it in the water, and it will float." Only after attaining this state of jivan-mukti, did a devotee fervently pray: "O Krishna, even though I be born among insects, birds, beasts, reptiles, demons, ghouls, or whatsoever, still through your grace may I have unshakable and unwavering devotion to you." [Prapanna Gita]

So it is seen in the final analysis that everyone will have to give up avidya [ignorance]. The world which is made out of ignorance does not last forever. You have mentioned ignorance, faultfinding and other things in your letter — these are innate in human nature and are experienced by all. This is called avidya. As long as it exists, one cannot attain knowledge and devotion. Therefore, how can one suddenly experience the world as the manifestation of Brahman? If you want to realize "All this is verily Brahman" [Chandogya Upanishad, III.14.1], you will have to abandon the idea of the world. Without renunciation, neither knowledge nor devotion can arise in the mind. First one will have to attain knowledge or pure devotion through renunciation, then one has a choice — either to take another birth or to attain nirvana. Still, it is better to be born as a companion of the Lord for the good of mankind than to attain nirvana. Undoubtedly, this is the view of the Master and Swamiji.

The other view: You will not have to give up anything in this world; enjoy everything to your heart's content and see

Brahman everywhere; the knowledge of Brahman is easy to obtain. Although such statements sound sweet and alluring, they cannot be worthwhile and acceptable — because they contradict the scriptures, reason, and the experiences of the great souls.

Once I heard a person arguing in front of our Master, saying that this world is real. After listening to him, the Master said: "Ram, why don't you say in simple words that even now you have the desire to enjoy the sour dish of hog-plum [the worthless pleasures of the world]! What is the need for all this vain argumentation?" What response could have been more forceful and irrefutable? The truth is that if one has attachments one is afraid to renounce the world. But to hide this attitude and imagine that one can realize God without giving up attachments, only indicates one's natural inner weakness.

Regarding this tree of worldly existence, the Gita says, "Having cut down this firm-rooted Ashvattha tree with the strong axe of detachment, then that goal should be sought for." [XV.3-4] This teaching of Lord Krishna cannot be contradicted in any way. It is needless to say that those who, out of their attachment, disregard the scriptural teachings on renunciation, consider worldly life to be the goal, and declare renunciation, which is the final conclusion of the unerring Vedas, to be unnecessary — their approach may be daring, but it is not reasonable. If I have any opportunity in the future, I shall try to discuss this subject again. This much for today.

Your well-wisher,
Turiyananda

Varanasi
2 March 1920

Dear Kha. Maharaj,

Revered Swami Turiyanandaji has received your letter of February 17. I am writing whatever he dictated to me upon listening to the questions from your letter.

Knowledge is of two kinds: 1. *Sva-samvedya*, or that which is known by oneself; 2. *Para-samvedya*, or that which is known by others. Sva-samvedya — the knowledge which comes from one's own experience — is true; and undoubtedly it can be verified with the scriptures and the signs of an illumined soul. As he is established in Brahman, his experience of oneness never changes, although externally his lifestyle may seem to be incongruous. Para-samvedya — the knowledge which comes from studying the scriptures and from other sources — is based on external signs. As the person of indirect knowledge has no personal experience, he cannot properly ascertain Self-knowledge and the state of liberation-in-life.

As one cannot make a child understand the sex experience before attaining puberty, similarly, a spiritual aspirant experiences the truth through an evolutionary process. Having faith in the words of the scriptures and the guru, as the aspirant continues his sadhana [spiritual practices], in the course of time the knowledge of Brahman dawns in his heart.

In this connection, there is a story in the Vedantic tradition. After a virgin girl married, she returned from her husband's home. Then her unmarried virgin friends asked her, "Tell us, how much pleasure have you gotten from your husband?"

---

*This valuable letter was dictated by Swami Turiyananda and written by his assistant Swami Dhruveshwarananda.

She answered, "A lot of pleasure." But her friends could not understand. In the meantime, another newly-married girl arrived there. Listening to their questions, she smiled from her own experience of pleasure; but the other girls could not understand. Likewise, he who has attained the state of liberation-in-life, he truly understands; whereas others only guess and can never be free from doubt.

They are called *jivan-mukta*, or the knowers of Brahman, who have attained unitive knowledge while living and are not bound by past, present, or future. Due to prarabdha [the result of past karma], a jivan-mukta lives in the body and experiences the functions of the body. In other words, he may look happy or unhappy because of the contact of good or bad things; but he never loses his even-mindedness because he has the knowledge of his true nature [that is, he is Brahman — beyond the pairs of opposites]. This state has been substantiated in the Gita where Krishna mentioned the characteristics of a man of steady wisdom merged in samadhi: "He who is not perturbed by adversity, who does not long for happiness" [II.56] and other verses.

An illumined soul has clear knowledge of the real and the unreal, therefore his mind is never identified with unreal objects; whereas, an ordinary person is identified with the unreal objects through "I and mine." As a result of this ignorance he suffers from unending miseries.

Ignorance is bondage and knowledge is liberation. When this unitive knowledge dawns on a person, he becomes jivan-mukta, or liberated-in-life. In the Yoga Vashistha Ramayana [Nirvana, CXX.1-13], seven stages have been described for a spiritual aspirant according to his evolution. The first to third stages are called the realm of an ascetic, and the fourth to seventh stages are called the realm of knowledge. The state of jivan-mukti starts at the fourth stage, which is also called the state of dream. There the world seems to be unreal, but the mind has not yet attained complete tranquility. The fifth stage is called the state of dreamless sleep. In this state, the mind is devoid of thought-waves, has attained full rest, and can awaken itself from samadhi. The sixth stage is the intensified form of the fifth stage. It is also called the state of deep dreamless sleep. At this stage the yogi cannot awaken from samadhi without the help of others. The seventh stage is called *turiya,* or the transcendental state. At this stage the yogi cannot awaken from samadhi even with others' help. He remains absorbed in blissful Brahman and his body lasts as long as his prarabdha continues. An ordinary yogi cannot come back from this stage; but a great soul, like an avatar, through God's grace comes down to the realm of "I and mine" for the good of mankind. The Master used to say, "A great soul can move back and forth from the lower stage to the seventh, and live in this world holding some good desires, such as, 'I am a devotee, or I am a jnani [man of knowledge].'" . . .

Yours affectionately,
Dhruveshwarananda

125

Varanasi
10 April 1920

Dear Nirmal [Swami Madhavananda],

I have received your letter of April 7. . . . Neither this person nor that person is the cause of anything; at the root of all is God. Everything has emerged from him. Never forget him "from whom has streamed forth this eternal activity." [Gita, XV.4] Fix your mind on God. If he is pleased, there is no more anxiety or fear of anybody's displeasure. Don't pay much attention to external causes; rather, practise to see everything within. "Your lover is in yourself, and your enemy too is within you." [A Hindi saying] "He himself is his friend, and he himself is his enemy." [Gita, VI.5] "The Atman, indeed, is all this." [Chandogya Upanishad, VII.25.2] "There is no diversity in the Atman." [Brihadaranyaka Upanishad, IV.4.19] It is not enough to read these teachings from the scriptures. Now you will have to realize them by yourself. Now or never. . . .

Your well-wisher,
Turiyananda

126

Ramakrishna Mission
Varanasi
15 April 1920

Dear Bashi [Bashiswar Sen],

I have received your letter of April 11. . . .

You have mentioned that in my last letter I wrote that "we should remain in this world as witnesses." Yes, it is absolutely true. This not only applies to you but to all of us. If we can live in this world as witnesses, then we can enjoy fun and merriment, otherwise not. But it is extremely difficult to remain as a witness in everything we do. We identify ourselves with our activities, and as a result experience happiness and misery. May the Divine Mother always keep us close to her and not allow us to run away and get entangled in the meshes of maya. I shall be blessed if, by her grace, I get the opportunity to pass the remaining days of my life as a real witness. . . .

Your well-wisher,
Turiyananda

127

Varanasi
19 April 1920

Dear Ramesh,

I have received your letter of Vaishakh 1 [April 1920]. . . .

Doubts in the mind cannot be removed by correspondence or by studying books; one has to make an effort. One should follow the instructions of the scriptures and the guru; thus one develops faith, and from faith comes purity of heart. Only then are all doubts dispelled from the mind. This is what Krishna taught Arjuna in the Gita: "Therefore with the sword of knowledge cut asunder this doubt about the Self, born of ignorance and residing in your heart, and devote yourself to yoga. Arise, O Bharata!" [IV.42] The Lord says, "Arise and practise yoga"; in other words, follow the injunctions of the scriptures. Doubts have to be cut asunder by the sword of knowledge; this cannot be done only by listening to instructions. Practice is necessary; and practice leads to perfection. The truth is: "Keep your mind fixed on God, and gradually you will be united with him." One has to keep on practising.

Meditation invariably produces results — whoever may be your ideal. One should think of the object of meditation as Brahman. Saint Ramprasad mentioned steadfast devotion to the Chosen Deity in some of his mystical songs: "According to the different modes of worship, O Mother, you have made the main deity into five; now when the aspirant dissolves the five into one, how will you survive?" "Knowing Kali is Brahman, I have renounced both virtue and vice." "Ramprasad says, 'She is the ultimate Reality whom I address as the Mother. O my mind, can't you follow my intention? Shall I have to unveil this mystery publicly?'" One should have steadfast devotion; that does not mean one has to be dogmatic. Sri Ramakrishna frequently cautioned his devotees on this point.

One should not listen to anybody and everybody. One should follow the instruction of his own guru, and that brings success. Tread your own path with a one-pointed mind. By listening to the words of many or by diverting one's attention to this and that, one ruins one's spiritual life. It does not help at all.

The Master used to say, "Books are like knots" which bind a soul. One should give up this wild-goose chase and follow this teaching of the Gita as the only goal: "O Arjuna, make only one resolute and unwavering thought [for Self-realization]." [II.41] Some, even after liberation, take birth as the companions of the avatar or divine incarnation. They are ever-free souls. They have been referred to in the Bhagavatam: "Such are the glorious qualities of the Lord that the sages whose only pleasure is in the Self, and from whom all fetters have fallen off, even they love the Supreme Lord with motiveless devotion." [I.7.10]

Try to be thoughtful and make a decision after pondering the pros and cons. What more is there to say?

Your well-wisher,
Turiyananda

128

Varanasi
24 April 1920

Dear X,

I have received your letter of Vaishakh 2 [April 1920]. . . .

Because you understand everything, you must now do what is best for you. Weakness is an innate tendency in human beings. If you say, "I am weak, I am weak," the weakness will not go away. Rather, a person can become strong by wholeheartedly cultivating positive thoughts: "Why should I be weak? I must be strong." Try to implement the teachings of your teacher into your actions; merely listening to advice does not produce any result. The Master used to say: "A person does not get intoxicated by merely uttering the word 'siddhi, siddhi' [hemp]. First you collect siddhi, make a paste, and then drink it. Thus you will get the joy of intoxication."

Why do you say that your prayer and meditation are not going in the right direction? Please take effective measures — that is my advice to you. By all means one should continue one's sadhana; superficial tasting does not work. Momentary zeal does not bring success — try to make it permanent. You are not a child. In this respect, I do not have to say anything more to you. Shun that thing immediately which you think makes you weak. Accept that thing with earnestness which you think will make you strong. I have nothing else to say. . . .

Your well-wisher,
Turiyananda

129

Varanasi
10 May 1920

Dear Gurudas [Gupta],

I have received your letter of May 8, 1920. . . .

I am glad to learn that your anxiety about initiation is gone. Whatever you have written in this respect is undoubtedly pertinent and reasonable. Initiation is definitely helpful in spiritual life. The omniscient Lord makes everything favourable for one who has resolved to sacrifice his life for God. That person will not have to make any special effort for initiation.

The main thing is to have intense longing to attain God, and to engage oneself wholeheartedly in that task. Then success will come automatically. God, as a guru, initiates and teaches everything. God is the only guru; others are mere instruments. This does not mean that I intend to prove that initiation is unnecessary. Many people get benefit from initiation, and it is necessary for the majority of people. But only one's own steadfast devotion is very effective — that I intend to say.

I am delighted to hear that you are studying the Gita. The Gita is the embodiment of all scriptures. It destroys man's rebirth in this mortal world. The Gita is the heart of the Lord. It has no parallel. A person who practises the teachings of the Gita, his mind becomes pure and he develops the power of right understanding in every subject. That person attains supreme peace.

I am really pleased to know that you realize that your understanding is becoming clear. Surrender yourself to the Lord. He will make you do what is good for you. Don't be impatient. He will show you the way. Wherever you are, if you hold onto God, there is nothing to fear. Holding a pole, if you whirl, you will not fall. One who completely surrenders himself to God becomes free from duty. The Bhagavatam says: "He who has shunned the ego, the sense of agency, and has taken refuge in God wholeheartedly, no longer has any debt or obligation to the deities, sages, creatures, relations, men, and manes. He is the servant of none else but the Lord [and being so, he fulfills his obligations to all and is free from the sin of failure to do his duty]." [XI.5.41]

Do not worry. Move on as before. Offer your past, present, and future to him. Do not plan for yourself. You will see, he will arrange everything for you. . . .

Your well-wisher,
Turiyananda

130

Varanasi
31 May 1920

Dear Gurudas [Gupta],

I was pleased to receive your letter of May 28. It is not a small thing that gradually you are becoming more aware of yourself. Thus you continue your journey from outside to inside and gradually reach the inmost Self. If you can experience your true nature, then the purpose of your life will be over. Your life will be blessed attaining that state: "It is the Ear of the ear, the Mind of the mind, the Speech of speech, the Life of life, and the Eye of the eye. Having detached the Self [from the sense organs] and renounced the world, the wise attain to Immortality." [Kena Upanishad, I.2] Experiencing the Self in all, "he cannot hate anyone." [Isha Upanishad, 8]

As long as one has a connection with the body, senses, and mind, one has knowledge of good and bad. When one is strongly connected with the Supreme Self, the pairs of opposites do not exist. In other words, good and bad cannot perturb him anymore. "If a man knows the Self as *I am this*, then desiring what and for whose sake will he suffer in the wake of the body?" [Brihadaranyaka Upanishad, IV.4.12] If a person has the knowledge "I am the Atman," then in spite of physical and mental afflictions he can remain in bliss experiencing his true nature. As he has separated himself from his body and mind, their afflictions do not affect him.

Thinking "I am the body, I am the body," I become identified with the body. Then why should I not be the Atman if I think "I am the Atman, I am the Atman"? The cause of our suffering is the acceptance of untruth as truth. If we could know the truth as truth, then all of our misery would go away and happiness would come to us. To experience the Truth, one needs long practice with infinite patience. Practice and renunciation are the main supports. If one has steadfast devotion, everything becomes easy by God's grace.

The study of the Gita will help you to understand the Truth easily. "O Bhagavad Gita, you destroy man's rebirth in this mortal world. O Mother, I meditate on you." [Meditation of the Gita, verse 1] What more is there to say? This is the goal in life as well as in death.

Never forget these sayings of the Master: "One match stick can destroy one hundred years' darkness in a moment. One drop of God's grace removes all ignorance which accumulated through birth after birth." Longing is essential because it quickly leads to perfection. In fact, I am really happy, knowing you are making good progress.

In the beginning, contrition and mortification might have some necessity, but they are harmful if anybody harbours them excessively for a long time. Therefore, one should shun them. Holding to them needlessly is called tamasic firmness. Krishna says in the Gita, "The firmness by which a stupid person does not give up his sleep, fear, grief, despondency, and sensuality — that, O Partha, is of the nature of tamas." [XVIII.35] Repentance finds fulfillment when a person gives up his bad habits. Otherwise, what can one achieve by only repenting for one's bad deeds? Manu says, "He who has committed a sin and has repented is freed from that sin; but he is purified only by the resolution of ceasing to sin and thinking 'I will do so no more.'" [Manu Samhita, XI.231]

Your well-wisher,
Turiyananda

131

Varanasi
27 June 1920

Dear X,

I am in receipt of your postcard of June 25. I receive almost daily reports of the Holy Mother's condition. It now depends on the Lord's grace to make things take a turn for the better. . . .

"For a sage who wants to attain yoga, action is said to be the means; but when he has attained yoga, serenity is said to be the means." [Gita, VI. 3] This passage of the Gita describes clearly the stages of a yogi's life. The meaning is that those who want to attain yoga must do so through work; while for those who have already attained this state, work is no longer necessary. Rather, it should be slackened so as to maintain an unbroken current of thought. Work, either internal or external, must go on. For it has already been distinctly stated that "no one can remain even for an instant without doing work." [Gita, III.5]

First, external work is needed; then internal work — meditation and the like — is necessary. Therefore in the very next verse Krishna sets forth the characteristics of one who has attained yoga: "When a man has no attachment to the objects of the senses or to works, and when he has wholly renounced his will, he is said to have attained yoga." [Gita, VI. 4] Sri Ramakrishna illustrated this verse through his example of the mother-in-law who gradually reduces the duties of her pregnant daughter-in-law. Later when she gives birth to her child, she has absolutely no duties. She only attends to her child.

In the beginning all work is done to realize God; after attaining him, further work is done for his sake only. One is then full to the brim and has no more needs. The work which is done in that state is not for any selfish gain, and is therefore not classified as work. Realizing the Lord, one no longer has to practise spiritual disciplines or to concentrate his mind on God. That person is concentrated under all circumstances. The work which King Janaka or Swamiji did was not for their own sake. All personal concerns had ceased for them, so whatever they did in that state was for all. They had realized the truth that they were one with all. They had verily realized the state described in this verse: "With the heart concentrated by yoga, viewing all things with equal regard, he beholds himself in all beings and all beings in himself." [Gita, VI.29]

Those who have not attained this state are forced to do work, for they have the need to do something for themselves. Therefore, Krishna advises people to work without motive as far as possible. This will gradually purify the mind so as to enable one to see oneself in all. And when one fully beholds oneself in all, there will be no more work. In other words, even while working one will realize that one is not the doer.

Work and other such things last only as long as there is egoism. "All trouble will be over when the 'I' is gone." The devotee does all work in the spirit of "Not I, but Thou." While the jnani [follower of the path of knowledge], knowing himself to be the Atman, has realized that the body, mind, and intellect alone work, and never identifies himself with any action. That is all.

Take my word, nowhere do the scriptures advocate a stupefied state, a cessation of all activities, and mechanical withdrawing of the hands and feet from work. In the state of ignorance, people work with the idea that it is *their* work. When one attains knowledge and devotion, one gets rid of that egoistic idea. The devotee works for the Lord. The jnani, even while working, knows that he is not the doer and is at perfect rest. He sees that "the senses are busied with their objects." [Gita, V.9] This much for the present.

With love and best wishes to you all.

Yours affectionately,
Turiyananda

132

Varanasi
13 July 1920

Dear Gurudas [Gupta],

I have received your letter of July 8. . . .

It is a matter of regret that holy company is so rare! Krishna said in the Gita, "Among thousands of men, one, here and there, strives for perfection." [VII.3] Most people in this world are drawn to sense enjoyment. Who wants to renounce? People intend to have all enjoyment and no misery. But they do not realize that it is impossible to have happiness without misery. Such is the maya of the Great Enchantress that it does not allow people to have Self-awareness.

The Gita is the embodiment of all scriptures. May you attain your goal by studying the Gita — that is my prayer.

Practise meditation on the Gita. Whatever you read, reflect on that all the time — even while walking, sitting, eating, and lying down. Then the meaning of the Gita will be revealed in your heart, and that will give you peace. If you practise the Gita, you will get the fruit — this is a gospel truth.

Liberation is inevitable for a person who has achieved the state above the three gunas [sattva, rajas, and tamas], as mentioned in the fourteenth chapter of the Gita. The marks of a person who has transcended the gunas and how he rises above them have been clearly stated there. Krishna says, "He who worships me with the yoga of undeviating love rises above the gunas and becomes fit to be one with Brahman." [XIV.26] He also mentioned the reason, "For I am the abode of Brahman, the Immortal and the Immutable, and of the Eternal Dharma, and of Absolute Bliss." [XIV.27] Therefore, if you only practise and experience this fourteenth chapter of the Gita, you won't need anything else.

What Krishna described as the signs of a man of steady wisdom in the second chapter of the Gita [verses 55 to 72], he narrated a little differently in the fourteenth chapter [verses 22 to 27] as the signs of a man who has risen above the three gunas. Again, in the twelfth chapter [verses 13 to 20] Krishna has elaborately described the signs of a true devotee who is endowed with the signs mentioned in the second and fourteenth chapters. Remember, the Lord mentioned these signs again and again so that people could compare them with their own lives. . . .

Your well-wisher,
Turiyananda

133

Varanasi
17 July 1920

Dear Nirmal [Swami Madhavananda],

I have received your letter of July 13. . . .

Struggle alone does not lead to peace; one must surrender and submit. Through the grace of the Lord everything will gradually be resolved. . . . One should continue spiritual practices on a regular basis. It is important to follow a routine. But one must try to maintain the spiritual current within constantly. At first, theory and practice are separate, but later they become one. Theory itself turns into practice. Then spiritual life becomes easy and natural. This is what is called *sahajavastha*, or the natural state. One no longer has to make an effort to practise spiritual disciplines; his mind always dwells in God.

It is really troublesome if one cannot make one's mind spiritual. The mind becomes saintly by constant spiritual practice; then the mind does not feel the need for external holy company, because it enjoys constant communion with God. . . .

Your well-wisher,
Turiyananda

134

Varanasi
27 July 1920

Dear X,

I have received your letter of Thursday. . . .

It is true that the mind and the Atman are not the same thing. As soon as the mind becomes pure, the Atman manifests there and the mind ceases to function. The universal mind exists as long as the universe exists. As the universe is not infinite, so the universal mind cannot be infinite. Only the Paramatman, or Supreme Self, is without beginning and without end, and nothing else. If you think deeply, you will understand this. . . .

Your well-wisher,
Turiyananda

135

Varanasi
26 August 1920

Dear Gurudas [Gupta],

I was pleased to receive your letter of August 20. . . .

Progress in spiritual life comes little by little, and that is good and desirable. One should create one's own environment. Everything takes place in the course of time. It is true, without knowledge one cannot be detached; but one can practise nonattachment. It dawns on a person automatically if he practises sincerely for a long time. One should offer the fruits of one's action to God for his satisfaction. Later, when a person is convinced that he is working for God, he develops love for him. This is called *bhakti*, or devotion.

A mother suffers so much for her children. She does so many things to make them happy and comfortable, but she does not feel that she is doing any karma [action]. That is the way a mother gets her joy; and for that reason, it is not karma, but love. When one develops such love for God, that is called bhakti. If one can love God and make him one's own, then one's life becomes blessed; because God is the Life of our lives, the Soul of our souls.

With love and best wishes,
Turiyananda

136

Varanasi
12 April 1921

Dear Dinesh [Swami Nikhilananda],

I received your long letter a few days ago. . . .

Why did you make such a big fuss? When you call on God, then only you and God will know about it. If you make a mistake, he will correct it. God is omniscient. We only need sincerity and earnestness in spiritual life. Remember the Master's story about the pilgrim who went to visit Lord Jagannath in Puri. He did not know the way, but his genuine love for the Lord led him to the temple.

You have received initiation from the Holy Mother, therefore, you have nothing to worry about. You have mentioned the method of your meditation; that sounds wonderful to me. The purpose will be served if you can unite the guru and the Chosen Deity. Don't be impatient. One is supposed to practise for a long time. Maintain your equanimity in success and failure. Continue your spiritual practices and watch how long your mind dwells on God. If the mind runs away from God, make an effort to bring it back to him. Is it a task of two or four days? You will have to devote your whole life to it. What else can you do? If you consider God your all-in-all and attaining him is the goal of your life, then engage yourself fully in that task. Do the best you can. Don't be restless.

However, if one has hidden desires for name and fame, one tries to realize God hurriedly and then becomes restless to achieve name and fame. But this does not work. Rather, first fulfill your desire for name and fame, and then try to realize God. Again I remind you of the words of the Master: "A thread cannot pass through the eye of a needle if the tiniest fibre sticks out. Therefore, first all fibres are to be moistened and made one-pointed by rubbing; then the thread will pass through the eye of a needle." Giving up all desires, one should call on God with one-pointed longing. Krishna says in the Gita, "In this [karma yoga], O scion of Kuru, there is only one resolute and unwavering thought; but the thoughts of the irresolute are many-branched and unending." [II.41] This will give you the idea of what I mean to say.

Continue your sadhana [spiritual practices]. It will surely bear results. The saint Tulasidas said, "Whatever way you sow the seed in the soil, pointing either up or down, its sprout will rise upward." Similarly, if you practise your sadhana wholeheartedly, it will produce good results even though your means may not be perfect. If you have real devotion in your heart, the Lord will see it; he does not count human imperfections. The Lord knows our inmost thoughts. There is a saying: "The prayer of an unlettered person may be grammatically wrong and the prayer of a learned man may be correct, but both prayers will render the same virtue; because God accepts only the inmost feelings." Therefore, don't worry whether your meditation is going in the right direction or not. At first, one should meditate on the guru; there is no definite method regarding the meditation on the Chosen Deity [Ishta]. However, you go on practising your sadhana; God will set everything right for you.

There are two kinds of sadhana: preparatory and spontaneous. Those who have desires for the results of their actions are drawn to preparatory sadhana. On the other hand, those whose goal in life is to attain devotion to God don't like to be slaves of rules and the injunctions of the scriptures. They strive wholeheartedly to develop love for God. The Master used to say, "It does not matter whether the fodder of the cow is good or bad, if it is mixed with oil-cake, the cow gobbles it down greedily." Similarly one might have some flaws in the mode of one's worship, but if it is performed sincerely, God accepts that worship. What more shall I say? This much for today. . . .

Your well-wisher,
Turiyananda

137

Varanasi
17 April 1921

Dear Jivan,

I was glad to receive your letter of 1st Vaishakh [April 1921]. I hope that through the grace of God you are living happily and in good health in the holy bosom of the Himalayas and passing your days in the thoughts of God. . . .

Is your mention of various physical ailments and mental disturbances a hint that you desire to go elsewhere? I could not make anything out of it. Will your mind be steady by itself unless you make it so? Whether you go to a secluded part of the Himalayas favourable to spiritual practices or anywhere else, the mind will always be with you. It will be of no use if you do not succeed in controlling the mind and directing it towards God. And this you will have to do by exerting yourself. No one can do it for you. Of course it helps one a good deal to have a favourable place and holy company. Undoubtedly, bringing the mind under control takes hard self-effort.

You cannot say that you have had no past good karma, for you have had enough opportunity. One accomplishes much in this very life by dint of special effort and care. Man suffers in various ways because of his own foolishness. But one can minimize these sufferings if one succeeds in purifying the mind. Everyone experiences happiness and misery and no one can escape from them. They remain as long as the body lasts; but one is no longer overcome by them if one becomes devoted to God. They come and go. The wise person ignores them and keeps himself engaged in sadhana. Their influence ceases when one becomes rooted in spiritual practices. Then the mind is absorbed in the bliss of devotion and enjoys peace. Worship the Lord; the mind will be calm automatically. Without depending on a place or a person, take refuge in the indwelling Self. Try to purify the mind with all your heart and soul. Curb your outgoing tendencies and make an effort to be indrawn. And shunning all worldly desires, direct yourself towards God. Then you will no longer go astray due to the vain promptings of your mind; and you will be endowed with peace and goodness by the grace of the Lord. . . .

Your well-wisher,
Turiyananda

138

Varanasi
6 May 1921

Dear Dinesh [Swami Nikhilananda],

Yesterday I received your long letter. This letter repeats the same old story of your previous letter. Nevertheless, you have mentioned that you cannot express in words how much benefit you have derived from my advice. But I do not understand what benefit you have derived. I see the same old complaints and lamentations there, without any change. How shall I understand by this that you have been benefitted?

All work is to be learned through practice. It seems to me that you people do not admit that practice is necessary for spiritual disciplines and control of the mind. You want to be a great yogi or a great devotee by practising meditation for a couple of days or repeating japam for four days. You are prepared to exert yourself and wait for results regarding everything else, but in spiritual matters you cannot withstand the slightest delay. You become overly impatient.

However, human character is formed by practising disciplines in life after life. But without comprehending this, you people want success within three days. What else shall I say? It seems that you did not read my letter attentively. If so, you would not have questioned me again in the same old fashion. Is it so easy to control the mind? How can you do that without exerting yourself? I think I mentioned this in my previous letter. Now I have nothing more to write. . . .

With best wishes,
Turiyananda

Courtesy: Vedanta Society of Northern California

Meditation Cottage at Shanti Ashrama, California, c. 1901

SECTION II

Letters Written in English

Courtesy: Vedanta Society of Northern California

Swami Turiyananda, Varanasi, India, c. 1921

1

Los Angeles
California
1901

My Dear Gurudas [Swami Atulananda],

Don't get discouraged or disheartened. Why should it be always sunshine and good times? Let Mother's will be done. Never mind sunshine or rain, we must not forget Mother at any time. Even if we don't see her, why should we lose heart? She appears again in our view. She knows what is best for us. Once we have given [ourselves] over to her, what right have we to think of ourselves again? It is not so easy to do as to say — of that I am sure, but there is no other way out. Whether we see or don't see, Mother is our only place of rest. There are ups and downs in all hearts, but we should not give way to them.

Real, genuine sympathy alone works wonders. That is the one thing omnipotent in this world of sorrows and weaknesses. Ask of Mother for that and you will have it. Think not about yourself but only for others. That is renunciation, that is religion, that is all. You have died, why do you think of yourself? Have you not given everything over to Mother? Why then think of yourself again? Never care for position. Give up all such ideas. Work is worship. Everything is in the life we live, not in position. Mother knows the heart and sees the heart and arranges things accordingly. Let your light so shine that everybody can see it. Let your work be silent and in secret and your Mother who seeth in secret shall reward thee openly. The fowls of the air have their nests to rest, but the Son of man had nowhere to lay his head. Jesus had no position, and millions and millions of hearts are his place, or he is the place where millions of weary souls go for rest. Go on my dear boy; live the life. Pray for it earnestly and sincerely.

It pleased me immensely to read the account of the celebration in the [Shanti] Ashrama of Sri Ramakrishna's birthday anniversary. We observed the day here in talk of him and prayer. May Sri Ramakrishna arouse in us the real spirit of renunciation and love for Mother, whose very personification he himself was.

* * *

Be strong, my dear boy! Don't give in to anything whatever. It is not good to be weak; the weak must go to the wall. This is the law of the world. But what have you to do with the world anymore? Mother's child, good or bad, weak or strong, you have no other to look up to but Mother! Others, who do not know, may think of temporal help. But you can never think that way, I am sure!

* * *

Sri Ramakrishna is the concrete embodiment of the Vedantic Truth, because in his life he manifested in full all the subtle truths that we read in the Vedanta philosophy. Pray for unflinching love and devotion and you will have everything.

* * *

There is no world outside. It is what we project outside. But how difficult it is to understand this, and how much more difficult to remember it always, even after understanding it.

We feel unhappy when we make ourselves small. We feel miserable when we think of ourselves as finite. That is the bane. Yet we forget and are in the whirlpool of maya ever once again. But thanks to the grace of Mother, we remember it again soon. "There is no happiness in that which is finite; that which is finite is perishable. That which is universal is Blissfulness Itself." [Chandogya Upanishad, VII.23.1, 24.1] Know the universal! That is thy real Self.

May we never lose sight of this our real Self, which is the Self of all, our dear Mother, whose children we are.

Turiyananda

2

Shanti Ashrama
California
2 June 1901

My dear Mr. R—,

I have been so happy to receive your kind letter. I have been thinking of you very much for the past few days. I am glad you are all doing well now. My health was not satisfactory, but is now all right. It is gratifying to know that you are doing better every day. I am always with you in Spirit. Give my love to [ ] when you see her. She is so kind and good. I heard about the person you speak of. It is all right. She is Mother's child too. If she ignorantly does anything that is not proper Mother will forgive her. She will not do the same thing again when she knows better, you need not feel anxious for her. Be steady in what you have known to be Truth and that is all. If you cannot bear anything in her better do not take notice of it. That is the best way to avoid all unpleasantness. Truth stands on its own merit and does not need any prop to support it. Vedanta has no quarrel with anyone. It includes all and is not at all personal. You go on in your own way. Mother will take care of you. My love to your boy and wife and Miss [ ].

With best wishes and love,

Yours in the Mother,
Turiyananda

3

Shanti Ashrama
California
20 August 1901

My dear X,

Your kind letter containing the remittance came duly to hand. Many thanks for the same. But I must ask you not to feel constrained to send money. I know how you love me and how you like to help my work. Mother is taking care of everything. I am so glad you all are doing well and liked Swami Abhedananda. He came here and stayed for one week only. I felt sorry he could not stay longer. It has been so hot here and he left for Yosemite. You will see him again in San Francisco before he goes to Los Angeles. I had a very nice visit and talk with him. I am feeling very much tired and some of the students here are asking me to go somewhere for rest. I have not come to any conclusion yet. I am glad to know you are memorizing Gita. Try to understand the spirit of it as well and live up to it. There is nothing like Gita. It is the cream of all Vedanta Philosophy. Yes, the translation by Mahadev Sastri is considered best, for it contains the commentary of Sri Sankaracharya. My love and best wishes to all please. I think of you all often and anon.

Wishing you all well and joy,

Yours in the Mother,
Turiyananda

4

Buchanon Street
c/o Mrs. C. F. Peterson
San Francisco, California
18 November 1901

My dear X,

I thank you for your good letter I received day before yesterday. I was so much concerned and sorry to learn about Miss B—'s illness. Will you please let me know how she is doing now by return of post. May she get well soon and feel hale and hearty. Remember me to her please and give her my love and best wishes. I received your card you left the day you came to see me. That was the first time I went out for a walk after my recovery. I am feeling almost all right now, and hope to be myself again soon under the good and kind care of [ ]. I am glad to know that you have moved the children and you are all feeling well. Hoping to hear from you soon about the well-being of Miss B—.

With best wishes and love,

Yours in the Mother,
Turiyananda

5

1309 Buchanon St.
San Francisco
18 November 1901

My dear X,

I have received your good letter and the book you sent yesterday. I thank you very much for them. It pleased me immensely to learn that Miss B— is out of danger and improving steadily. I saw this book when I was at Cambridge near Boston. I saw and was introduced to its author too in the same place where he came to lecture on St. Francis. I liked him very much. Especially his simple, unassuming attitude I noticed with great satisfaction and pleasure. I think he is an advanced thinker of this country and tries to live the life as best he knows. I think too he has not come in close contact with the Vedanta Truths yet. However, he seems very free and liberal in his ideas. I will read the book with care this time. I thank you again for the book. I shall be so glad to see you whenever you shall find it convenient to come. I am feeling well and strong again. Trusting you are all doing well, with best wishes and love,

Yours in the Mother,
Turiyananda

6*

Belur Math, India
20 September 1902

My dear Ujjvala,

Your affectionate letter is to hand. I am glad to know you are all doing well. Everything here is topsy-turvy to me, but I hope Mother will turn things better. I was laid up after I came here and I am not quite well yet. The blow was too severe and I have not recovered from its shock. One redeeming feature is that Swamiji has got the rest he needed so badly. What he has done for the world, let the world realize that and be benefitted by for ages. He gave up his body in samadhi and it was not an ordinary death. It was conscious passing out [of his body]. Of course, it is calamitous to us, but we must

---

* This letter was written after Swami Vivekananda's death, July 4, 1902. Swami Turiyananda received the sad news in Rangoon on his way back to India.

learn to submit to Mother's will. Before I reached here he left. That is a grief I shall never be able to forget in my life. I am not sure yet as to my future career, but I trust Mother will show me the way. Swami Trigunatita will be on his way to San Francisco soon. He is a very beautiful soul and will prove helpful to many in spiritual matters. I am sure you will spare nothing to make him comfortable and at home when amongst you. I have heard from [ ] and others. Kindly remember me to all the friends there. My best wishes and heartfelt love for them as ever. Convey my loving regards to your mama please. May the grace of Sri Ramakrishna be with you all always. May you all live prosperous and happy by doing what is considered right according to the light you have received from his teachings through his servant and son,

Turiyananda

I shall be so happy to hear from you from time to time. You have heard by this time about the news here from others I have written to. I was so much delighted to read your letter full with the genuine spirit of loving devotion. May Mother bless you and keep you in her care and never allow you to turn away is the earnest and sincere prayer of yours in the Mother,

Turiyananda

P.S. I was so glad to receive a few beautiful lines from [ ]. There was no mention of her address in the letter. Will you kindly remember me to her and convey my feelings of gratefulness and sincere best wishes and love when you see her. She is one of the foremost of my true friends in America. My best wishes and love to her dear sister and niece as ever.

T.

7

Belur Math
Howrah, India
16 October 1902

My dear Joe [Miss Josephine MacLeod],

It was with greatest satisfaction that I received your very affectionate letter the other day. It consoled me a good deal to be told that Swamiji was not disgusted with me but was satisfied with my loyalty and devotedness to his cause. It was extremely unfortunate that I could not see him again. But we must learn to bear what cannot be mended. I received the sad news [Vivekānanda's passing away] from a fellow passenger when the steamer was leaving Rangoon. At first I could not take it as true and thought it might be a rumour like the others we came across when in America through the newspaper columns. But when I was given the authenticity of the melancholy event the shock was too severe for me to stand. It stunned me outright and I have not been able to recover from its effects yet. I have improved physically a good deal but my brain is very very weak still. I cannot even think of doing any missionary work just at present. I feel I need a complete rest (mental specially) which I find is so hard to obtain. I have been asked by Swami Ramakrishnananda to come to Madras where he says he shall take every care to make me feel rested. Mrs. Sevier has also been very kind to invite me in the mountains. I do not know where should I go. I have a tendency at present to be quite alone and altogether free from all associations of work — I mean the religious teaching, etc. I [would] like to be in perfect communion with Mother for some time at least before I can take up my line of work again. I hope and pray Mother will arrange something in that direction if it is her will to do so.

As about Swamiji I can assure you it was no death to him. He passed out [of his body] as you may say consciously and willingly in samadhi. There might be other reasons for it. But it was true he needed rest very badly and this world could never have given him that rest. It is therefore a consolation to think that he will have that rest now to prepare himself again for the task he took upon himself to perform — the regeneration of the world. The world is justly mourning over his untimely departure and now awakening to the appreciation of his great work unique in the world's history. It will go on realizing the fact more and more as the time rolls on.

With affectionate regards and love to yourself as ever.

Yours in the Mother,
Turiyananda

8

Vrindaban, India
20 January 1903

My dear Ujjvala,

Your affectionate letter came to hand a few days ago. It was redirected to me here from the Math. I have been living here for about two months. I left the Math nearly four months ago and visited some holy places on my way. This place is about one thousand miles from the Math. Here was born Sri Krishna, the divine teacher and preacher of Bhagavad Gita. This is considered one of the greatest pilgrimages of the Hindus. I am feeling much better here, though not quite well yet. I hope the new Swami has become old with you all by this time. You must be enjoying his company and teaching to your profit. I am glad you all kept up the meditation at Dhira's all this time and continue it still regularly. May Mother bless [ ] and you all her dear children, and may she give you understanding to discern things as they really are and not as they appear to be. Be strong, U—, and do not depend upon what this or that one would say about you, but consult the Mother within and act according to her dictates. Be sure whatever binds is not of Mother and that which makes one free is of her. Abide by the same with your whole heart. Have no private selfish end but have sincere love for truth and piety and Mother shall speak from within you. How are you getting on, U—, flaming upwards? Are you becoming "butter,"* or spending your time and energy in social nonsense? Never let go your Ideal, but hold on to It with a firm grip and you will be led rightly to the goal which is the one and same for all. You must not ask me questions like one you have asked me in your last letter. I always like to see Mother in all. You know that. Kindly remember me to all Mother's children there. I have received kind letters from many, but I am sorry I cannot write to all of them, but nevertheless do remember them all. My best wishes and love to all. Kindly convey my loving regards to your mama. With best wishes and love to yourself as ever,

Yours in the Mother,
Turiyananda

9

Vrindaban
26 January 1903

My dear Miss MacLeod,

I received your kind letter of the 18th November redirected to me here on the 16th December 1902. I cannot

*Referring to Sri Ramakrishna's parable: As the butter floats when the milk is churned, so when one attains devotion, he floats and becomes separated from the ocean of maya.

sufficiently thank you for the same. I am very sorry I could not write to you any earlier.

Your one suggestion as to my going to work has been an inspiration to me. I used to feel so much worried about it. But your advice: "Do not hurry about beginning your work. Plans need you — you do not need plans" settled me. May Mother bless you my dear Joe. I am getting reconciled gradually. It pleased Mother to ordain so, that Swamiji would depart and that I would not see him again in flesh here! What can you or anybody else do? But there is one consolation that comes to me often whenever I think of him and that is that Swamiji is now in perfect peace and rest which he needed so very badly and which this world could never have given him.

They have celebrated the birthday anniversary of Swamiji for the first time this year at the Math and it was a success. You will hear from Swami Saradananda of it I am sure. Madras, Varanasi, Allahabad and many other places observed that day with festivals. May whole India learn to exult in it. May Guru Maharaj [Sri Ramakrishna] be glorified in the life of Swamiji forevermore. It is the appreciation of such souls and showing devotion and respects to them that make humanity exult morally and spiritually in all climes and nations. . . .

Yours sincerely,
Turiyananda

10

Vrindaban, India
29 April 1903

My dear Ujjvala,

I received your long letter of the 2nd March, redirected here from the Belur Math on the 16th April last, and I thank you for the same. I am glad to find you are working so well and are so very much pleased with the work of Swami

Trigunatita. I have received a letter from Mrs. [ ] and another from [ ]. Will you please thank them for me? It is so nice you had the celebration of Sri Ramakrishna's birthday in the new rooms of the Vedanta Society first. It augurs so auspicious and lucky for the Society. I am glad you have sent a description of the celebration there to the Math, but I have not seen it. I live at about a distance of one thousand miles from the Math and I hear so seldom from there. It is good you have become rajas [active], but you must not stop there. Mother wants you to be *butter* and nothing short of it will satisfy her. *Never forget this.* Mother's baby, remain baby at heart and you will not have to be afraid of any temptation whatever, for be sure Mother takes good care of her babies and not so much of her grown-up children.

I hear from G— often. He is all alone in the [Shanti] Ashrama just at present. I know he is a brave and faithful soul. Yet try to encourage him in every way you can. Kind and loving words even from the hearts of near and dear ones do a good deal to cheer up a soul which is not in its high spirits. Mind this well. It is thousand times far better and more humane to console and sympathize with a fellow brother than to please oneself by visiting distant lands. Learn to be unselfish, my dear baby, really and truly, and take heed to avoid all sophistries which lie so subtly in its way. May Mother bless you.

Yes, I have heard about C—'s marriage. . . . My best love to S— please. I think so much of her. She is my mother, but she does not seem to take any notice of her time. Can you tell me something of C—? Sometimes I like to know about her. I hope she is quite well now. How is your mama doing? She must be really glad that you have stood up on your own feet and feel so much independent now. Try to make her happy as best as you can. I suppose that is your first human duty to perform. My loving regards to her please. Remember me to all the friends and students there and give them my best wishes and love. I am feeling much better now, but I have not begun work yet in right earnest. Mother will settle that for me and I know she shall engage me in the right thing and place as she shall think best. It is all she that is working in this universe, whether we know it or not. But of course one must know it through realization to become free. Please write to me more often and in more detail without expecting replies always if you can. Treat my letters always as personal and if possible confidential. Pray for me constantly as you pray for yourself. My love and blessing to you as ever.

Yours in the Mother,
Turiyananda

11

Vrindaban, India
27 May 1903

My dear X,

Your kind letter of April 18 I believe is to hand. It contained a kind note from Miss B— also. I received your other beautiful and affectionate letter you wrote to me in the month of October 1902. I thank you ever so much for both of them. And my thanks are also due to Miss B— I am sorry I could not write to you so long. I had been suffering more or less from something or other all this time and am not quite free from complaints even now. I think my nervous system has undergone a terrible shock under all those severe tests of life that I have gone through during the past few years. And it will take a considerable time, I believe, before it can come to its natural condition of health if it ever comes at all in its present lease of existence. I have been very glad to hear that Swami Trigunatita has done such good work in San Francisco and that you all like him so well. But I do not hear from anybody any detail of the work done as you think I do. I like to hear so much of it and will be so glad if you will let me know the full account of the work. But our letters will be between you and me.

I understand that there is one Swami Ram [Tirtha] amongst you for some time. I would like to know something of him from you. It is so nice you have seen the photos of other swamis with me in the group. Will you send me a copy of the same if you can? I like to see it. Kindly send it to my Vrindaban address. Nothing pleases me so much as to know that you are treading on and on in the path of religion you have once begun and that you are following your Ideal as best as you can. May Mother bless you all and keep you close to her embrace.

It gave me great satisfaction to learn that you are in correspondence with [Gurudas]. What a noble soul this dear [Gurudas] is. He is now all alone in the Ashrama. [Gurudas] is true to his name in the very real sense of the term. He is indeed blessed. Kindly remember me to Mrs. [ ] and Miss [ ] and give them my best wishes and regard. I feel really glad to know their feelings for me expressed in their words and writing and to know about their spiritual advancement. All love to [ ]. . . . May Mother keep him and bring him up after her own choice. My best wishes and love to all the friends please. With prayer and love for you as ever,

Yours in the Mother,
Turiyananda

12

Vrindaban, India
24 June 1903

My dear Miss MacLeod,

Your very affectionate letter of May 5 from Switzerland

was most welcome. I was so happy to learn that you had been feeling better. I hope you are quite well now. . . .

May Mother's work started by Swamiji flourish everywhere. May Mother's children come unto Mother. Yes, Joe, I quite agree with you. The people in India are alive with the spirit that never dies and that sustains them. But for all that their condition has become very deplorable just at this moment and the sudden disappearance of Swamiji from amongst them is an enigma to me still. Swamiji seemed at least to have solved the problem and his whole life was only for the amelioration of that wretched condition of poor India. However, Mother knows what is best and we do not. May we only submit to her decree knowing that to be the best and may we never forget Mother.

With affectionate regards and love to you as ever.

Yours sincerely,
Turiyananda

13

Vrindaban, India
12 August 1903

My dear Ujjvala,

Your letter of the 10th June came duly to hand. I was very glad to know you all had been doing so nicely. I received a letter from D— by the same mail. I have written to her already in reply to that letter. I have received another letter from her which I could not reply yet. I have been waiting for your letter which you promised to write to me in your last letter giving me information about C—. However, I hope everything is well with her. I got a letter from C— . . . of late. It was nice and of cheerful tone too, but in it also she didn't write anything as regards her own health and so forth. It was full of sentiment only. I have not written to her in reply yet. Will you please convey my loving regards to her when you write to her. Yes, it is more than one year, my dear Ujjvala that I left your shores, but it seems much longer than that to me. Mother alone knows where she is going to keep me, but of one thing I can assure you that wherever I might be, I will have the interest of you all at heart and that I will never be slow to pray for the spiritual development of you all to Mother. May you all cling close to Mother and be helpful and loving to one another. I hear of [ ] often. May Mother protect him always. How faithful and like a hero he is at his place in the Ashrama, and to be sure a right man in the right place. I need hardly tell you much about him, I know. He speaks so beautifully about you, how helpful you are to him and so forth. I am really glad of it. My loving regards to S—. It doesn't matter if she has 15,000,000 desires, still she is my mother.

I hope Swami T. [Trigunatita] is again amongst you with fresh ardour and vigor this time and you are enjoying his lectures and his company with more zest than before. I am glad to know that you try to help him as best as you can. I am delighted to know that S— is learning stenography. She will be another hand to help the swami there. It pleased me very much to learn that S— is well again and is to live with [ ] and [ ] in Camp Taylor after her recovery from such a dangerous operation. My love to them, please. What is the matter with F—? You never follow my requests closely, I see. Write me openly please. I guess there is a feeling now towards the [ ] people which is not very friendly amongst the members of the Vedanta Society. Is that true? Well, I would ask you never to identify yourself with any party spirit, Ujjvala. Keep always aloof of it if you want to be happy. Try to see Mother in all. That is the secret. I am doing much better now. Hope you are all doing well. My love to M— and

S— and all the friends who care for it. With wishes and love to you as ever,

Yours in the Mother,
Turiyananda

P.S. Will you please give me some account of the work Swami Ram [Tirtha] is doing there and if possible of the doings of Dharmapala, when you write to me again. Try to give me important news that would interest me.

14

Vrindaban, India
16 August 1904

My dear Mr. X,

I thank you for your kind letter of July 4th which was replete with the news of you all. It was so good of you to write to me such a long descriptive letter. Your money order has also duly reached. I am sorry that you have sent it to me out of your income which I know is scarcely enough for your own requirements. However I wish to tell you here that you should not strain yourself for me in any way. For that would hurt me much. I got a letter from Miss [ ] a few weeks ago in which she told me how Mr. [ ], the children and herself were in the [Shanti] Ashrama and how they enjoyed the peaceful atmosphere there and were benefitted thereby. Her letter delighted me exceedingly. Will you kindly thank her for me? I am sorry I cannot write replies to all the letters I got. But I know Miss [ ] will understand it and will excuse me. I am doing much better now. Physically I have improved a good deal. But my nerves are not restored to their proper condition yet. I still feel nervous debility at times and my head is not quite free from the weakness either. Mother alone knows what she is doing with me. But that she is doing the very best for me, I have not the least doubt about it. It does not matter where and how she keeps me, but it would give me infinite delight if I can hear that you all are keeping close to Mother and have made her the sole aim and end of your lives here and hereafter.

It is such a pleasure to learn that [ ] is doing better and that he is liked and loved by you all so much. It would be nice if he can come to the city at least for a little time. He has been living in one place for quite a length of time. A little change may prove beneficial to him in more ways than one. But he is so considerate and will do what is proper and good I feel sure. I could not understand very well about the "petition" you have mentioned in your letter. But whatever it might be you need not be so much concerned and sorry for signing it. It should not be given so much importance at any rate. I apprehended some misunderstanding that was going on in the city with regard to me some time ago. Of course I could not understand the nature of it. However I immediately stopped writing letters to my friends there, which I thought might be the cause for it. I am for peace and harmony and would sacrifice anything to keep them. Life is already full of vexation and troubles and we need not try to add to them any more. May Mother bless you all. May you all stick to nothing else but Mother. "Sufficient unto the day is the evil thereof," never forget this. Hold onto Mother and whatever tries to obstruct it reject the same altogether forthwith. . . . Your growing spiritual condition on account of the mantram has delighted me beyond all description. May it be with you evermore. My blessings and love to your very dear children and best wishes and love to [ ] and [ ].

With best wishes and love to you as ever,

Yours in the Mother,
Turiyananda

15

Rishikesh
17 February 1914

Dear X [a California student],

The life of renunciation is the only life that can make us truly happy. No other life can ever do so. It is certain that one day we shall have to give up everything whether we want to or not. It is much better to give it up gladly and freely before we are compelled to do so. But if one cannot do that, the next best course is to turn everything over to Mother and abide by her decree. Know her to be the only guide in life under all conditions. Pleasure and pain pass away. They do not last long. We gather knowledge through experience; and by not identifying ourselves with pain or pleasure we gain freedom. Be always content with what Mother ordains. She knows what is best for us. Such a life also brings peace and consolation; and then the world can do us no harm.

You are Mother's children; you need not be afraid of the world. Be devoted to her and she will take care of you. She alone is Real. All else is vanity and vexation. Did not Jesus say, "What shall it profit a man if he shall gain the whole world, and lose his own soul?" Mother is the Soul of our souls. If we have her we no longer care much for the things of this world.

The world goes on in its way and will continue to do so for all eternity. But he who sees Mother in everything and knows for certain that it is all her play will have rest for his soul and peace within. May we see her hand and guidance in everything. May she bless us.

Yours in the Mother,
Turiyananda

16

Ramakrishna Cottage, Almora
7 October 1916

My dear Doctor,*

Just now your very kind letter of the 2nd instant is to hand. I have been thinking so much about you these days. I am very sorry that you too fell ill and are suffering still. Inscrutable are the ways of Providence. But He is good and kind to us and we have to admit that. May we not lose faith in His dispensation, no matter how we are situated. Let us not think selfishly, but be satisfied with His ordainings knowing full well that whatever He does, it is all for our good only. For in that thought we shall have peace of mind at least.

I feel very very sorry for your father. Of course you are doing everything to bring him round, and that is not a little consolation for him. May he recover from his malady soon. I shall wait anxiously to hear about your own well-being as early as possible. . . .

I shall be very happy to see you at Almora when you come after seeing your father well. I am so thankful to Mother for giving you such nice faith in her even at such hours of travail and trial as you are undergoing just now. Your present attitude of mind is very favourable for spiritual advancement

---

*Doctor D'Mello, an Indian medical doctor who was later temporarily employed in Rangoon. He certainly met Swami Turiyananda at least once, and as we shall see, also went later to Mayavati and spent seven or eight weeks in June and July of 1919. Obviously the swami was fond of him because the doctor seems to have possessed sincere spiritual aspiration. These letters — not originals but legible copies — came into our possession years ago and have not so far been published. Though we are unable to trace the originals, it will be evident to anyone reading these letters that they are genuine — the power and spiritual contents are characteristically profound. —Editor, *Prabuddha Bharata*, May 1975.

indeed. You need not try to make yourself free by taking to means; that is not fair. It is the will of the Mother you shall feel free even where you are now situated without having to stir a little for further efforts. Stick to your present resigned attitude tenaciously. . . .

Hoping this will find you hale and hearty. With best wishes and love,

Yours affectionately,
Turiyananda

17

Ramakrishna Cottage, Almora
23 October 1916

My dear Doctor,

I was very glad to get your letter dated 18.10.16 and to learn therefrom that your father had been feeling better. May he recover soon his power of speech and his former health by the grace of the Mother. . . . I am really very sorry to understand that you are troubled again with the idea of possessing woman. I hope it has come to take leave of you forever, never to return again. You have discrimination enough to guide you aright. Besides I feel sure Mother will take care of you, and not allow you to go astray. I have been very much pleased to read the soliloquy to Mother in your letter. That hinted to me that Mother is not unmindful about you. If you can talk this way to Mother within you with earnestness and sincerity she will not let go of you so easily, but will hold you in check. Who is this Sadhu Siddharudha* you mention in your letter? Is he a Buddhist monk or a Hindu Sannyasin? What he spoke to you in advice is very nice, full of reason

*A renowned Hindu saint who lived near Hubli, in Karnataka, South India.

and truth. But Mother will not allow you to take sannyasa [monastic vows] to disgrace it. If once you could give up the idea of sex entirely, and could not find the trace of it in your heart of which you are quite conscious, be sure you will have that state of mind again if you try to bring it back in right earnest; anyhow never yield but hold on to your ideal of sannyasa. For once you give in there will be no chance for you again to take your stand.

Khir [Condensed or thickened milk. Sometimes it also means milk pudding.] is one thing and woman is quite another. Don't believe in the theory of quenching lust by giving vent to it. Practise self-control as much as possible, and pray with all sincerity to Mother for further help. Take heart and the help is sure to come. May Mother give you full strength to conquer the beast in you completely.

I shall be very glad to learn that you have secured some position for yourself. Of course it would give me great pleasure to see you here. But you can come after securing a post, no doubt. I do not know yet for certain if I will go to the plains during the cold weather. I am doing pretty well.

Hoping you are hale and hearty, with my best wishes as ever,

Yours in the Lord,
Turiyananda

18

Ramakrishna Cottage, Almora
3 November 1916

My dear Doctor,

Many thanks for your kind letter of the 28th ultimo. Glad to know that your father can sit up now. He may regain his former health gradually.

You need not take to such awful measures to get control over your passions. Such drastic and cruel means are for the tamasic — *mudha* [a person of animal nature]. Mother will not put you to such violent methods in order to gain mastery over carnal desires. They will go away of themselves when your desire for realizing the Mother would increase, as a man would not care to have treacle after he has tasted candy. So when you get real taste for divine pleasure all craving for sense pleasure will cease to trouble you anymore. One thing that is needful for you just now is to think of Mother and Mother alone and to look to nothing [else] for help or guidance. Have absolute faith in Mother that she will protect you and lead you aright, and you will be saved for certain.

Svadharma in the Gita does not mean Christianity or Hinduism, or any ism for the matter of that, but the duty of one's own status in life. Arjuna was a kshatriya prince, and his duty was to fight, but he wanted to take to the life of a brahmin, and give up fighting, and that is why the Lord declared unto him, "Better is death in the doing of one's own dharma; the dharma of another is fraught with peril." [Gita, III.35] However, I admire the spirit of self-restraint that you have written about in the life of the Saint in your letter. That kind of punishing oneself may be necessary and helpful to some. But for you is the path of love and not torture. Love for Mother will take away the love for the flesh from your mind. And that is going to be in your case sooner or later, may it be sooner than later.

What are you doing now? Not trying to secure any post? It is no good sitting idle. I shall be very happy if I hear that you are doing something. My best wishes and love to you as ever.

Yours in the Lord,
Turiyananda

19

Ramakrishna Cottage, Almora
26 November 1916

My dear Doctor,

I have been very much anxious to hear from you, and it was with great satisfaction that I received your so long and beautiful letter of the 19th instant the day before yesterday.

It pleased me so very much to learn that you have been feeling much better these days, and no adverse thought disturbs your peace of mind with regard to spiritual advancement as it used to do before. You need not thank me, but thank Mother, and be grateful to her if you need be to any. For it is she who blesses us with everything that we want in earnest from her. Only I am exceedingly happy to note that you think that Mother has made me an instrument to bring some solace to you. I feel so grateful to her for the same if it is really so. Yes, she made me to understand that yours was the path of love, and not that of self-torture, though the latter may have use for some.

I am glad that you keep yourself engaged always and never allow the time to hang heavily on you. Yet I pray that you may have some work for your own provision and for that of others who depend on you. It is well that you are trying for a post, and I trust you will secure one before long. I am sorry your father has not improved much as yet. I am afraid you are quite right when you say that he may not be his old self again. For he is too old for that now. But what could be done? What cannot be cured must be endured, as the adage goes. It is a matter of regret that you could not come to Almora as you wished. But never mind, we shall meet again in proper time by the grace of the Mother. I have been urgently requested by S—, [Swami] Shivananda and others to come to Varanasi as early as possible. I think I shall have to go down to Varanasi very shortly. Let us see how the Mother ordains it.

The course of meditation that you are following now is all right. You go on in that line and you will have your object realized therein. Very natural and excellent are your ways. Go on with them till you have become filled. This will purify your heart, and make you see the bottom of it which you want to do May Mother bless you always. With my best wishes and love to you as ever,

Yours in the Lord,
Turiyananda

20

Belur Math, India
6 March 1917

My dear Doctor,

Your kind letter of the 1st instant has delighted me. I am very, very glad to see that you are now in Almora again and living in the Ramakrishna Cottage with brahmacharins there. How nice. How grand! Yes it would have been nicer if I could be there just now. But it is all right. The Mother will see to everything you need, I feel sure of that.

Why do you welcome miseries and troubles? They are over now. Now you think of Mother and Mother alone. You need not search for Mother anywhere else but in your own self. She is the Self of all. While you cannot doubt about your own existence, how can you doubt about the existence of Mother? She is the Existence of all existences. She is the basis of all. "He shining everything shines after Him; by His effulgence all this is illumined." [Mundaka Upanishad, II.10] She shining everything shines; through Her splendour all else is illumined. First Mother, then everything else. Nobody can know her but through her mercy. Wait and watch and in her good time the light dawns on you, driving away the darkness that intervenes, to see her face within your own heart. Abide by her. Don't you see her hand that is drawing you nigh to her? You are now only to look up to her in patience. It is not that you have no belief in her. But you want to be convinced, and that you are going to be presently. You have come a long way, and there is not much delay. Have patience and work on diligently and the success is yours. . . .

May Mother give you success here and now in temporal as well as in spiritual things, and may she make you fit to be her instrument in carrying success to others by all means in your power, is the fervent prayer of your ever well-wishing and everloving Turiyananda.

My best wishes and love to Br. Nabochaitanya and Br. Rama. I am doing tolerably well. Hoping to hear from you soon again,

Yours in the Lord,
Turiyananda

21

Belur Math, India
18 March 1917

My dear Doctor,

I thank you for your kind letter of the 13th instant just to hand. . . .

You need not be so anxious for your mental condition in these days. Go on calling upon Mother's grace fervently and the light shall dawn on you in good time as the Mother would think it right and proper for you. You throw yourself heart and soul at the feet of the Mother, and she will take care of you, and you shall feel free. I am glad you all are doing well there. The swamis and brahmacharins here are doing nicely also. My best wishes and love to you as ever.

Yours in the Lord,
Turiyananda

22

Belur Math, India
2 April 1917

My dear Doctor,

. . . You are right; the best way to forget the past is not to think of those events again. Better think of Mother if you are to think anything. That way by her grace one may become lost in her thought entirely. . . .

Why not address me as 'Dear Swami' instead of Guru Maharaj. That will please most. Our Master used to hate being called 'Guru' and 'Father'. . . .

With my best wishes and love to you all as ever.

Yours in the Lord,
Turiyananda

23

Belur Math, India
15 April 1917

My dear Doctor,

. . . You need not be anxious for the ups and downs in your devotional attitude of mind. For that way it goes not only with you but with everyone before it takes any firm hold and gets settled. You go on with your devotion and prayer, and be sure Mother will grant you your wishes in her own good time. . . .

With my best wishes and love to you as ever and with prayer to Mother for your real prosperity.

Yours in the Lord,
Turiyananda

24

Belur Math, India
9 May 1917

My dear Doctor,

. . . I am glad to find that you are no more nervous to go to Burma, but are confident of your internal strength. That is very well. But at the same time you must be very careful and not too much overconfident. Yes, better to wear out than rust out. So it would be nice if you can get something to do when you have the mind to do so and the circumstances require it too. Yes, Rama and yourself are quite right, and I am also not different in opinion with you both. I trust Mother will help and protect you wherever you be and will not let you go astray. . . .

Trusting this will find you well and prosperous, with sincere prayer to Mother for your true well-being.

Yours in the Lord,
Turiyananda

25

Sashi Niketan, Puri
28 June 1917

My dear Doctor,

I am in receipt of your kind letter without date just this morning. I received your other letter dated 14.6.17 duly. I thank you for both of them. You are so very kind to me. But the Mother has not freed me yet from earache fully. Sankarananda and myself went to the Government dispensary here this morning, and saw the Civil Surgeon for medical advice. Let us see how we get the benefit of it. We have been doing almost everything that you have asked us to do in your letter since these twenty days. But who can take away the suffering before it is completely endured? I must wait till Mother is pleased to relieve me in her good time. . . .

How I long to see you and like to be with you! But Mother's ways are different. She knows as you say what is best and let us abide by her decrees. I know she is very kind to us all and will do the needful to take us to her arms. Wishing you all success, and trusting this will find you well and prosperous and with my best wishes and love to you as ever,

Yours affectionately,
Turiyananda

26

Sashi Niketan, Puri
9 August 1917

My dear Doctor,

You need not trouble yourself about freedom from work so soon. Mother knows well when it would suit you and she shall arrange it that way in her good time. Of course, you should have time for meditation above everything else. You must have time to think of Mother without which none can get along all right. I know you will be able to make time for that anyway. Some way will open for that no doubt. Wait and see how it works in that direction. I felt uneasy when you were without employment, and I am so glad to find you now in the midst of work. What does it matter whether you be in Rangoon, or Madras, or in Naini Tal so long as you are well and prosperous, and under the care of Mother? May Mother keep you always in her arms and protect you evermore. . . .

Swami Brahmananda is feeling not very well at Puri this time. He may take a change in Bhubaneshwar shortly. Bhubaneshwar is a very healthy place indeed, and he may feel all right there. You will be pleased to hear that about five acres of land have been purchased in Bhubaneshwar by the swami only recently in order to start an Ashrama there before long. It would be nice to have a place there so near to the Math and so healthy and beautiful at the same time. The swami has an idea of raising a few rooms on the land presently to make it habitable just now. . . .

Hoping this will find you free from all ailments and troubles and in the enjoyment of sound health, and peace of mind, with my best wishes and love to you as ever,

Yours affectionately,
Turiyananda

27

Sashi Niketan, Puri
22 August 1917

My dear Doctor,

. . . You need not be anxious for making any plans. Mother will show you the way in time and direct you which course to follow. I am so glad you have time for meditation, and that you do take advantage of it. How excellent that is. It is meditation alone that shall keep you in direct touch with Mother. . . .

Yours affectionately,
Turiyananda

28

57 Ramkanta Bose St.
Calcutta
1 August 1918

My dear Doctor,

I am in receipt of your kind letter of the 21st ultimo just now. I received your other letter also dated 7.7.18 duly. I am sorry I could not write to you in reply any earlier. Swami Premanandaji, you will be grieved to hear, is now no more. He left his mortal coil on Tuesday evening at quarter after four and his body was taken to Belur Math where it was cremated after proper ceremonial.

His end came so suddenly. On the previous Saturday morning he was brought here from Deoghar where he had showed signs of increased ill health. When he came here, he was in a very bad plight. The Doctor after examination found that he was suffering from advanced pneumonia. There was no lack of treatment or nursing or diligent care, but nothing was of any avail. Baffling everything, he expired and went to eternal peace, leaving all sorts of pains and sufferings — due to the long illness that he underwent — behind him altogether.

The loss which the Math and the circle of devotees sustained from his absence is irreparable; but what could be done? The Lord's will comes to pass every time. All are in mourning now, and I cannot describe to you how they are feeling at this moment. His exalted soul must be enjoying unspeakable bliss with the Lord, but his friends here are sorely dejected for not finding him in their midst. But the influence which he has left behind will be fresh in their mind for all time to come. I cannot write you much just now. I hope you will excuse me for this. I shall try to answer you again when I feel better. The Holy Mother and the swamis are doing physically well.

My best wishes and love to you as ever,

Yours in the Lord,
Turiyananda

29

57 Ramkanta Bose St., Calcutta
12 October 1918

My dear Doctor,

I have received your letters of 30.9.18 and 1.10.18 together yesterday, and [am] glad to find that you are now free from all physical complaints and are doing well. I also was anxious for not hearing from you. It is gratifying to know that Swamiji's words in his epistles did so much for you. Yes indeed, Swamiji's words are very powerful and life-giving; they are not only able to remove ailments of body, but they can and do purify souls and lead them God-ward. You have experienced how powerful his words are in doing away with physical pains. May you experience his power which leads people to the realization of the Godhead and perfect freedom. . . .

With my best wishes and love to you as ever,

Yours in the Lord,
Turiyananda

30

Varanasi, India
12 June 1919

My dear Doctor,

I am very glad to get your letter of the 8th instant this morning and it has given me great satisfaction to know that you have safely arrived at Mayavati after all. Never mind for the troubles on the road, but that you have reached your destination and have so much been pleased with the fine sceneries and surroundings of your much coveted place, is something beyond and above all complaints.

May you now engage yourself in the meditation of her, who is the Mother of us all and whose single grace can make our lives full of bliss and free from all turmoils and vain vexations. May you be fortunate to gain your ends which you have in your mind and be blessed by the grace of the Mother for whom you have so much devotion and love. Throw yourself at her feet wholly, and she will take you up in her arms as a mother does her child when in extreme helplessness and bewailing.

I thought of not disturbing you with any letter at this moment but anyhow you have my cordial blessings and heartfelt love.

Yours in the Mother,
Turiyananda

31

Varanasi, India
23 June 1919

My dear Doctor,

Yours of the 18th instant came duly to hand. I am glad to learn that you are enjoying the company of the swamis there to your advantage and benefit. It is not always that we can retain the ardour and zeal that come in us from spiritual advancement, but we should not feel disheartened, or lose courage but should engage ourselves the more and never give up the game. It is through the grace of Mother that we get such heightened states of spiritual fervour. It may disappear for a time, but it can never vanish. It must reappear if you are after it. Nevertheless if you feel dry and lack all enthusiasm even then if you keep on praying to Mother tenaciously, she is sure to send you light and comfort that will fill your heart again with love and devotion. Think yourself as Mother's child always that you really are, and never cease asking her for what you aspire to have, and sooner or later they will come to you sure as morning follows the night. . . .

Trusting this will find you well and happy, with my best wishes and love to you and to all the members of the Advaita Ashrama,

Yours affectionately,
Turiyananda

32

Varanasi, India
21 July 1919

My dear Doctor,

Your very kind letter of the 18th instant is to hand. . . .

It has given me very great pleasure to understand that you are enjoying the reading of Upanishads in that quiet and holy place and have felt uplifted by their influences. But why have you expressed so pitiably about yourself in it [the letter]? Why do you care so much about your past samskaras [latent impressions]? You do not concern yourself much for the dreams from which you have awakened though very bad they might have seemed when dreaming. So why should you think so seriously about the samskaras which are now no more, but are the things of the past? Look on them as past dreams from which you have awakened.

Numerous thoughts may come in the mind during meditation, but why take note of them? Let them come and go. Be yourself a witness of them, and have nothing to do with them. Engage your mind with nothing but thinking of the Ishtam [the Chosen Deity], whatever It might be, and try to "dilute" yourself with It. Do not identify yourself with any samskara at all, and you shall feel free. What you shall think that you shall become. That is the secret. So if you think of Christ, then Christ you shall become inwardly, and as long as you don't become that, don't give up thinking about your Ishtam as deeply as possible. You must have patience. Rome was not built in a day. You never forget that.

May you succeed in attaining your end is my sincere prayer. Kindly remember me to all the members of the Advaita Ashrama and give them my heartfelt best wishes and love. With my best wishes and love to you as ever,

Yours affectionately,
Turiyananda

33

Varanasi, India
10 October 1919

My dear Doctor,

I am in receipt of your kind letter of the 1st instant. I have been very glad to learn that you have improved in health and strength by the change in Maymyo [in Burma]. May you get on well. It is nice that you have sent applications to different places. I wish you may get some appointment soon. Of course, I can understand your feelings very well, but that won't do; you must work still for some time at least to put your daughter in a fair way of prosperity. When you have done that you will have time to think of giving up the wretched worldly connection once for all. Then you shall feel free to retire permanently with a conscience at once free from all responsibilities. But if you give up the world now probably you will not have that peace of mind which comes from renunciation. May Mother give you strength to do that which seems your duty to the world first and then giving up everything devote yourself wholly to Mother when you have finished that duty. You are intelligent enough and I need hardly speak more on this subject. No haste, have patience and Mother will do all for you which is right in right time. . . .

Trusting this will find you hale and hearty, and with my best wishes and love to you,

Yours in the Lord,
Turiyananda

34

Varanasi, India
24 October 1919

My dear Doctor,

I am not quite happy to be informed that you could not get any favourable reply to the applications you sent. Let us see what becomes of the other applications that are yet unreplied. You can go on with your meditation even when in service, and you need not give up everything for that just at present. Your mind has told you what is true under the circumstances that you are now in. You are really not fit for that state which you think you are prepared to accept, viz., the state of absolute poverty. Therefore don't call your mind a rogue or insincere, but it seems to me that it has proved your true friend by giving you advice to ponder over the subject with a profound silence. I hope Mother will furnish you with a post that is suitable to you very shortly, and will give you ample opportunity for meditation and thinking of her sincerely and with love. My best wishes and love to Delicia dear, and to yourself.

Yours in the Lord,
Turiyananda

35

Ramakrishna Mission
Luxa, Varanasi
21 December 1919

My dear Doctor,

Yours of the 14th instant is to hand. . . . I am so glad to know that you will get a chance soon to leave Rangoon for India, where you hope to secure an appointment. May you get the post at Ooty [Ootacamund, South India] and be in India once again. . . .

You need not be disheartened, but be of good cheer remembering the answer which Sri Krishna gave to Arjuna that "the doer of good never comes to grief," in the sixth chapter of the immortal Gita. If you are not fit for the life of sannyasa [renunciation] just now, there is no reason for you to be depressed.

For are you not the son of the Mother anyhow, and devoted to her already? What if you are not a sannyasin? You are Mother's child just the same and are no less dear to her. You only look up to her for everything and love her with all your heart and soul. She knows better where to keep you and in what manner than you can possibly do yourself. Only stick to Mother and never forget that you belong to her. Do your duty manfully in whatever station of life you may be put and prove yourself a Mother's child by bringing all sorts of circumstances under your feet, having full consciousness that you are above them all, and they have no power to frighten you, far less to gain ascendancy over you in any way. May Mother give you strength and vigour to accomplish this. . . .

Yours in the Mother,
Turiyananda

36

Ramakrishna Mission
Luxa, Varanasi
14 February 1920

My dear Doctor,

Many thanks for your kind letter of 4.2.20 received day before yesterday. I was very glad to know therefrom that you were doing very well spiritually. Try to be in touch with Mother always and she is sure to protect you and lead you aright without fail. It gave me very great satisfaction to learn from your letter that you could understand Mother's play [which] she had with you — to rouse you to your senses, when you went astray in thought — by giving a shock to you. That was very nice. Be on the alert now as to how you should think things that are not congenial to Mother. . . . It pleased me immensely to note that you have got a friend in the person of Mr. Raj Krishna, a native of Punjab who is so helpful to you in matters spiritual. It is nice to have such a companion to whom one can open his heart and get response.

You must fight your case to a finish by all means. You must do it fully. For things done by halves are never done right. Only do it, trying to remain unaffected, using your efforts in full, giving the results over to Mother. Know that you are engaged in doing it for somebody else. Know yourself to be the witness always, and not a participant. That is the secret of doing *nishkama karma* — unselfish work.

I think "*mithilayam pradagdhayam na me dahati kinchana*"* is complete in itself. If it has another part I am not aware of the same. What a grand idea of unselfishness expressed in that one line! . . . It is so difficult to be rid of the "*Aham*" [the sense

*"Even if the whole of Mithila burns down, nothing that is mine burns." These are the words of Janaka, King of Mithila, to a sannyasin.

of 'I'] that is so deeply implanted in the human mind. But by the grace of the Mother someone can eradicate it if he works hard, sincerely and with unbounded patience. Mother herself obliterates it with her own hand, if the aspirant gives himself up to Mother fully and unconditionally. . . .

Trusting you are hale and hearty, with my best wishes and love to you and dear Delicia,

Yours in the Mother,
Turiyananda

37

Ramakrishna Mission
Luxa, Varanasi
22 March 1920

My dear Doctor,

I received your kind letter of the 13th instant duly. I have been exceedingly happy to learn that you have secured a post in Ooty where you are going to join it very soon. I think you have done right in choosing the post that is permanent to avoid unnecessary anxiety and exertion after some time by joining one that is temporary. Never be mindful of pecuniary gain only. You shall have other advantages in the post you have accepted such as time for meditation and communing with Mother which is indeed so vitally indispensable for spiritual development. Besides the climate of Ooty is so inviting, and that means a good deal no doubt.

What nonsense have you written about your Kundali [horoscope], and the reading of your palm, etc.? Don't you believe in such nasty things at all, leaving aside your faith in Mother. Mother alone is omnipotent. She can do anything and everything if she wills it. She is able to do away with fate even if there be any such thing as fate. Don't be credulous.

Don't lose faith in Mother. If you have a desire for marriage that is another thing. But if you are determined to lead a single and spiritual life there is no power on earth or above it to dissuade you from your noble purpose. Be sure about it. If you marry you shall do it wilfully and there is none else to decide it for you. If you have a tendency or leaning towards marriage that is a different thing altogether. But if you are sincerely averse to it, if you really want to remain free, you shall have all help from within. This is hypnotism pure and simple that you are told by way of prediction. Throw it off by implicit faith in Mother and in your own soul, which is always free and independent. If I hear that you have married I shall know that it is your own will that has made you marry and not any outside influence that has acted on you. Be cautious and strong. Don't be weak and yield to any persuasion whatever if you want to make yourself really happy and peaceful. If Mother has been pleased to bring you out of the mire of samsara [worldly existence] you should not willingly get entangled in it again and prove yourself wretched. . . .

Trusting this will find you well and prosperous with my best wishes and love, and asking you again to be strong and wary,

Yours in the Mother,
Turiyananda

38

Ramakrishna Mission
Luxa, Varanasi
25 April 1920

My dear Doctor,

You will be very sorry to learn that Swami Adbhutananda, our Lattoo [Latu] Maharaj is now no more. He breathed his last on last Saturday at ten minutes after twelve in the morning. His expiration was a wonderful thing, and I cannot describe to you the beauty of his face after he gave up his body. It was so serene, so affectionate, and full of light and cheerfulness, as if the result of his lifelong sadhanas stood revealed at that moment. He began to remain in meditation from the very beginning of his illness, and continued to be in that quiet state to the end, till he expired. Whoever saw him then was struck with admiration and had to exclaim, "How grand it is to be a real sadhu [holy man], and to quit the world in the way he did!" Indeed his life was an exemplary one, and thrice blessed. Blessed be the Lord, whose heavenly influence made us realize the spiritual truth expressed so vividly in the life of this saint, a most devoted and dear servant of Sri Ramakrishna. After the observances of the timely rites that were required to be performed, we took his body to Manikarnika [the famous cremation ground in Varanasi], decorated with flower garlands and other holy things, to be immersed in the sacred water of the Mother Ganga for jala-samadhi.* Now we are going to make the last ceremonial by feeding the sadhus and the poor Narayanas [poor and destitute people considered as forms of God] on the thirteenth day of his ascension, at the Advaita Ashrama here. We have lost a great soul, a spiritual giant, in the person of Lattoo Maharaj. The Lord be blessed.

Others of both the Ashramas here are doing tolerably well.

Trusting you are well and prosperous, with my best wishes and love to you and to dear Delicia as ever,

Yours in the Mother,
Turiyananda

---

*Literally, burial in water. The usual practice in north India for the disposal of the body of a dead monk is to sink it, tied to a heavy weight, in a holy river like the Ganga.

39

Ramakrishna Mission
Luxa, Varanasi
10 August 1920

My dear Doctor,

I am in receipt of your kind letter of the 3rd August after quite a long time. It was my thought-force perhaps, that made you write this letter. For I have been thinking of you so very much of late. . . .

Holy Mother has left us all but she won't be able to leave the hearts of her devotees. There she will abide forever, and continue to bless us all for all time to come.

My health is not satisfactory. I suffer from terrible pains in my legs and I am not free from other complaints arising from diabetes. But what could be done? I must bear them patiently to avoid further disturbances that may result from restlessness and useless anxieties.

Trusting this will find you well and prosperous, with my best wishes and love to you all,

Yours in the Lord,
Turiyananda

40

Varanasi
21 March 1922

My dear Doctor,

You want to see the Lord in everything. Why then do you not begin to see the Lord in everything even from now? *Just try and you shall succeed.* If you don't try even from this moment you shall never be able to see him in everything at any time. You must do it and nobody else shall do it for you.

Therefore go on seeing him that way, and practice will make you perfect. Whole-hearted sincerity — that is what we need most.

I see you are sorry, for your wretched habit of suspiciousness is still lingering in you. If you don't like to have it really, then don't give vent to it anymore. What is habit but the repetition of a thing over and over again? Don't indulge in repeating 'suspecting' things and you will be free from the habit of suspecting others. Here also you yourself will have to work it out, and nobody else would do it for you.

My best wishes and love to swamis and brahmacharins there.

With my best wishes and love to you as ever,

Yours in the Lord,
Turiyananda

41

Varanasi, India
12 May 1920

My dear Miss MacLeod,

I received your kind letter of March 31st. . . . I am extremely sorry to let you know that Swami Adbhutananda [Latu Maharaj] is now no more. He breathed his last on the 24th of April last. His passing out was indeed very wonderful. He began to be in meditative state from the very first he fell ill and absorbed in that meditative state he gave up his body.

He had a small blisterlike something on the ankle of his right leg and being operated [on] it developed into gangrene in a few days. All the best local medical help was requisitioned but to no effect and in ten or twelve days he expired. He showed no signs of pain or trouble during his illness, and the wonder of all wonders was that after his death when we made him sit to make some rites for the occasion we found him looking so beautiful, so serene, so full of peace and bliss. His face beaming with light and intelligence unspeakable as if he were taking leave from his friends for the last time with an exhortation of affectionate benediction. Really it was a sight for the gods to see.

We chanted the name of the Lord for three continued hours and then took his body decorated with flower garlands, sandalpaste, etc. in procession to the Ganga side and carried [it] to Manikarnika by boat to be immersed in the holy waters of the Mother Ganga after due performance of the last rites necessary for the occasion of jala [water] samadhi. Latu Maharaj entered into peace eternal and another son of Sri Ramakrishna joins with him making us feel poorer for the loss irreparable. Indeed we have lost a spiritual giant in the person of Latu Maharaj whose illiteracy and unsophisticated life helped him most to become what he was — a genuine and ardent devotee of Sri Ramakrishna. . . .

The West must be spiritualized or there is no hope for its peaceful existence. . . .

Yours affectionately,
Turiyananda

GLOSSARY

Abhedananda, Swami (also Kaliprasad Chandra) — 1866-1939, a monastic disciple of Sri Ramakrishna.

Abhyasa — repeated practice of spiritual disciplines.

Adbhutananda, Swami (also Latu Maharaj) — ?-1920, a monastic disciple of Sri Ramakrishna.

Advaita — nonduality. Also the name of a school of Vedanta philosophy which teaches the oneness of God, the soul, and the universe. The main exponents of Advaita Vedanta were Gaudapada and Shankara.

Anahata — a sound which may be heard in meditation at a certain stage of spiritual unfoldment. It is referred to as the music of the spheres. *See also* Kundalini

Arjuna — one of the five Pandava brothers and hero of the epic Mahabharata, one section of which is called Bhagavad Gita. In the Gita, Sri Krishna speaks to mankind through spiritual instructions to Arjuna.

Asana — place or mat on which a spiritual aspirant sits for meditation. Also, position or posture of the body, as the various asanas prescribed for health in Hatha Yoga.

Ashvattha — fig tree considered holy by Hindus. The Tree of Life, represented as having its roots above and its branches and leaves below. The tree symbolizes cosmic existence, which has its roots in the transcendent realms, while its branches extend into the world. The roots of the Ashvattha symbolize the unmanifest Absolute aspect of Brahman; its trunk and branches symbolize manifest being.

Atman — the Self, or the soul. Also denotes the Supreme Soul, which, according to Advaita Vedanta, is identical with the individual soul.

Atulananda, Swami (also Cornelius Heijblom, Gurudas Maharaj) — 1870-1966. Born in Holland, he came to the United States in 1892. He heard about Vedanta and met Swami Abhedananda in 1898 in New York. In 1900 he joined Swami Turiyananda and other devotees in California at the Shanti Ashrama. In 1923 he took the vows of sannyasa from Swami Abhedananda, becoming Swami Atulananda and lived in India until his death.

Bhagavad Gita — lit., the "Song of God." Considered the practical scripture of Vedanta philosophy, the Gita consists of the teachings of Sri Krishna to the warrior Arjuna on how to realize God while carrying on one's duties. It is part of the sixth book of the Indian epic poem, the Mahabharata.

Bhagavatam or Bhagavata-Purana — the famous devotional Hindu scripture, attributed to Vyasa. The Bhagavatam illustrates religious truths through the life of Sri Krishna and stories of ancient India's saints, seers, and kings.

Brahman — the Absolute. The supreme reality of Advaita Vedanta.

Brahmananda, Swami (also Rakhal Chandra Ghosh) — 1863-1922, considered the spiritual son of Sri Ramakrishna.

Brahma Sutras — an authoritative treatise on the Vedanta philosophy, ascribed to Vyasa. The Brahma Sutras interpret through reasoning the spiritual experiences described in the Upanishads.

Dharma — a comprehensive term used to refer to that which determines our true essence; the basis of human morality and ethics, the lawful order of the universe, and the foundation of all religion; righteousness. Dharma also refers to duty. One's own duty in life is based on one's true nature, and is called Svadharma.

Divine Mother — the dynamic aspect of the Godhead, which is usually represented in female form. The Divine Mother appears under many different names as the divine consort of Brahma, Vishnu, or Shiva. Some of her names are Kali, Durga, Tara, Parvati, and Shyama.

Dualism (Dvaita) — a school of Vedanta, which teaches that God and the individual soul are eternally separate, and that the world is real.

Gunas — sattva, rajas, and tamas. The three gunas make up the universe of gross and subtle matter. Sattva represents calmness and purity; rajas, activity and restlessness; and tamas, inertia and stupidity.

Guru — a spiritual teacher. *Gu* = darkness, *ru* = destroyer. The guru is one who destroys the darkness or ignorance of the disciple. According to Swami Vivekananda, a guru must know the essence of the scriptures; he must be pure; and he must teach selflessly, without desire for name, fame, or wealth.

Hanuman (also Mahavir) — leader of Sri Rama's army and a hero of the Ramayana. Hanuman is revered in India as an ideal devotee because of his ecstatic love for Sri Rama.

Ishtam — one particular manifestation of God which appeals to the heart of a spiritual seeker, to whom he offers his worship and on whom he meditates.

Ishvara — lit., "lord of the universe"; the concept of a personal god; Brahman with attributes.

Japam (also Japa) — repetition of one's mantram as instructed by the guru. Repetition may be audible, silent with only the lips moving, or mental. The aim of japa is to purify the mind and achieve one-pointed concentration on the object of meditation.

Jiva — lit., a "living being." The individual soul, which is in essence one with the Universal Soul.

Jivan-mukta — lit., "one liberated while still alive"; one who is still in the body but has freed himself from the bonds of ignorance. He has given up identification with body and mind and has attained liberation. As the Self he knows he is one with Brahman.

Kabir — 1440-1518, an Indian poet and mystic.

Kali — A name of the Divine Mother. Kali is usually pictured as dancing on the breast of Shiva, her husband, who lies inert, symbolizing the transcendent aspect of Spirit, whereas she symbolizes the dynamic aspect, the power of Brahman. *See also* Divine Mother

Kali Yuga — the fourth world period, through which mankind is said to be passing at present. The first three world periods are: Krita or Satya (the ideal golden age); Treta (when righteousness begins to decline); Dvapara (when desires and diseases surface and injustice grows). In the Kali Yuga spiritual efforts slacken, knowledge is forgotten, and evil dominates.

Karma, nishkama — unselfish action. Such actions are done without expecting any return.

Karma, prarabdha — lit., *pra* = before; *arabdha* = begun; *karma* = deed; the results of deeds that were begun in former lives and are now working themselves out in the present one. Such consequences are the harvest of ripened fruits; the resulting events cannot be prevented, just as one cannot call back an arrow that has already left the bow.

Krishna — an incarnation of Vishnu. He is the best known of all the Hindu deities. He is prominent in the Mahabharata, and in the Bhagavad Gita section gives instruction to mankind through his disciple Arjuna.

Kundalini — the spiritual energy lying dormant in all individuals. There are six centres of consciousness or chakras (also called lotuses) which parallel nerve plexuses: Muladhara (between anus and sexual organ); Svadhishthana (at base of sexual organ); Manipura (at navel); Anahata (at heart); Vishuddha (at throat); Ajna (between eyebrows). In the cerebrum is the Sahasrara, the highest centre.

Mahabharata — lit., "the great epic of (the battle of) the descendants of Bharata." The most voluminous epic of Indian literature, it contains over 100,000 verses, the authorship of which is ascribed to the sage Vyasa. The Bhagavad Gita is part of the sixth book of the great epic.

Maharaj — lit., "great king"; lord, master. A title of respect used to address Indian holy men, either instead of the name or following the first name. Swami Turiyananda and his brother disciples sometimes addressed Sri Ramakrishna as Guru Maharaj.

Mantram (also mantra) — the particular name of God, corresponding to the Chosen Deity (Ishtam) of the disciple, with which he is initiated into spiritual life by his guru.

Mukti — final liberation and release from all worldly bonds, from karma and the cycle of life, death, and rebirth, through union with God or knowledge of ultimate reality.

Nirvana — final absorption in Brahman, or the All-pervading Reality, through the annihilation of the individual ego, desire, and passion. It also means liberation.

Pancadasi — a 14th century treatise on nondualistic Vedanta by Sri Vidyaranya Swami.

Paramahamsa — lit., "greatest swan"; a monk who belongs to the highest order of knowers of Brahman; a term often applied to Sri Ramakrishna. Also, a monk who belongs to a particular sect of the Shankara Order of India.

Paramatman — the supreme Atman (or Self); Cosmic Soul. As absolute consciousness, it is identical with Brahman.

Patanjali — second century BC, author of the Yoga Sutras (or Raja Yoga), one of the six systems of orthodox Hindu philosophy.

Prahlada — a great devotee of Vishnu, whose life is described in Hindu mythology. In spite of various forms of torture inflicted on him by his father, Prahlada remained steadfast in his love for Vishnu. Vishnu then appeared in the form of a man-lion and killed Prahlada's father.

Prana — the sum total of primal energy, from which all mental and physical energy has evolved. Prana manifests, for instance, as motion, gravitation, magnetism, the vital principle which sustains physical life, thought force, and bodily action.

Pranayama — lit., "control of prana," it consists of breathing exercises, which may be combined with the practice of a mantra. Pranayama is the fourth of the eight limbs of raja yoga.

Prarabdha Karma — *See* Karma.

Prasad — food or any other gift which has been ceremonially offered to God or to a saintly person; it is usually afterwards given to devotees. A recipient of prasad considers himself blessed and purified.

Premananda, Swami (also Baburam Ghosh) — 1861-1918, a monastic disciple of Sri Ramakrishna, and regarded by him as an Ishvarakoti (or ever-pure, ever-free soul).

Qualified Nondualism (Vishishtadvaita) — a school of Vedanta, which teaches that the soul and nature are modes of Brahman, and that the individual soul is a part of Brahman.

Rama (also Ramachandra) — one of the most popular divine incarnations of Hinduism; king of Ayodhya; hero of the Ramayana. His wife was Sita.

Ramakrishna, Sri — 1836-1886, a Godman of India, considered by many to be an avatara, or incarnation of God. His life inspired the modern renaissance of Vedanta. After practising intense spiritual disciplines and realizing his union with God through various paths within Hinduism, as well as through Christianity and Islam, Sri Ramakrishna proclaimed, "As many faiths, so many paths."

Ramayana — lit., "the life story of Rama." The oldest epic in Sanskrit literature, it contains 24,000 verses, the authorship of which is attributed to the sage Valmiki.

Ramprasad (also Ramaprasad) — 1723-1803, one of the most important Bengali saints and poets. A worshipper of the Divine Mother Kali, his inspirational songs are sung throughout Bengal.

Sadhana — a set of spiritual disciplines, such as japam, meditation, and selfless action.

Sadhu — a holy person.

Samadhi — the superconscious state in which man experiences his identity with the ultimate reality.

Samsara — the relative world. Also, the relentless cycle of birth, death, and rebirth to which a person is subject as long as he remains ignorant of his identity with Brahman.

Samskaras — lit., "impression, consequences," they are impressions, tendencies, and possibilities present in consciousness that have arisen through one's thoughts and actions, including those of earlier births. One's character is the result of the sum total of these Samskaras.

Samkhya (also Sankhya) — one of the six systems of orthodox Hindu philosophy. It teaches that the universe arises through the union of prakriti (nature) with purusha (consciousness). It believes there are as many souls and units of consciousness (purushas) as there are living beings.

Sannyasa — lit., "renunciation," it is the giving up of selfish interests and worldly things and devoting oneself to the realization of God. One who renounces is known as a sannyasin, or a monk.

Sarada Devi (also Holy Mother) — 1853-1920, wife or spiritual consort of Sri Ramakrishna.

Saradananda, Swami (also Sharat Chandra Chakrabarty) — 1865-1927, a monastic disciple of Sri Ramakrishna. He authored the monumental biography *Sri Sri Ramakrishna Lilaprasanga* (*Sri Ramakrishna, the Great Master*).

Satchidananda (also Satchitananda) — Absolute Existence, Absolute Consciousness, and Absolute Bliss. An epithet of Brahman, the ultimate reality.

Sat-sanga — holy company; associating with spiritual adepts and devotees, to purity and uplift the mind.

Sha, Sha, Sa — forbear. Sri Ramakrishna once said, "In the Bengali alphabet no three letters are alike in sound except the three sibilants Sha, Sha, and Sa, and they all mean 'forbear.' This shows that even from our childhood we are made to learn forbearance through the very alphabet. The quality of forbearance is of the highest importance to every man."

Shankara (also Shamkara or Shankaracharya) — 788-820, one of India's greatest saints and philosophers; the main exponent of Advaita Vedanta.

Shivananda, Swami (also Taraknath Ghoshal) — 1854-1934, a monastic disciple of Sri Ramakrishna.

Shraddha — faith, love, self-confidence, and strength all combined. Shraddha is not blind faith. It is an inner conviction that the words of the teacher and of the scriptures are true.

Shraddha Rites — a religious ceremony in which food and drink are offered to deceased relatives. It is held on the day after the period of family mourning is over and is observed annually thereafter.

Shukadeva — the son of Vyasa, and the narrator of the Bhagavatam. He is regarded as an ideal monk of India.

Shyama — a name of the Divine Mother.

Suradas — a medieval mystic saint of India.

Sushumna — the hollow canal which runs through the centre of the spinal cord. It is flanked on the left by the Ida and on the right by the Pingala — the main channels through which the afferent and efferent nerve currents travel. When the Kundalini (or spiritual energy) awakens, it passes through centres of consciousness which are located in the Sushumna. *See also* Kundalini

Svadharma — *See* Dharma

Swami — lord, master, spiritual teacher. The word swami, a title of the Hindu monk, may be used instead of the name or preceding the name.

Tantra — a religious philosophy, the central theme of which is the dynamic aspect of the Godhead (Brahman), usually regarded as feminine.

Trigunatitananda (also Sarada Prasanna) — 1865-1915, a monastic disciple of Sri Ramakrishna.

Tulasidas (also Tulsidas) — 1532-1623, an Indian mystic and poet. His Hindi version of Valmiki's Ramayana (*Ram-charit-manas*) is the most beloved and influential book in North and Central India.

Turiya — the superconscious. Lit., "the fourth," in relation to the three ordinary states of consciousness — waking, dreaming, and dreamless sleep — which it transcends.

Upadhi — all names and forms of ignorance that are taken up by the Atman (or Self) when it is identified with the body, mind, senses, and ego. The term refers to everything that is superimposed on and conceals Brahman.

Upanishads — the sacred scriptures which contain the philosophical aspect of the Vedas. Lit., *upa* = near; *ni* = down; *sad* = sit. Upanishad means to sit down near one's teacher and hear about God, the main subject of all Upanishads. They are regarded by orthodox Hindus as records of the spiritual experiences of ancient sages of India. There are about one hundred and eight Upanishads, of which eleven are considered major.

Vedanta — lit., "the end of the Vedas," Vedanta means the highest wisdom. It is one of the six systems of Hindu philosophy, and is based mainly on the teachings of the Upanishads, the Brahma Sutras, and the Bhagavad Gita.

Vedas — lit., "knowledge"; the most ancient and sacred of Hindu scriptures, regarded by orthodox Hindus as having been revealed to ancient seers who wanted to know about God.

Viveka-chudamani — lit., "crest jewel of discrimination"; an important work on Advaita Vedanta by Shankara.

Vivekananda, Swami (also Narandranath Datta) — 1863-1902, monastic disciple and chief apostle of Sri Ramakrishna. In 1893 Vivekananda represented Hinduism at the Parliament of Religions, held in connection with the World's Columbian Exposition in Chicago.

Vyasa — the compiler of the Vedas and the author of Vedanta Sutras and the Bhagavad Gita.

Yoga — lit., "yoke"; the union of the individual soul with the Supreme Soul. Also, the discipline by which such union is effected. Four of the best known yogas are: karma yoga (the path of selfless action); bhakti yoga (the path of love); raja yoga (the path of self-control and concentration); and jnana yoga (the path of knowledge).

Yoga Vasishtha Ramayana — a poetic work of 32,000 verses, attributed to the sage Valmiki, who also composed the Ramayana. The Yoga Vasishtha is presented as a lively and colorful dialogue in which Vasishtha teaches Advaita Vedanta to his student, Prince Rama.

INDEX

action, desireless, 76
Adbhutananda, Swami, death of, 272-73, 275-76
Advaita, of Ramakrishna and Shankara, 45
Atman: pure mind knows, 111-12; different views of, 113
avidya: explained, 60; must give up, 208

body: as machine, 122; connection with, 218; don't identify with, 90
bondage, becoming free of, 35
Brahman: householders attaining, 129; is all, 115; vision of, 134

careful, person, not subject to grief, 31
chakras (spiritual centres), location of, 51
character, formation of, 34
Chosen Deity, same as guru, 199
creation, not real, 115
criticism, why bother about, 143

days, good and bad, 150
desire: for devotion, 76; for enjoyment, 75; getting rid of, 182; for Mother only, 181; for name and fame, 226
devotees, real, don't ask for anything, 93
devotion: cultivation of, 118; desire for, 76; is rare, 140
difficulties, need perseverance, 47
disciple, who is, 55
disciplines, spiritual (*see also* practice, spiritual; sadhana): purpose of, 163-64; regular practice of, 88-89, 151-52
disease, minimizing, 70
Divine Mother: and I, best attitude, 111; in everything, 45; brings fearlessness, 103-4; the only guide, 251; protection of, 64; the Self of all, 257; worship of, 80
doubts, removing, 214
dualism, 114; vs. nondualism, 73; Vedantic school of, 205

ego: eliminate through work, 186; if it doesn't go, 189
enthusiasm, need for, 91

faith: importance of, 68; leads to peace, 103
fear, devotee doesn't, 184
food: discrimination about, 158; for spiritual life, 155-56
forbearance, need for, 81
friendship, need of, 34

ghost, seer of, 137

Gita: destroys rebirth, 217; meditation on, 222; quintessence of, 65, 67; value of studying, 31
God: absorption in, 171; –consciousness, through steady practice, 154; as doer, 78; is everything, 79; focus mind on, 158; with/without form, 122; known only by grace, 160; and guru within, 149; makes everything known, 130; need love for, 134; –realization, in human life only, 145; no other refuge, 153; seeing, 135; seeking, 135; source of all goodness, 130
grace: attaining God through, 37-38; through patience, 146
guna, sattva, enhancing, 88
gunas, state above, 222
guru: and God within, 149; same as Chosen Deity, 199; who is, 55

holy company: advantage/benefit of, 127, 142; best means to God, 160; having, 48; not having, 40
human body, result of merit, 94
humility, aids improvement, 44
hypocrisy, giving up, 138

ignorance, explained, 60
illumined soul, signs of, 211
impurity, bars God's vision, 137
instructions, spiritual, how to give, 44
instrument, think yourself, 67

japam, practice of, 50
jiva: evolution of, 115; incarnation of, 83
jivan-mukta, signs of, 211
jivan-mukti (liberation-in-life), 63

karma: nishkama, secret of, 270; past, not for liberated, 176; rajasic, 86
knowledge, two kinds of, 210
kundalini, awakening of, 51-52

liberation, inevitable above gunas, 222
Lord: only good for us, 167, 177; singing name of, 162
lotuses (spiritual centres), location of, 51
love, needed for God, 134
lust, problem with, 119

mantram: as seed, 56; identical with deity, 58; purpose of, 55
meditation: higher than japam, 50; instructions for, 190-91; steadfast practice of, 59
mind: calming, 185; calmness of, not important, 37; control of, 192-93, 228; fluctuations of, 179; importance of, 70; improving, 49; purification of, 152; root of trouble, 52
money: desire for, 50; don't put mind on, 201; for holy causes, 170

nondualism, 114; through discrimination, 71; through dualism, 71, 73; qualified, 114; Vedantic schools of, 205

opposites, pairs of, 81

para-samvedya, defined, 100, 210
parents, service to, 42
passions, control of, 255
patience, succcess through, 98-99
peace, attainment of, 96
perseverance, need for, 47
practice, spiritual (*see also* disciplines, spiritual; sadhana): love best form of, 162; steady, attains God, 154
Premananda, Swami: death of, 263; letter to, 126, 131-32, 142
purity, vs. impurity, 130

Ramakrishna, Sri: as Ishvara, 205; no liberation for, 204; parable, milkmaid on water, 73; philosophy of, 195-97
— sayings of: affliction and body, 26, 69, 82, 139, 170; as many faiths, 195; make butter, 208; cannot buy God, 50; desire for devotion, 76; endure and survive, 175; fight from fort, 128; food and oil-cake, 77, 227; forbear, forbear, 82; Gita repeated, 66; go east, leave west, 12, 38, 147; be gold, 208; grace of one, 136; grain merchant and mice, 102; grant pure love, 77; great soul in world, 212; grief pierces body, 137; hereditary farmer, 37; hide and seek, 107, 208; hold pole, 208; imitation custard-apple, 98; no intoxication by words, 58, 216; jackals howl same, 103, 150; japam better than ritual, 50; karma softened, 137; learning insignificant, 108; longing and grace, 133; match destroys darkness, 219; unite mind and speech, 52; monk and snake, 171; Mother and I, 111; mother keeps kitten, 92; none remain unfed, 110; adept parcheesi player, 107; pith and sheaths, 197; pregnant woman, 67; scriptures like shopping list, 13; squeezing almanac, 109; one step toward God, 118; ten steps towards God, 163; syrup and treacle, 117; thorn pricks, 72; thread can't pass needle, 192, 226; tie knowledge in cloth, 197; water comes and goes, 170; zeros added together, 196
recollectedness, cultivate within, 47
refuge, in God, 144
renunciation: necessity of, 208-9; of ego, 182-83
rules, obstruct progress, 41

sadhana (*see also* practice, spiritual; disciplines, spiritual): in adversity, 69; continuing, 226; in all conditions, 166; results of stopping, 199-200; needs sincerity, 73
samadhi: for householder, 96-97; three states of, 212
samskaras, do not dwell on, 266
Saradananda, Swami, letter to, 34
scripture, need to follow, 43
self-effort, need for, 84-85
self-esteem, low, 148, 156

self-surrender: practising, 67; signs of, 100-101
senses, control of, 117-18
service: opportunity for, 119; to parents/father, 42-44; privilege of, 141; right spirit of, 124; as worship, 129
shraddha: importance of, 68; leads to peace, 103
shraddha ceremony, value of, 53
simple soul, God near to, 138
singing name of Lord, 162
sleep, true, in samadhi, 33
soul: evolution of, 115; incarnation of, 83
story: king who pretended, 138; renunciation of ego, 182-83; virgin girl, 210
suffering, is inevitable, 82
surrender, no other way than, 39
sva-samvedya, defined, 100,210

talking, no escape from, 50
Turiyananda, Swami, 20-21; American work of, 19, 25; childhood of, 11; death of, 27; first meeting with Ramakrishna, 11, 187-88; itinerant years of, 16, 18; last years of, 25, 27; pictures of, 2, 10, 28, 30, 232; Ramakrishna's training of, 12; reminiscences of Ramakrishna, 14-15; way of teaching, 22, 25

Vedanta: exposition of, 112, 114; knower of, 114; principal books on, 48; schools of, 114, 205
Vedas, basis of Hinduism, 57; origin of, 54
vigilance, importance of, 32
vision: during another's death, 136; impurity bars, 137; of Brahman, 134
Vivekananda, Swami: catholic feeling of, 53; death of, 238, 241; memories of, 132-33; nonattachment of, 46

weak, never think you are, 36
weakness, removing, 215
witness, live as, 213
women, attitude towards, 87
work: becomes worship, 36, 120-21; for the Lord, 62, 82; how to, 59; necessity/need for, 36, 220-21; unselfish, secret of, 270-71
world: no happiness in, 174; not real, 92
worthless, don't think you are, 46

yoga: attaining, 220; defined, 194; paths of, 74, 206; signs of attainment, 220; and work, 221